Complete Book of

Model
Railway
Electronics

Complete Book of

Model Railway Electronics

Roger Amos

Patrick Stephens Limited

WARNING! ELECTRICITY CAN BE DANGEROUS!
The electronic projects in this book are, to the best of the author's knowledge and belief, both accurately described and safe. However, great care must always be taken when assembling electronic circuits, and neither the publishers nor the author can accept responsibility for any accidents which may occur.

© Roger Amos 1998

First published in 1990
Second edition published 1998

British Library Cataloguing-in-Publication Data:
A catalogue record for this book is available from the British Library

ISBN 1 85260 591 X

Library of Congress catalog card No. 97-76833

Patrick Stephens Limited is an imprint of
Haynes Publishing, Sparkford, Nr Yeovil, Somerset, BA22 7JJ

Tel.: 01963 440635   Fax: 01963 440001
Int. tel.: +44 1963 440635   Int. fax: +44 1963 440001

E-mail: sales@haynes-manuals.co.uk
Web site: http://www.haynes.com

Haynes North America Inc.
861 Lawrence Drive, Newbury Park, California 91320 USA

Printed and bound in Great Britain by
Butler & Tanner Ltd, Frome and London

Contents

Introduction

In 1979–80 when I wrote *Practical Electronics for Railway Modellers*, my intention was to break new ground. In its Introduction I observed that whereas the average railway modeller is a competent *electrician*, skilled in the wiring and switching that is an essential part of most model railway layouts, paradoxically he finds the subject of *electronics* a 'closed book'. Perhaps this is because he likes to see things move. Switches and relays have visible moving contacts, not unlike the railway turnouts (points/switches) with which he is so familiar. Electronic devices, in contrast, have no moving parts. What goes on inside the little black plastic packages is a mystery hidden from human eyes.

I had found that electronics solved a multiplicity of problems in railway modelling, but in order to 'pass on' my experience in a form that was useful to other modellers, it was necessary to produce a book that assumed no prior knowledge at all. *Practical Electronics for Railway Modellers* contained a set of appendices giving fundamental theoretical and practical information that allowed its use even by readers having no prior experience of electronics.

To say that that book revolutionized the world of railway modelling may be an exaggeration, but its sales certainly exceeded expectations and unquestionably it *did* lead many modellers into using electronics for the first time. Undoubtedly its timely appearance when both railway modelling and electronics were enjoying an upturn in fortunes contributed to the decision of the model railway magazine editors to publish occasional electronics-oriented articles, which they had been loath to do in earlier years (and not without reason).

And, oddly enough, the book also found a niche outside of regular railway modelling circles! I heard recently of a school that adopted *Practical Electronics for Railway Modellers* as the basis of its electronics syllabus; they found that building projects that could be put to work on a model railway stimulated the pupils' interest in a way that conventional experiments, often isolated from 'real life' situations, failed to do.

I deliberately avoided any use of integrated circuits (ICs or 'chips') in *Practical Electronics for Railway Modellers*; this was for two reasons. Firstly, my aim was to keep the book with its projects as simple as possible. Secondly, as I claimed in the Introduction, in five years of model railway experience I had never found a chip that was useful.

This second reason did not stay true for long. Having gained a grounding in the 74-series of TTL (transistor/transistor logic) chips, I found that instead of making life more complex, they greatly simplified many projects especially in signalling which is of necessity a thoroughly 'logical' discipline. So in 1985 *Practical Electronics for Railway Modellers 2* was published. This followed a similar sequence to *Practical Electronics for Railway Modellers*, but assumed a fundamental knowledge of electronics and included a long appendix on TTL.

Since writing *Practical Electronics for Railway Modellers 2* there have been two main developments in my personal model railway electronics writing story. One was the ill-fated magazine *Model Railway Electronics* which ran for just four quarterly issues in 1984. The other was the book *Computer Projects for Railway Modellers*, jointly authored with Martin Cock, published in 1987. Inevitably both have generated new ideas and led me to a better understanding of the subject.

So when I was approached to produce a single volume revising the first two books, I leapt at the chance. Indeed almost as soon as I had finished writing *Practical Electronics for Railway Modellers 2* I had felt a need to combine its contents with those of the first book to give a more comprehensive overview of electronics. In fact the current book does more than that. It also includes some of my own material from *Model Railway Electronics*. And I have taken the opportunity to eliminate some projects which have now become impossible owing to non-availability of components and others which present problems which only emerged in the light of readers' experience.

The overall result is what must be one of the most comprehensive treatises on model railway electronics ever written, suitable for beginner and experienced dabbler alike. Hence its title, the *Complete Book of Model Railway Electronics*. I do hope that you find it helpful.

May I repeat the tributes at the end of the Introduction to *Practical Electronics for Railway Modellers 2*:

'I must acknowledge my gratitude to many organizations and persons for their assistance in the preparation of this book. I name especially Westinghouse Signals Ltd for information on prototype signalling systems, Maplin Electronic Supplies Ltd for permission to reproduce TTL pinouts from their catalogue and RCA Corporation for permission to reproduce the information found in Appendices 14 and 15 of this book.

'I owe an incalculable debt to my father, S. W. Amos, who nurtured my interest in electronics from an early age and is still a source of the most helpful criticism and advice. Finally, and by no means least, I salute my long-suffering wife, Jennifer, who has endured unreasonable desertion while I have been "playing with wires and trains" in preparation for this book.'

Roger S. Amos
Rugby

Preface to the Second Edition

I am grateful for this opportunity to introduce some changes to this book. Most of these are minor corrections and improvements. Thankfully most of the components specified in the first edition are still obtainable; I have specified suitable alternatives to the few that have become obsolete. Also, I have added the Maplin order codes for semiconductors and other critical components.

I have amended some of the signal driver circuits in Chapter 15 to give greater flexibility or to suit substituted components. A new Appendix 16 details the model railway electronic project kits available from Maplin. The kits vary widely in their complexity and the simpler ones provide an ideal introduction to the exciting possibilities that electronics offers to railway modellers. I acknowledge my continuing gratitude to Maplin for their cooperation.

On a more sombre note I must draw readers' attention to the provisions of the Electromagnetic Compatibility Directives (Ref 89/336/EEC). These have made it a more serious offence to operate equipment which may interfere with radio, television or other equipment. The only circuits in this book which may cause such interference are the high-frequency lighting circuits described in Chapter 31. Before operating these, please read and heed the warning given in that chapter.

Roger S. Amos,
Rugby

Part 1: Introductory projects

Preamble

The first two projects in this book have been especially chosen to serve as a practical introduction to electronics for readers who have no previous knowledge of the subject. Nevertheless, experienced readers may also find them useful. Chapter 1 — a protection circuit for sidings — must represent the simplest possible electronic circuit since it consists simply of one silicon diode. Not only does this simplest-of-all circuit provide the railway modeller with a useful security system, but it also introduces him to the high-technology world of the semi-conductor.

Chapter 2 is an add-on unit for Chapter 1, an indicator using a light emitting diode (LED). Lighting up when the train has arrived, this is useful when the siding is out of sight of the operator. It also introduces the LED, another kind of semi-conductor diode of immense practical value to the railway modeller, and the resistor, one of the 'nuts and bolts' of electronics.

In these two projects the reader will therefore have encountered resistors, silicon diodes and LEDs, components widely used in model railway electronics. The chapters describe the circuit, its functioning and application and draw attention to any special features. Step-by-step instructions are *not* given for two reasons. Firstly, the intended readership consists of railway modellers who will be accustomed to assembling projects, albeit not electronic ones. Secondly, instructions are boring and it is futile to say, 'Solder A to B' when it is obvious from the circuit diagram that A must be joined to B and soldering is the accepted means of doing so. Guidance on soldering and methods of construction will be found in the Practical Appendices that make up Part 9 of the book.

Readers with no previous experience of electronics are advised first to *read* through Chapters 1 and 2, then Appendices 1 to 3.

Chapter 1

Diode protection for sidings

One of the petty irritations in model railway operation is the disruption caused by derailments when a train at speed hits the buffers at the end of a siding — or, worse, runs off the track if the siding is bufferless. This is especially likely to happen if the siding is out of sight of the operator. One way of preventing this sort of accident is to isolate the end of the siding by means of a rail break or an insulating fishplate and to connect the power to the isolated siding end by means of a switch on the control panel. The power is switched off as the train approaches the end of the siding, so the train will stop as soon as the last set of wheels fitted with power pick-ups crosses the rail break. Of course, to get the train out of the siding the switch must be operated to restore the power to the siding end. This demands a switch and a length of twin-flex wire; both are cumbersome and expensive.

The same effect can be achieved automatically and cheaply by replacing the switch with a silicon diode of suitable rating (see Figure 1.1). The train will always stop as soon as the last power pick-up has crossed the rail break but, on turning the controller to reverse, the train will run out again normally. The diode acts as an automatic switch, blocking 'into-siding' current, but allowing 'out-of-siding' current to pass. It is, of course, important to ensure that the diode is connected the right way round. If it is connected the wrong way round, the train will not be stopped as it runs down the siding and turning the controller to reverse will fail to bring it back. If this happens, take the diode out, turn it round and put it back into the circuit.

How it works

It is a gross oversimplification to say that the diode conducts electricity in one direction only, but for practical purposes this is near enough to the truth. The diode has two terminals or leads called the *anode* and the *cathode*; the cathode is usually marked by a spot or a band on the body of the device; alternatively the cathode end may have a wide 'lip' to it. Inside the device is a tiny piece of silicon which has been 'doped' with two different impurities to give it a negatively charged n-zone (the cathode) and a positively charged p-zone (the anode); the interface between these zones is called the *junction*. Electrons, which are the 'carriers' of electric current, find it easier to pass from the n-zone to the p-zone than in the opposite direction. So, when the anode is connected to a higher voltage (ie, a voltage more *positive*) than that on the cathode, the diode will conduct current quite freely; under these conditions it is said to be *forward biased*. But when the anode is at a lower voltage (ie, less positive or more negative) than that on the cathode, the diode blocks current; only a negligible leakage current passes. The diode is now said to be *reverse biased*. However, if the reverse voltage is great enough, the junction 'breaks down' and reverse current will flow freely.

Choosing the right diode for the job

It is essential to choose a diode whose 'peak inverse voltage' (PIV) rating is high enough for the application. For this project a minimum PIV of 50 V (volts) is sufficient. Too low a PIV could mean that under certain conditions junction breakdown would occur, causing malfunction of the circuit. Also the current that can pass through a diode is limited by the area of the junction; too high a current will cause it to overheat. It is therefore also essential to choose a device capable of handling the current which it will encounter in its application. In this project the minimum current rating permissible is 1 A (Amp). Any of the 1N4001 series of rectifier diodes would be suitable.

Figure 1.2 relates the internal structure of a silicon diode to its external appearance and also gives the symbols used in circuit diagrams.

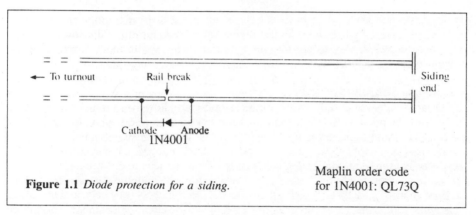

Figure 1.1 *Diode protection for a siding.*

Maplin order code
for 1N4001: QL73Q

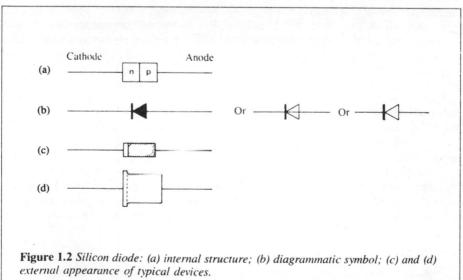

Figure 1.2 *Silicon diode: (a) internal structure; (b) diagrammatic symbol; (c) and (d) external appearance of typical devices.*

Chapter 2

LED indicator for protected siding

If the diode-protected siding in Chapter 1 is out of sight of the operator, he will have no way of knowing when the train has arrived and been stopped at the end of the siding. It is, however, easy to arrange for a simple visual indication to be given using a light-emitting diode (LED).

Light-emitting diodes (LEDs)

LEDs are invaluable to railway modellers as miniature, long-lived sources of coloured light. In later projects we shall see how they can be used in colour-light signals and as train headlamps and tail lamps. Their simplest use, however, is as indicators. The diode used in Chapter 1 was a silicon diode; LEDs resemble silicon diodes in some respects, but the semi-conducting material from which they are constructed is an alloy of gallium, phosphorus and arsenic, the proportions of which determine the colour of light emitted. Like silicon diodes they conduct electricity one way only, and of course, it is when conducting electricity that they emit light. The circuit diagram symbol (Figure 2.1a) is as for a silicon diode, but the parallel arrows suggest light being emitted. They are, however, highly susceptible to damage by reverse voltages (as low as 3 V) and by overheating. Extreme care must be taken in the design of the circuits using LEDs to preclude the possibility of reverse voltages; care must also be taken when soldering connections to LEDs to avoid overheating them and to ensure that the LED is being connected the right way round. Often the cathode is adjacent to a notch in the body of the device (Figure 2.1b), but it is best to test the device first using a 3 V battery via a 100 Ohm resistor to check which lead is which. When the train has been stopped on the diode-protected siding, the silicon diode is reverse biased and so blocks the current to it. If we now connect the LED so that it is parallel to the first diode, but anode to cathode, the LED will light as soon as the train arrives.

In practice it is not quite so simple. The LED would overheat and burn out at once. For most LEDs the maximum current that can be passed is 30 mA (milliAmps — 1 mA = 1/1,000 Amp), cf, the typical current taken by a model locomotive, around 250 mA. So a resistor must be added in series with the LED both to limit the current to a safe level and to ensure that the train is stopped.

Resistors

A *resistor* is an electronic component which allows a limited amount of current to pass; the current is in fact proportional to the voltage applied and the ratio of current to voltage for each resistor is known as its *resistance*. Resistance is measured in Ohms (abbreviated Ω or R); high resistances are in KilOhms (KR or just K — 1 K = 1,000 R); even higher resistances are in MegOhms (MR or just M — 1 M = 1,000,000 R or 1,000 K). Now 1 R is the resistance which allows 1 A to pass for each volt applied.

It just happens that the maximum voltage available from most controllers is around 20 V and so the resistance needed for this application is 20 V/20 mA = 1 K. So we need a 1 K resistor to protect the LED. Some resistors are marked with their value in figures, but most use an internationally accepted colour code (see Appendix 4). For those not wishing to memorize the code at this stage 1 K is brown-black-red (starting with the band that is nearest to one end of the device).

Figure 2.2 shows the circuit diagram for the siding protection system with LED indicator. The rectangular symbol is the resistor; this symbol is a new international standard, but many publishers still use an older symbol, which is a zigzag line; readers should recognize this when they see it.

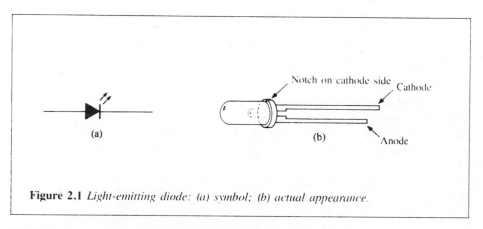

Figure 2.1 *Light-emitting diode: (a) symbol; (b) actual appearance.*

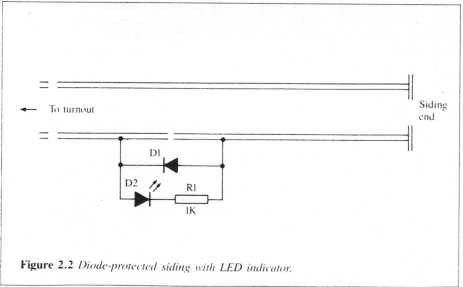

Figure 2.2 *Diode-protected siding with LED indicator.*

How the circuit works

When the train crosses the rail break silicon diode D1 blocks the heavy current which it needs as before. But LED D2 can conduct current via resistor R1 and the train motor. This current will be limited by the resistor to a maximum of about 20 mA — enough to light the LED brightly, but not enough to keep the train running. As long as the controller is left set 'forwards' (ie, into the siding) the LED will remain lit up, indicating that the train has arrived and been stopped. When the controller is turned to stop or reverse, the LED will be extinguished. On turning the controller to reverse, the train will run out of the siding normally, as before. Incidentally the silicon diode protects the LED against inverse voltages; the forward voltage across D1 (which is also the inverse voltage across D2) cannot exceed around 1 V.

Although the circuit diagram in Figure 2.2 suggests that the LED is physically adjacent to silicon diode D1, this need not necessarily be so. If the siding is out of sight of the operator, the LED may be mounted on a control panel or mimic diagram to give the operator immediate indication of the arrival of the unseen train. This may, of course, necessitate the use of long leads under the baseboard.

Part 2: Controllers

Preamble

The purpose of a controller is, of course, to regulate the direction and speed of a model train. An ideal controller would give infinitely variable control of speed from a barely perceptible crawl — a scale 1 mph, say — to full speed, which may be a scale 100 mph or more for a modern express passenger train. Moreover it should give prototypically smooth starts and stops.

Until the advent of transistorized circuits, controllers were of two types. Commonest was the *rheostat* type in which a heavy-duty rheostat (variable resistor) in series with the locomotive motor provided some control of current and therefore of speed. Rheostat controllers have either a simple rheostat with a separate changeover switch for direction or a split-track rheostat, direction control being combined with the speed control, which has a central 'stop' position. The latter is more complex and expensive, but easier to use and more reliable. Switches are a frequent cause of faults in controllers and their use is best avoided wherever possible.

The other type of controller uses a *variable transformer*, in which the magnetic coupling between primary and secondary windings is adjustable, providing a means of varying the output voltage and therefore the speed. Both types of controller are still made and widely used. The controllers provided by the ready-to-run model railway manufacturers are generally rheostat types.

However both types of controller pose problems with which the reader will probably be only too familiar. Imagine your train standing in the station ready to leave. You advance the speed control and nothing happens. You advance it further and still nothing happens. You advance it to perhaps 75 per cent of full power when suddenly the train bolts from the station with the abruptness of a bullet leaving a gun! You can now turn the speed control down to 25 per cent, say, of full power and reduce the train's speed to a reasonable level but it is too late; the illusion has been destroyed. Prototype trains — even electric types with brisk acceleration — pull away smoothly and take appreciable time to accelerate to normal cruising speed, an effect which is often difficult to reproduce in miniature using a conventional controller.

The reason for this lies in the characteristics of model locomotives and of conventional controllers. A stationary train — even if it consists only of a 'light' locomotive — has considerable inertia. To overcome this and set the train rolling demands considerable power and therefore a high current. This is why the train will not begin to move until the speed control is well advanced. As soon as the inertia has been overcome, and the train has begun to roll, rather less power is needed to keep it moving.

So unless the speed control is turned down as soon as the train begins to move —
and there is no practicable way of knowing exactly when to turn it down and how far
— the train will race away in a thoroughly unprototypical manner.

Model railway manufacturers have attempted to tackle this problem from the motor
end rather than the controller end. Permanent-magnet motors have gentler characteristics
if the armature windings are small relative to the size of the magnets. So either a conventional small magnet is used with an armature having five, or even seven, small
poles or a conventional three-pole armature is completely enclosed between a pair
of massive permanent magnets; the latter is known as a ring-field motor. Even with
these, however, it can be difficult to achieve realistic smooth starts with a conventional
controller.

Transistors provide precise control of electric currents and transistor technology has
made possible great advances in electric motor control. Electronic controllers fall into
two categories. In a *closed-loop* controller the circuit compares the voltage across the
locomotive motor with a control voltage set by the speed control. Any potential deviation in speed arising from a change in voltage across the motor (due to a variety of
reasons) is prevented by the closed-loop controller which automatically introduces compensation, thus holding the speed steady. In a *pulse-width modulation* (PWM) controller, the output consists of pulses of full power and speed is controlled by adjusting
the length of the pulses; for low speeds the pulses are kept brief, while for higher
speeds the pulses are longer and the spaces between them correspondingly shorter.
A PWM controller may incorporate the kind of feedback-loop found in a closed-loop
controller and a closed-loop controller may well, by using an unsmoothed power supply, deliver a pulsed output, which assists in smooth starts.

Four circuits for controllers are given in this section: two closed-loop types and two
PWM. Chapters 3 and 4 describe simple closed-loop controllers ideal as beginner's
projects but capable of giving an excellent performance. Chapter 5 describes a simple
PWM controller and Chapter 6 a more sophisticated design combining PWM and
closed-loop techniques.

Chapter 3

Simple closed-loop controller

In a closed-loop controller the voltage across the motor, ie, that at the output of the controller, is compared with a control voltage set by the speed control. To perform this comparison we need to use a *transistor*.

Transistors

We made the acquaintance of silicon diodes in Chapters 1 and 2. Transistors allow for even more precise control of electric current. Whereas a diode has only two terminals, a transistor has three; they are called the *collector*, the *emitter* and the *base*. The current flowing between the collector and the emitter (called the *collector current*) is controlled by the current flowing between the base and the emitter (called the *base bias*). When there is no base bias, there will be no collector current, except for a negligible leakage current. The base bias is generally much smaller than the collector current which it controls — under ideal conditions the collector current may be as much as 500 times as great as the base current controlling it, but conditions are rarely ideal and 100 is a more typical figure. This figure, the current gain or α, varies widely with conditions, with the transistor type used and even between individual transistors of the same nominal type.

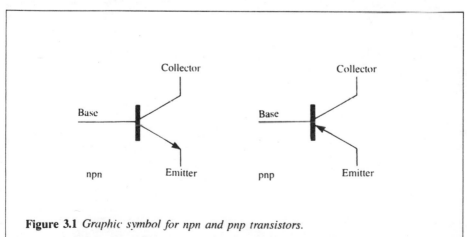

Figure 3.1 *Graphic symbol for npn and pnp transistors.*

The transistors for our project are an npn general-purpose type, such as a BC 337, and an npn power type. In an npn transistor both the collector and the base need to be kept positive relative to the emitter. (There are also, however, pnp transistors whose collector and base must be negative relative to the emitter.) Figure 3.1 shows the circuit diagram symbols for npn and pnp transistors. Note that the emitter is distinguished from the collector by an arrow and that the direction of the arrow indicates whether the transistor is an npn or pnp type. The arrow (like the arrow in the diode symbol, forward bias assumed) points towards the negative terminal of the power supply or battery.

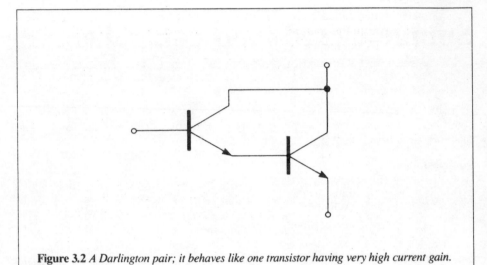

Figure 3.2 *A Darlington pair; it behaves like one transistor having very high current gain.*

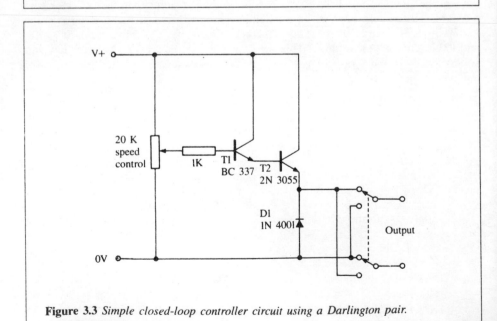

Figure 3.3 *Simple closed-loop controller circuit using a Darlington pair.*

We have seen that the collector current of a transistor is controlled by the generally much smaller base bias, both currents emerging on the emitter. If this combined current is used as the base bias for a second transistor, the resulting pair of transistors will give a very high current gain. Known as a *Darlington pair*, this circuit and its variants are widely used in electronics; the basic circuit is shown in Figure 3.2. A simple but effective closed-loop controller can be made using a Darlington pair whose input is derived from a *potentiometer* across the supply and whose output is taken from the emitter of T2. Figure 3.3 shows the practical circuit for this controller.

Potentiometers

Potentiometers (often called 'pots') are among the most familiar of electronic components, since they form the volume, tone, brightness and contrast controls in domestic audio, radio and TV equipment. A potentiometer consists of a circular (or sometimes straight) carbon track having a specified resistance. It has three terminals; one at each end of the track and a third making electrical contact with a slider which can be moved by means of the control knob to contact any point along the length of the carbon track. Figure 3.4 shows the construction and external appearance of a typical rotary potentiometer.

Its circuit diagram symbol and mode of operation is shown in Figure 3.5. As the symbol suggests, it may be thought of as a resistor with an adjustable tapping. In the circuit of Figure 3.5, when the slider is at the top of the track, the output voltage will equal the input voltage. When the slider is at the bottom of the track, the output voltage will be zero, ie, equal to the 'ground' or 'earth' side of the circuit, to which it is now short-circuited. When the slider is at an intermediate position between the ends of the track, an intermediate output voltage will be obtained; any output voltage between zero and the input voltage can be obtained by moving the slider to the appropriate point.

Potentiometers are available with track resistances ranging from 1 K to 1 M and following linear (resistance proportional to distance on track) or logarithmic (resistance proportional to logarithm of distance on track) laws. They resemble rheostats but are in generally higher resistance ranges and are cheaper and more compact, providing a second advantage of electronic controllers over rheostat types.

How the controller works

The circuit as shown in Figure 3.3 must be connected to a suitable power supply, which we will consider in more detail later on. The potentiometer P1 is, of course, the speed control and is used as a source of base bias (via the current-limiting resistor R1) for the Darlington pair T1/T2. In an npn transistor the base voltage must be positive relative to the emitter if conduction is to occur. This is because the transistor contains (between its base and emitter terminals) a pn junction resembling that in a diode; in an npn transistor the base behaves as the anode. While this junction is forward biased, base bias will flow stimulating collector current, but if the base/emitter junction is reverse biased, base bias is blocked and so collector current will also stop.

Now apply this to the circuit of our controller. As long as the voltage on the base of T1 is heathily positive relative to the voltage on the emitter of T2, which is the voltage across our locomotive motor, the transistors will conduct and supply current to the track. However, if the voltage across the motor rises, eg, if the motor begins racing and develops extra back EMF, so that the voltage on the emitter of T2 approaches that on the base of T1, the current being delivered to the track will be reduced and may even be cut off altogether, slowing the train and compensating for the burst of speed.

The controller is therefore what electronics buffs would call a 'voltage follower'.

The output voltage follows the input voltage, ie, that set by the potentiometer. In practice it is generally about 1.4 V lower; there is a loss of about 0.7 V across a forward-biased silicon junction. We shall meet this 'diode drop' again and again. By adjusting the speed control any output voltage between zero and the supply voltage (less 1.4 V) can be obtained and the motor is free to draw as much current as it likes at any voltage — provided certain limits (such as automatic cut-out thresholds) are not exceeded.

Diode D1 protects the circuit from the effects of 'inductive overshoot'. This is a pulse of power generated by a motor just after its external power supply is turned off. When a motor forms the emitter load of a transistor, inductive overshoot can bias the transistor forward even when the speed control is at zero; this has sometimes caused acute embarassment to experimenters who suddenly find that for some seemingly unaccountable reason they cannot stop their trains! The diode, which under normal circumstances is reverse biased and therefore has no effect on the circuit, harmlessly short-circuits

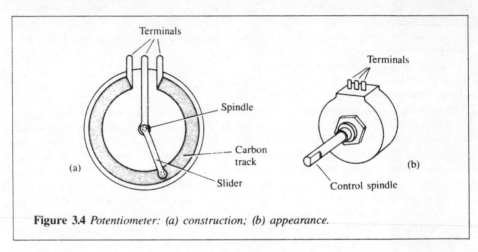

Figure 3.4 *Potentiometer: (a) construction; (b) appearance.*

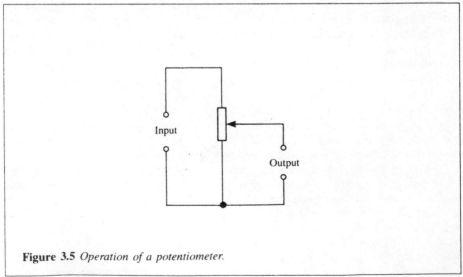

Figure 3.5 *Operation of a potentiometer.*

inductive overshoot so that it cannot interfere with the operation of the transistors.

Circuits like this one are used in some practical controllers and will in general give better results than conventional types. But there are a number of disadvantages. One that we have already noted is that the maximum output voltage is 1.4 V less than the supply voltage. Another disadvantage is that the 'controllability' at low speeds, eg, on starting, is poor. This is because at low speeds the motor back EMF is very small and this circuit is simply not sufficiently sensitive to detect it and make use of it for autoregulation.

Power supply

Beginners to electronics should not construct mains supply units; these can be purchased quite cheaply ready made. With a 12 V to 16 V smoothed supply there will be ample power, but poor control at low speeds for the reason given above. Better low-speed control will be obtained if an unsmoothed supply is used, but a higher voltage (16 V to 20 V) will be needed for full power.

A controller (or its power supply) *must* incorporate some kind of overload cut-out mechanism to protect its own circuitry, also the transformer and the locomotive from damage by overheating in the event of a short circuit or jammed mechanism. This could be a thermal device incorporated in the power supply unit or an electronic circuit — a suitable electronic circuit is described in Part 3.

The transistors used

The average model locomotive at medium speed and moderate load draws about 250 mA, but a worn-out loco may draw as much as 1 A; two of these double-heading a train will obviously draw 2 A, the threshold of many overload cut-out systems. The *output transistor* (T2) in our controller must therefore be a type that is capable of delivering 2 A without burning out. Since a safety margin is always sensible the ideal device for this job is the 2N3055 or its plastic derivatives (eg TIP 3055); this is the 'industry standard' high-power npn transistor, well known to students of hi-fi amplifiers; rated for 15 A, it is sufficiently robust to withstand rough treatment, both electrical and physical. It should be mounted on a heat sink, ie, a block of finned metal to conduct away excess heat. *In closed-loop controllers the output transistors tend to run hot.*

The *driver transistor*, ie, the pre-output stage (T1) also needs to be carefully selected, as its collector current may on occasion exceed 100 mA. In this position use a type rated for 1 A; the BC337 would be a suitable choice.

Components used

Maplin order codes are as follows: BC337 QB68Y, 2N3055 YH98G, TIP3055 QH56L.

Chapter 4

High-performance closed-loop controller

This controller, which uses only six components (excluding those in the power supply), originated by accident when I was adapting a sophisticated cassette-recorder motor control for model railway use. This circuit used the 723 voltage regulator IC with a power Darlington as its output stage. It worked quite well for a while and then failed. Investigation showed that the 723 IC had 'burned out' although used well

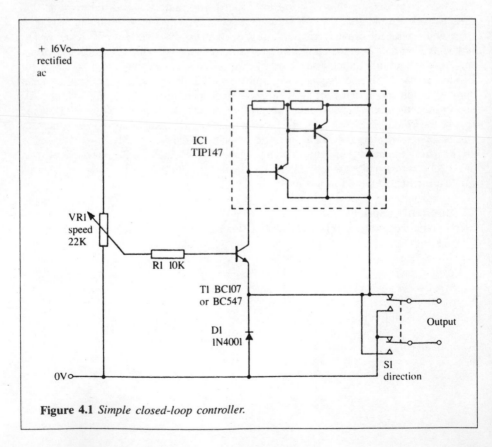

Figure 4.1 *Simple closed-loop controller.*

within its limits. To test the Darlington for damage I connected its base direct to the speed control potentiometer. The resulting simple controller performed even better than that using 723! A few refinements, such as T1, led to the circuit shown in Figure 4.1.

Transistor Tl is used as a comparator — it compares the output voltage (on its emitter) with the control voltage (on its base). Under normal conditions resistor R1 is unnecessary, but is included to protect T1's base/emitter junction against burn-out if the controller output should be short-circuited while the speed control is at maximum. The value of R1, like that of VR1, is uncritical. The nature of the feedback-loop ensures that the base/emitter junction of T1 is normally nearly reverse biased; consequently, the input resistance on the base of T1 is very high. This makes this controller ideal for use with voltage-control systems such as those in Chapters 8 to 10 of this book.

The diode D1 protects the base/emitter junction of Tl against inductive overshoot. Its omission would make it difficult to stop certain types of locomotive.

IC1 resembles an ordinary power transistor both in appearance and function but it is, strictly speaking, an integrated circuit incorporating in one 'chip' of silicon two pnp transistors in Darlington configuration, two bypass ('pull-up') resistors to ensure that the Darlington turns fully off when unbiased and a diode which provides additional protection from inductive effects. The overall current gain of the TIP147 is of the order of 3000. If you cannot obtain (or afford) a TIP147, you could use two discrete transistors instead, eg a BC557 followed by a TIP 2955. Connect a 1K resistor between base and emitter of the first and a 100 R between base and emitter of the second.

Power supply

You should use a full-wave rectified AC supply giving an indicated 16 V DC. The outputs obtained from many commercial power supplies are ideal. Lower voltages or half-wave rectified AC will give reduced power. If a *smoothed* supply is used, much of the controllability at low speeds will be lost and gentle starts may be impossible. The power supply must incorporate some form of overload cut-out rated at 1A to 2 A or, alternatively, fit an electronic cut-out such as that described in Chapter 7.

IC1, or T3 if a discrete transistor is used in the output stage, *must* be mounted on a substantial heat sink for, as in all closed-loop controllers, the output transistor is required to dissipate substantial power in the form of heat.

Performance

The combination of T1 and IC1 gives this circuit a current gain theoretically approaching 1,000,000. Consequently the speed regulation is excellent, extraordinarily so for a closed-loop controller. It produces better, smoother starts than many PWM controllers and, moreover, it does so with a silence that is eerie; the feedback system even senses lateral movement of the motor's armature and counteracts it so that locomotives which normally clatter now run silently. As a Hornby pannier tank coasts to a halt, the only sound is the drum of its wheels on the rails which is most satisfying! It is this, perhaps, as much as its low speed performance and absolute simplicity that has impressed many who have seen this controller in use.

Components

The TIP147 is available from Maplin (cat UJ31J). An alternative is the TIP127 (WQ74R). The TIP2955 pnp power transistor's catalogue number is QH55K.

Chapter 5

Unusual pulse width modulation controller

This controller is based on a design described in *Model Railway Electronics*, No 1, February 1984. It combines simplicity with a refreshingly different approach to pulse width modulation (PWM).

The principal advantage of PWM is the ease of control, particularly at low speeds and when starting. The motor receives brief pulses of full power and, because it is *full* power, there is sufficient torque to overcome friction and inertia and to get the train rolling. But because the pulse soon ends, the motor does not get the chance to go racing off as soon as it has overcome the forces that try to hold it back. A further advantage is that the output transistor, being used as a switch only, dissipates no power and therefore needs no heat sinkage.

However, PWM has two principal disadvantages. One is motor heating in most PWM systems, a considerable proportion of the controller output is dissipated as heat in the motor windings, especially at low speeds. Even if the windings do not melt and go open circuit, the heat has a demagnetizing effect. The second disadvantage is noise. The steep rise and fall of the power waveform causes the armature to rattle, so that the locos buzz angrily. With diesel-outline locos the sound can be remarkably realistic, but with steam- or electric-outline locos, it is disconcerting.

This new circuit eliminates the motor heating tendency by achieving a gentle rise in the output waveform but the cut-off is sharp, so the noise problem remains, although it is not so raucous as some PWM controllers.

At the heart of this controller is the inexpensive 555 timer 1C, which we shall meet again and again in this book. This device, which contains 21 transistors besides numerous resistors and diodes in a tiny package, is described in detail in Appendix 14. Also in this circuit we find the first application in this book of a *capacitor*.

Capacitors

A *capacitor*, as its name suggests, has an electrical *capacity* — it can store electricity. The earliest capacitors consisted of two metal plates separated by an insulator, which was often an air gap. This construction is suggested by the diagrammatic symbol shown in Figure 5.1a. If the two plates are connected to the terminals of a battery, current will flow while an electrostatic charge builds up between the plates. But as the charge builds up the current falls and, after a certain time, when the capacitor is fully charged, the current stops altogether. The capacitor may now be disconnected from the battery and yet retain its charge. It may be connected to a suitable circuit, when it will *dis-*

charge — the same electricity that charged it up now leaves the capacitor as a discharge current. This current gradually diminishes until the capacitor is fully discharged.

The unit of electrical capacitance is the Farad (F), but the Farad itself is a massive unit not normally encountered in electronics. In model railway electronics most of the capacitors have capacitances in microfarads (μF); (1,000,000 μF = 1 F). Many high-value capacitors are formed by a chemical process and are known as *electrolytic capacitors*. Unlike most other sorts of capacitor these are *polarized*, ie, the terminals are labelled positive and negative and for correct operation the component must be connected the right way round; the terminal labelled positive must be kept positive (or neutral) relative to the other terminal. Polarized capacitors are distinguished in circuit diagrams by the symbol shown in Figure 5.1b; the 'hollow' side is always positive.

Another feature to watch for in capacitors is the maximum working voltage. This is given on the side of the device and must not be exceeded or damage may result.

How the controller works

The 555 can be used as a timer in two ways. It can be set up as a free-running multi-

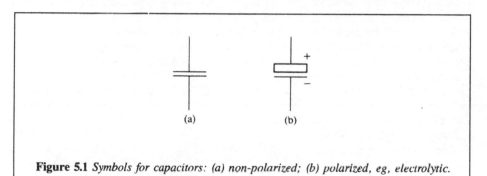

Figure 5.1 *Symbols for capacitors: (a) non-polarized; (b) polarized, eg, electrolytic.*

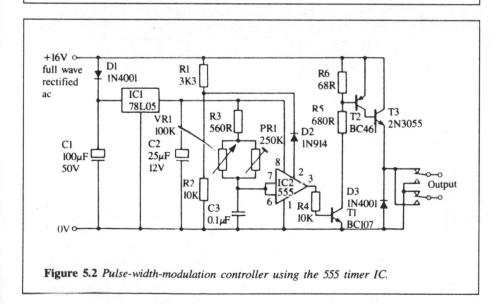

Figure 5.2 *Pulse-width-modulation controller using the 555 timer IC.*

vibrator, ie delivering a continuous stream of pulses, as in Chapter 22 of this book. It can also be used as an interval timer ('one-shot') which is how it is used in this Chapter (see Figure 5.2).

When used as a one-shot, the 555 operates a cycle as follows. In its quiescent state, the output of the device (pin 3) is held *low*, ie, close to the potential of the supply negative terminal. During this period the timing capacitor is held discharged by a conductive transistor in the 555 whose open collector is connected to pin 7. The one-shot starts its timing cycle when a negative-going pulse (ie a pulse at a voltage less than one third of the 555's supply) is applied to pin 2. Once triggered, the 555's output goes *high* (ie approaching its supply voltage) and the short circuit is removed from the timing capacitor, which begins to charge via the timing resistor network. When the charge on the capacitor reaches two-thirds of the 555's supply voltage the device trips, the output goes low, the short circuit is applied to the timing capacitor to discharge it and the device returns to its quiescent state until another trigger pulse is applied to pin 2. The 555 can control timed period from microseconds to hours depending on the values of the components in the timing circuit.

The 555 requires a smooth power supply between 4.5 V and 18 V. In Figure 5.2 IC1 (a 78L05) is used to provide a regulated supply at 5 V, but the 78L 12 IC could be used instead to provide a stabilized supply at 12 V. This variation of the operating voltage will not greatly affect the performance of the 555.

In this circuit the incoming waveform of the full-wave rectified AC supply is used to provide triggering pulses for the 555. (It is assumed that your mains supply is at 50 Hz. If it is at 60 Hz a slight adjustment will be needed.) If you operate the circuit

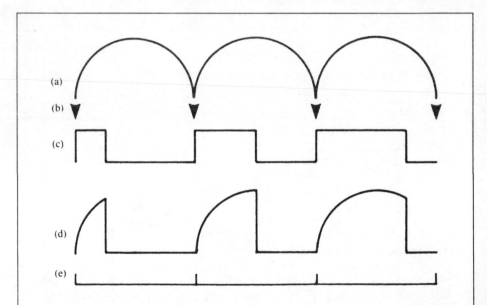

Figure 5.3 *How the PWM controller's unique waveform is derived: (a) the incoming full-wave rectified AC waveform; (b) trigger pulses applied to pin 2 of the 555 at the nulls; (c) output of the 555 at 25, 50 and 75 per cent duty cycle respectively, representing unprototypically abrupt acceleration! (d) controller output, effectively the product of (a) and (c); (e) time scale, each division representing 10 ms (50 Hz mains assumed).*

from a half-wave rectified AC supply considerable complications will ensue.

Diode D2 provides for the 555 to be triggered whenever the power supply voltage dips below about 1.3 V. Owing to the shape of this waveform, this means virtually at the nulls which, with a 50 Hz supply, come at 10 ms (millisecond) intervals. (See Figure 5.3.)

The 555's timing network is so designed that the interval timed is adjustable roughly over the range 0.2 ms to 10 ms. At the lowest settings of the speed control, therefore, the pulses will be about 0.2 ms long but, as the speed control is advanced, the pulses will become longer until at 10 ms they merge into each other, since as one pulse ends the next will begin immediately. The 555's output is fed to the array of transistors T2/T3/T4. These, it will be noticed, are supplied from the unsmoothed, rectified AC supply and there is a good reason for this. The output stage *could* be operated from a smoothed supply, whereupon the controller would deliver a square-wave PWM output, with all the usual motor heating perils. But by operating it from the raw unsmoothed supply with the pulses beginning at the nulls as the 555 is triggered, our controller gives a sinusoidal rise with a sharp cut-off at the end of the pulse. (This output wave form is the opposite of that obtained from controllers using thyristors; these become conductive at a stage during the cycle determined by the speed control and remain conductive until the null, when they are reset.) It is the sinusoidal rise of the output waveform that is responsible for the elimination of motor heating effects; at low speeds the motor is not subjected to the full supply voltage, as it is in square-wave PWM systems.

Resistor R3 is essential for, in conjunction with C3, it sets the minimum pulse duration. If it were zero, the minimum pulse duration would be infinitesimal since C3 would charge instantaneously, but then the transistor on the 555, whose duty it is to hold the timing capacitor discharged between cycles, would find itself connected straight across the 555's supply when the speed control is at zero. Not only would it short the 555 out, but also it would risk burn-out. So, a compromise is necessary. R3 protects the transistor but saddles one with a minimum pulse length which causes a complication in the output stage which, in turn, is resolved by the introduction of R6. The 555 is triggered whenever the power supply output, approaching the null, drops to about 1.3 V. With the speed control at a minimum the 555's output will be a pulse about 0.2 ms long, which is delivered to the output stage which therefore becomes — or attempts to become — conductive. Inevitably, there is *some* supply voltage available at this time that is duly delivered to the motor which sets it buzzing and may even be sufficient to turn it. The potential divider R5/R6, however, ensures that at these low power supply voltages the T3 receives insufficient base bias to bring it into conduction. Consequently, when the speed control is at maximum, the motor is not only stationary, but silent.

Setting the controller up

Set pre-set potentiometer PR1 to maximum resistance and VR 1 to minimum resistance (minimum speed). With a volt meter (25 V range), motor or lamp across the output terminals of the controller, switch the controller on and advance VR1 to maximum and back a few times, watching what happens to the output. You should find that the maximum output is delivered when VR1 is roughly at its mid point. Maximum output occurs when the one-shot's time interval equals the mains half cycle. Above this setting the output falls. Now set VR1 to maximum and back off PR1 until maximum output is obtained. You should now find that VR1 gives smooth control from minimum to maximum speed. PR1 should not need any further adjustment unless you move to a district having a different mains frequency.

Power supply requirements

As mentioned earlier, this controller circuit needs a full-wave rectified AC supply, which should be 12 V to 16 V nominal. If a half-wave rectified AC supply is used considerable modification to the timing components will be needed and a higher voltage will be needed for full speed.

The 555 must have a smoothed supply between 5 V and 18 V. The function of D1/C1/IC1 in Figure 5.2 is to provide a supply for the 555 stabilized at 5 V. Without IC1 the 555 would be subjected to a supply at about 23 V which might damage it. Needless to say, the power supply must be fitted with a current limiter or overload cut-out.

Options

This circuit is ideally suited to a number of optional extras, including use with a speedometer (Chapter 11). Figure 5.4 shows a simple modification to the timing circuit to turn the speed control into a 'straight' voltage control potentiometer. Consequent upon this modification the accessories described in Chapters 9 and 10 may be added to this controller.

Components

Maplin catalogue numbers are as follows: 555 QH66W, 78L05 QL26D, 7842 WQ77J, BC461 QB72P, 2N3055 YH98G.

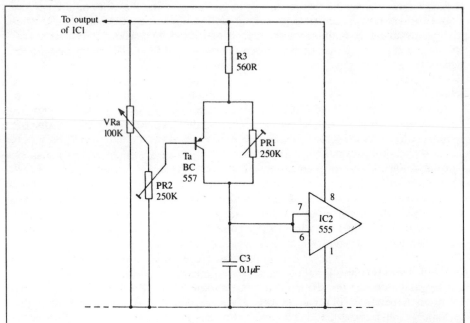

Figure 5.4 *Modifications to the circuit of Figure 5.2 to make the speed control a 'straight' voltage-control potentiometer. With the sliders of the VRa and PR2 both set to maximum (ie, away from supply negative) set PR1 for maximum speed. Then with the slider of VRa at minimum, adjust PR2 until the train just stops. VRa should now give smooth control from minimum to maximum. Consequent upon this conversion the accessories described in Chapters 7 to 11 can be added to this controller.*

Chapter 6

Sophisticated PWM controller

The electronic controllers described in the previous three chapters offer the benefits of comparative simplicity and a performance far exceeding that possible from conventional rheostat controllers. For many modellers they will be perfectly adequate. But they are not the ultimate!

Although they give gentle starts and fine control of speed, speed is still not absolutely *constant*; on uphill gradients and tight curves trains will still slow down and on downhills they will accelerate. It is theoretically possible to keep train speeds absolutely constant (within limits) despite gradients and curves, and that is what the controller described in this chapter does. It is complex and is not recommended for beginners!

Theory

Model train motors slow down on uphills and tight curves primarily as a function of their inherent electrical *resistance*. As the loco enters the upgrade it has insufficient torque to take the increased load so it slows; its 'back EMF' opposing the supply voltage from the controller falls and so it draws more current. The extra current passing through its resistance raises the potential difference (known as the IR) which is effectively in series with the motor and starves it of power.

What is needed is a means of sensing the fall in motor speed and effectively advancing the speed control a little to make up the loss. There are two ways of doing this and this controller takes the easier of the two.* Every motor also acts as a generator and, as it turns, generates a voltage (often called misleadingly the 'back EMF') which is proportional to speed and which opposes the supply voltage. On a PWM controller (or a closed-loop controller being run from an unsmoothed power supply) it is easy to arrange to monitor the voltage across the motor *between* power pulses. Since the controller output stage is off, whatever voltage is present must come from the motor itself and so must be back EMF. Since this is proportional to motor speed rather than controller output, it can be used in a feedback loop (servo) to give very tight control of motor speed. It can also be used in a speedometer circuit.

---

* The other method, widely used in industrial motor control systems, is direct IR compensation. The current drawn by the motor is monitored and multiplied by a constant representing the motor resistance to give a voltage that is added to the control voltage to compensate for the lost IR. The method has been used in model railway controllers but is fraught with difficulties.

Circuit description

The controller, which has been described in *Model Railway Electronics* and *Electronics Today*, employs both PWM and closed-loop techniques simultaneously. For this reason it has been called a PWAM (Pulse Width and Amplitude Modulation) controller and was designated The 'P WAyMan'. Its output is square-wave PWM but the pulse amplitude (height) is under direct closed-loop control from the speed control potentiometer. The pulse width is controlled by a servo which compares the speed control setting with the motor back EMF.

The circuit diagram is given in Figure 6.1. (For simplicity the reversing switch has been omitted). Although it looks complex, when considered section by section it is remarkably simple. For instance, the output stage around T3 and IC3 is almost the same as the closed-loop controller considered in Chapter 4 and the pulse generator circuit around IC2 is similar to that in the PWM controller in the last chapter. The only new parts are the sample-and-hold circuit for detecting the back EMF (T5-T7) and the comparator circuit around the operational amplifier IC4.

Operational amplifiers

Operational amplifiers (or 'op amps') are integrated circuits very widely used in electronics. Their essential features (besides positive and negative supply terminals) are two inputs and an output terminal. The two inputs are called the *inverting input* (distinguished in circuit diagrams by a negative sign) and, rather clumsily, the *non-inverting input* (distinguished by a positive sign). (Note that the polarity of the symbols on the circuit diagram has nothing to do with the polarity of the voltage or current on these inputs — it is just a 'shorthand' way of saying that the non-inverting input must be taken positive to make the output more positive and the inverting input must be taken more negative to make the output more positive.) The graphical symbol for an op amp and the pin-outs of the 741 and 748 ICs are shown in Figure 6.2.

These two terminals provide what is known as *differential input*, that is to say, the amplifier responds to the *difference* between the potentials on the two inputs. If you interfere with the inputs, doing the same to *both* inputs, the amplifier ignores it, a

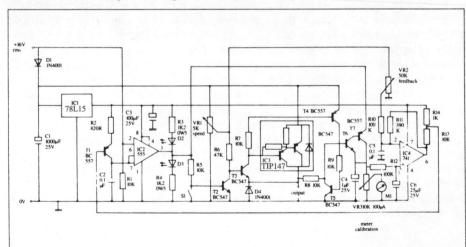

Figure 6.1 *Circuit of the 'P WayMan' controller; for simplicity the reversing switch is omitted.*

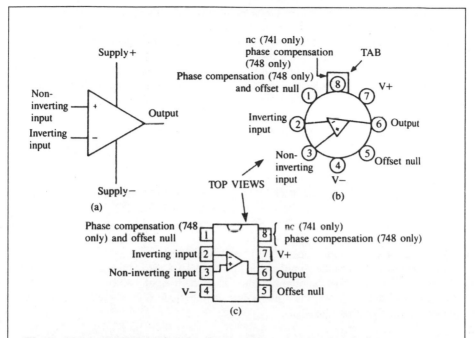

Figure 6.2 (a) Graphic symbol for an operational amplifier; (b) and (c) pin outs of the popular 741 and 748 op lamp ICs (top views); (b) gives the TO5 metal can version and (c) the 8-pin dual-in-line package.

phenomenon known as *common-mode rejection*, which makes op amps very useful in electrically noisy environments (eg adjacent to working model railways!) where such interference can cause problems. Instead, to make the output more positive, either the non-inverting input must be made more positive relative to the inverting input or the inverting input must be made more negative relative to the non-inverting input (which is another way of saying the same thing). The input resistance of op amps is very high (a few megohms) and so for practical purposes may be regarded as infinite. The voltage gain is also very high. That for the archetypal op amp, the 741, which we shall be using, is quoted as typically 200,000. Thus, a differential change of only 0.1 mV on the inputs would swing the output by an incredible 20 V! This is why *op amps are never used without feedback*.

Pulse width modulation system

The PWM technique is adapted from that used in the controller described in Chapter 5. The 555 timer IC is again used as an interval timer adjustable between nil and 10 ms and triggered automatically at 10 ms intervals (assuming a 50 Hz mains supply and full-wave rectification) by the nulls in the supply waveform. The 555 does not seem to mind having its trigger input taken to 23 V or so at the peaks.

Unlike the controller in Chapter 5, however, the 'on' period of the timer determines the length of the *spaces*, ie, the intervals between the pulses, rather than the length of the pulses themselves. When the timer is on, its output drives T2 which clamps to ground the input of the closed-loop controller. Since the output of the 555 is always high during the trigger pulses, it follows that even with the timed period set to minimum, the controller output will be subjected to brief (actually about 1.5 ms) interruptions at 10 ms intervals. This is useful since it ensures that there will always be spaces in the output during which back EMF can be sampled. (It also makes the controller compatible with live-rail track circuits — see Chapter 14.)

Length of the timed period is determined by the network R2/T1/C2 and in normal use is controlled automatically by feedback from the output of op amp IC4. R2 also protects the internal circuitry of the 555 against burnout.

Back EMF monitor and speedometer

The back EMF is monitored by the circuitry around T4-T7. T4 and T5 clamp to ground (via R8) the voltage across the motor during power pulses. Consequently T6 and T7 permit C4 to charge only during the spaces when the voltage present must be back EMF (D4 shorts away inductive kickback). The *quasi*-Darlington configuration of T6 and T7 minimizes offset loss and presents a very high input resistance.

C4 and VR3 (VR3 may be a fixed 10K resistor if the meter is omitted) are critical and must give a time constant (see Appendix 9) of 10 ms; shorter time constants give inadequate sampling; longer ones give spurious readings.

You may wonder why the complication of T4 and T5 was used when apparently all that is needed is a diode from the output of the 555 to the base of T6. The answer is that this was tried and did not work; the voltage drop on the diode was so great that T6 was not turned off and the strobing failed.

Comparator

The comparator consists of the circuitry around IC4, the 741 operational amplifier (op amp) which is set up as an inverting amplifier (from the control voltage viewpoint) having a gain of 4.9. This compares the motor back EMF (on VR3) with the voltage on the slider of the speed control potentiometer attenuated by another potentiometer VR2. This controls the feedback by varying the proportion of the control voltage that the op amp 'sees'.

As the motor back EMF rises relative to the control voltage (ie an unwanted acceleration) so does the 741's output voltage. This is fed via potential divider R13/R14 to T1, biasing it back and increasing the 555's timed period. The timed period, remember, represents the length of the *spaces* so that the motor is now starved of current, reducing its speed.

The ratio of R12 to C6 is important, although largely a matter of taste. In the prototype these ended up as 100K and 25µF giving a time constant of 2.5 s. Too brief a time constant causes the servo to effectively counteract the PWM that it is intended to control.

Setting Up

The two LEDs D2/D3 are useful here. They flash alternately at 100 Hz, so fast that they appear to be on together. If they are a well-matched pair, equal brightness will signify 50 per cent duty cycle. If D2 is brighter, the duty cycle is greater than 50 per cent, ie the power pulses are longer. These LEDs provide a useful visible indication of the controller's speed regulatory action.

With a train cruising at moderate speed adjust feedback control VRZ until the two LEDs appear equal in brightness (or the indicated voltage on pin 3 of the 555 is 7.5 V). You should now find that the duty cycle rises if the train climbs a gradient or negotiates tight curves or if you impede its progress with an unprototypical finger or if you advance the speed control suddenly. Similarly downhill gradients will reduce the duty cycle as will turning down the speed control.

The maximum duty cycle available from the controller is 85 per cent: when on maximum there is no 'headroom' for further upward speed compensation.

With a high value for C6 as on the prototype the speed compensating action is slightly delayed, which makes it all the more visible. As the train enters a down gradient it speeds up appreciably for a couple of seconds and then on go the brakes bringing it back to the set speed. Giving a train a helping pull on its way was followed by a slowdown or even a total stop, followed by a gradual resumption of the original speed.

The speedometer Ml is optional, but very useful. VR3 allows for it to be calibrated — it may need different settings for different locos but in my experience it has needed very little readjustment. A 100µA meter can be assumed to read 0-100 scale miles/hour. With a train running at an estimated scale 30 miles/hour adjust VR3 until the meter reads 30. You should now find that the readings are proportional to train speed. Stalling the loco (caution!) should bring the reading to zero. Lifting the loco off the track should also bring the reading to zero, but if you have track circuiting the track circuit voltage may interfere and cause a spurious reading (as long as the loco is on the track, it shorts out the track circuit voltage and the speedometer will read true).

Performance

The controller has been rigorously tested with a wide variety of loco types, old and new. Performance was generally excellent with the speedometer needing remarkably little adjustment between loco types. Speed compensation was excellent and there was no evidence of motor heating or motor noise because at low speed settings the pulse amplitude is also low.

Maximum speed is a little lower than on some controller types, being effectively 22 V at 50 per cent duty cycle, equal to 11 V. This was not noticeable in practice.

Optional switch S1, when closed, shorts out the bias to T2 disabling the PWM system so that the controller functions as a pure dc closed-loop type. This allows higher top speeds, but the speedometer and speed compensation systems do not operate.

Constructional notes

The output transistor (or Darlington) *must* be on a heat sink. Although this is a PWM controller, it is also a closed-loop type and the output device is required to dissipate power.

The power supply must be a proprietary type delivering 16 V ac into a full-wave bridge rectifier.

Speed is controlled by the voltage on the slider of VR1. The circuit is suitable for use with inertia systems and automatic control systems such as those described in Chapters 7 to 10.

Components

Maplin catalogue numbers are as follows: 78L15 QL27E, 555 QH66W, BC547 QQ14Q, TIP147 UJ31J, BC557 QQ165, 741 AV39N, 100µA panel meter RW92A.

Part 3: Accessories for controllers

Preamble

This section of the book describes accessory units that may be added to electronic controllers individually or in any combination. These are an overload cut-out, an inertia simulator, a bidirectional converter, which makes one-knob control of both speed and direction possible, an 'autostop' unit that can be used manually or electronically to provide automatic gentle stops and starts and, lastly, a speedometer. None of these units affect the *performance* of the controller to which it is connected in any way but each makes operation of the controller more interesting and challenges the model train operator to perfect the same skills that are demanded of the driver of the prototype!

Chapter 7

Overload cut-out

Every controller needs some form of overload cut-out to turn the circuit off if excessive current flows through it. Without such a cut-out a short circuit could burn out the output transistors, rectifiers or even the transformer. Many transformer units are fitted with integral thermal overload cut-outs (circuit breakers), which give adequate protection. The simple electronic circuit described in this project also provides suitable protection and will be useful to constructors not having a thermal device or wishing to build an all-electronic controller. The circuit shown in Figure 7.1 is for single-polarity controllers, such as those described in Chapters 3 to 6.

How it works
The current taken by the output stage passes through resistor R1, whose value should

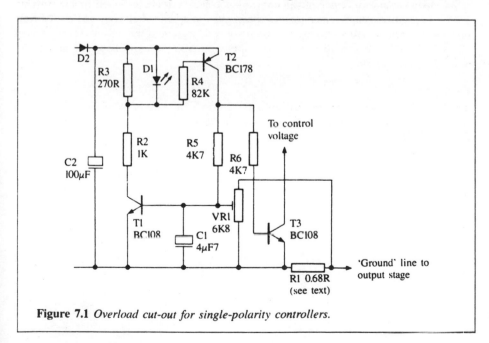

Figure 7.1 *Overload cut-out for single-polarity controllers.*

be chosen according to the following formula:

$$Rl = \frac{0.68}{I} R$$

where I is the current in Amps at which the circuit is to operate; for 1 A — a suitable trip point for most operators — Rl must be 0.68R. If you cannot find one, use three 2.2R resistors (making 0.74R) or four 2.7R (making 0.675R) resistors in parallel. In an overload, the voltage across Rl rises to 0.68 V, bringing T1 into conduction. Preset potentiometer VR1 (which may be 5 K, 6K8 or 10 K) allows for fine adjustment of the trip point. Capacitor Cl smooths the input voltage, which is essential on PWM controllers and types operating from unsmoothed supplies.

When T1 conducts, LED D1 lights, indicating overload conditions. T1 also provides base current for T2 which conducts, providing via R5 an alternative source of base current for T1. So both transistors will remain conducting even when the original overload conditions have disappeared. T2 also supplies base current via R6 to T3 whose collector is connected to the base of the first transistor in the controller circuit. When T3 conducts it short-circuits the input to the controller, effectively turning it off.

Resetting the cut-out

There are two ways to reset the cut-out (after first removing the short circuit or other cause of overload current). Either switch off the power supply to the controller for a few seconds to allow all voltages in the circuit to return to zero. Or momentarily short-circuit the base and emitter of T1 or T2 by means of a suitable push-button switch. (Such a switch, however, holds a hidden danger. It offers the temptation to hold the button down, disabling the cut-out circuit, on occasions when it is operating frequently, eg, when running-in a sticky loco. This is to invite the very type of mishap that the cut-out is intended to prevent.)

As the removal of its power supply resets the cut-out circuit, it must be operated from a *smoothed* power supply — an unsmoothed power supply is effectively switched off 50 or 100 times per second according to the kind of rectification. If the cut-out is being added to a controller having a smoothed power supply (such as those in Chapters 5 and 6) D2 and C2 may be omitted.

Components

You may use BC547s in place of BC108s and BC557s in place of BC 178s.
Maplin catalogue numbers are as follows: BC108 QB32K, BC178 QB53H, BC547 QQ14Q, BC557 QQ16S.

Chapter 8

Voltage control — 'inertia simulator'

The controllers described in Chapters 3, 4 and 6 (and 5 with the add-on shown in Figure 5.4) all require a single-polarity voltage at their input, ie, on the base of the first transistor. Normally this is provided from the slider of the potentiometer that forms the speed control. A high voltage gives fast running, a low voltage slower running and zero stops the train. This is why we have called this voltage the 'control voltage'.

There are other ways, however, of providing a control voltage which can greatly enhance operator interest. A favourite technique is to use as the control voltage the charge on a high-value capacitor. Separate controls are provided to regulate the rate at which the capacitor charges, the rate at which it discharges and the maximum voltage to which it can be charged. These are called the 'inertia', 'braking' and 'maximum speed' controls respectively. Also needed is a run/slow down function switch, as is an emergency stop switch. These may be separate, or they may be combined as a three-position switch (run/slow down/stop) or they may be combined with the direction control on a five-position switch (run forwards/slow down forwards/stop/slow down reverse/run reverse). Figure 8.1 shows one possible circuit using only a run/slow down and a separate stop switch; it is assumed that a separate direction switch is fitted

How it works
VR1 is the maximum speed control. The complementary pair T1/T2 transfer the voltage on its slider to control voltage capacitor C1 without passing on the internal resistance of VR1. When the capacitor charges, its charge current passes through inertia control VR2; when it discharges, the discharge current passes through brake control VR3 (or through bypass transistor T3 — see later).

Inertia control VR2 regulates the rate at which C1 charges and therefore the acceleration of the train. Set it high (ie, high resistance) for a heavy train, low for a light one. Note that acceleration will also be affected by the setting of VR1.

Brake control VR3 regulates the rate at which the train decelerates when 'slow down' is selected or when the maximum speed control VR1 is turned down. Set it high (nb, low resistance) for rapid deceleration or low for more gradual deceleration. The rate of deceleration will also be affected by the voltage on C1 when 'slow down' is selected. Half an hour's 'play' with the completed circuit will get the operator fully acquainted with the interaction of the controls.

You can now run trains 'semi-automatically' as follows. Select maximum speed, inertia and braking as appropriate. Set switch S1 to 'run'. As capacitor C1 charges, the train

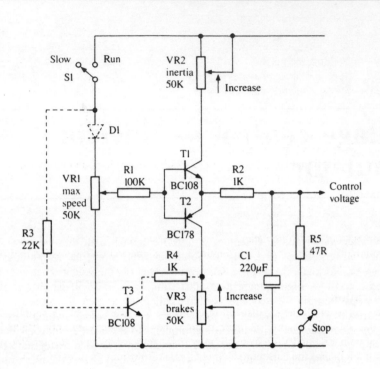

Figure 8.1 *Voltage control system. The components connected by dotted lines are optional (see text).*

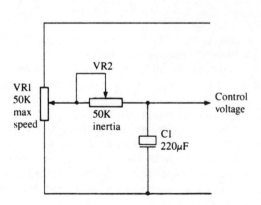

Figure 8.2 *Simplified voltage control system.*

will start and will accelerate at a rate determined by the settings of VR1 and VR2 until it reaches the maximum speed determined by VR1. To slow the train set S1 to 'slow down' and the train will decelerate at a rate determined by VR3 until eventually it stops. With the component values as shown in Figure 8.1, and the inertia and brake controls set to maximum *resistance*, the time taken to reach maximum speed from rest or vice versa is about 11 seconds, a useful time on an average layout. To stop the train instantly at any time operate 'stop' switch S2 which discharges the capacitor. The train will re-start, however, if S1 is in the 'run' mode when S2 is operated.

You can also run trains manually in the normal way. Turn inertia to minimum and brake to maximum and select the 'run' position of switch S1. The maximum speed control will now behave as a normal speed control. The train will stop if the speed control is turned to minimum. If the optional circuit containing D1/R3/T3/R4 is included it is not necessary to turn the brake control to minimum; the brake control will only take effect in the 'slow down' mode.

Cut-outs
The overload cut-out from Chapter 7 can be used with this control circuit without modification. The collector of T3 in Figure 7.1 is connected to the positive end of C1 in Figure 8.1.

Simplifications
If you do not want all the sophistication of Figure 8.1, there are many simpler circuits, such as that shown in Figure 8.2. Acceleration and deceleration are both affected by the settings of both VR1 and VR2. You will now find a noticeable lag in acceleration at lower settings of VR1 since the current to charge C1 must flow through most of the VR1 as well as VR2.

Components
You may use BC547s in place of BC108s and BC557s in place of BC178s.
Maplin catalogue numbers are as follows: BC108 QB32K, BC178 QB53H, BC547 QQ14Q, BC557 QQ16S.

Chapter 9

Bidirectional converter unit

Do you remember those rheostat controllers in which there was a single combined speed and direction control? There was a central 'stop' position; turning the knob to the left controlled speed in one direction and turning it to the right of 'stop' controlled speed in the other direction. It certainly made operation very easy and eliminated the troubles that can be caused by faulty direction-change switches. This type of rheostat controller is still available from some suppliers, as is at least one kind of electronic controller with a similar control arrangement. It is possible, however, to add on a converter unit to many types of conventional electronic controller to give this same kind of 'one-knob' control. Figure 9.1 shows one possible converter circuit.

How it works

Transistors T1/T2/T3/T4 form a bridge circuit. Since resistors R1/R2 have the same value, the voltage on the bases of T2/T4 equals half the supply voltage and the voltage on their emitters is held at about the same voltage. When speed/direction control VR1 is at its mid-point setting, the voltage on its slider is again equal to half the supply voltage. Consequently no bias is applied to any of the bridge transistors, no current flows through bridge resistor R3 and no control voltage appears across R5. Thus the train is stopped. Now, let us move the slider of the speed control towards the positive rail; we shall call this the *forwards* direction. The base voltage applied to T1/T3 rises, bringing T1 and (via R3) T2 into conduction. The conduction path is T1/R3/T2/R4/R5. As the speed control is advanced the current flowing through R5 raises a voltage across it which rises to about one-fifth of the supply voltage when the speed control reaches maximum. If the speed control is now returned through the central 'stop' position and on into the 'reverse' zone, so that the slider is now nearer to the negative rail than to the positive, T3 and T4 are brought into conduction instead of T1/T2. The conduction path is now T6/T5 (base/emitter junctions) T4/R3/T3/R5.

There is a reason for the inclusion of R4 in the collector circuit of T2. The bridge is not symmetrical. If R4 were omitted, the collector of T2 now being connected directly to R5 and the collector of T3, the maximum voltage obtainable across R5 (from which the speed control voltage for the controller itself is derived) would vary according to the direction selected. This is because the voltage applied to the base of T3 can vary over a wide range, whereas that on the base of T2 is held at half the supply voltage. Consequently, when reversing, the voltage on the base of T3 falls as that on its collector rises, the limit being when these are equal at about one-quarter of the supply voltage. When running forwards, however, the base of T2 is held at half the supply voltage and the voltage across R5 (in the absence of R4) could rise almost to this voltage. Resistor R4 'swallows' some of this giving a more even range of control voltages across R5.

So, turning the slider to either extreme raises voltage of constant polarity across R5, from which is derived a control voltage for the controller, but only in the *lower* half of the slider's travel is bias supplied to Darlington pair T5/T6. This has as its collector load the coil of a relay having (at least) double-pole, double-throw (DPDT) contacts which form the direction-change switch contacts. Thus, the train's direction is changed over half of the control range. Diode D1 kills inductive overshoot when the relay coil is de-energized. However, because the maximum voltage obtained across R5 is only about one-fifth (perhaps a little more) of the supply voltage, this must be restored to full range before being fed to the controller. This is the function of *quasi*-Darlington pair T7/T8. Resistors R6/R7 are chosen so that R6 equals four times R7. The output voltage is taken from across both resistors and this arrangement feeds back one-fifth of the output voltage to T7. That is to say, this circuit's output voltage equals five times its input voltage.

Use of this unit

The circuit as described may be used with any electronic controller requiring a positive-going input voltage; including all those described in Chapters 3 to 6 (the project in Chapter 5 will need the optional circuitry of Figure 5.4). It shares the controller's power supply, whether smoothed or unsmoothed. Pre-set resistors PR1 and PR2 should be adjusted so that full speed is just reached at the limits of travel of VR1's slider.

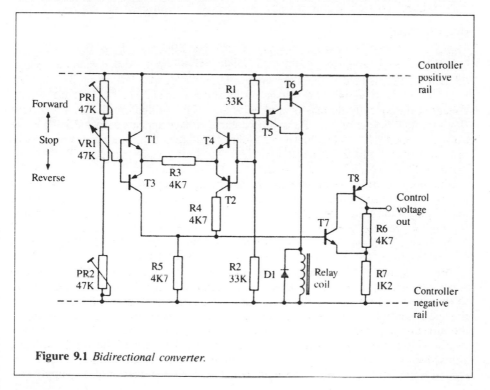

Figure 9.1 *Bidirectional converter.*

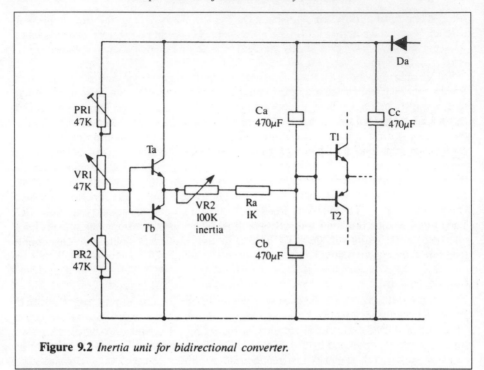

Figure 9.2 *Inertia unit for bidirectional converter.*

Inertia unit

An inertia unit may be added to the bidirectional converter unit. Its circuit is shown in Figure 9.2. With the component values shown, the response time to changes of the speed control setting is variable over the range 0.5 to about 50 seconds. Shunting at high settings of the inertia control is great fun! A rapid flip from, say, moderate forwards to moderate reverse gives a gradual deceleration to a standstill followed by a gradual restart in the opposite direction, which is very realistic to watch. It is also a real test of the 'driver's' skill judging the braking distances. Exactly as on the prototype!

The inertia circuit *must* have a smoothed power supply. If the rest of the controller has an unsmoothed power supply, incorporate D1 and C3 as shown. Otherwise, they may be omitted.

Components

The relay *must* have double-pole changeover contacts rated for 30V minimum; the coil must be suitable for transistor operation. In the Maplin catalogue the unit numbered YX98G is ideal. The bypass diode must be a 1N4001 (QL73Q) or better.

All npn transistors are BC547 (QQ14Q) and all pnp transistors BC557 (QQ16S).

Chapter 10

'Autostop' unit for automatic gentle stops and starts

It is very easy to arrange for trains to stop dead and suddenly restart. All that is necessary is to interrupt the electrical feed to the section of track on which the train is running. Several manufacturers sell what they call 'automatic signal kits' in which the switch that sets the signal to danger also isolates a short stretch of track on the approach and clearing the signal restores the power. So, the train approaching the danger signal stops dead very unprototypically and restarts, with equally unprototypical abruptness, when the signal clears.

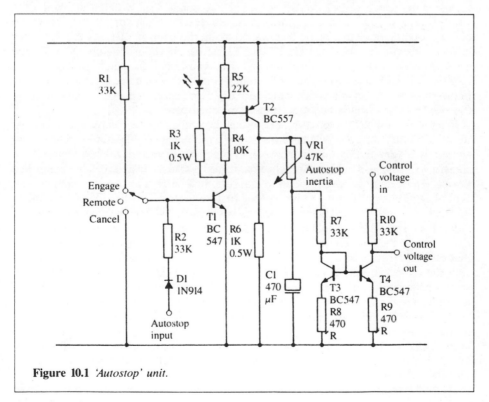

Figure 10.1 *'Autostop' unit.*

The only way to achieve fully-controlled automatic stops and starts is to gradually reduce the control voltage to zero at the input of an electronic controller and then to gradually restore it to its former level. That is the function of the 'autostop' units described in this Chapter. The comprehensive unit whose circuit is given in Figure 10.1 was developed for use in conjunction with the interlock system described in Chapter 26, but has many other possible applications, eg timed station stops (Chapter 27).

An input terminal is provided for remote controlled operation, but the unit can also be operated manually. A three-position switch, which may be a single-pole double-throw switch having a centre 'off' position, controls its functions. When this switch is put in the 'engage' position, the train will gently decelerate and stop. When the switch is put in the central 'remote' position, the train will stop if a positive-going voltage is applied to the remote input terminal; otherwise it will continue to run or, if previously stopped using the 'engage' mode, it will gently restart and accelerate to the speed set by the controller. When the switch is put in the 'cancel' position, the train will run normally or will restart gradually if previously stopped by the unit, even if a positive-going voltage is still being applied to the remote input. The rate of slow-down and acceleration is determined by a special inertia control quite independent of any already fitted to the controller.

How it works

A positive-going voltage on the base of T1 drives it into conduction, lighting the optional 'autostop' indicator LED 1. It also biases T2 into conduction, whereupon nearly the whole of the supply voltage appears across R6. Inertia capacitor C1 now begins to charge, the rate of charge being determined by inertia control VR1. As this capacitor charges, the current being fed via R7 into T3 increases proportionately. Now T3 and T4 form what is called a 'current mirror'. This is a circuit in which the current fed into the collector of one transistor (T3 in this circuit) causes an equal current to flow in the collector circuit of another transistor (T4). For a current mirror to work properly the two transistors must be an accurately matched pair.

In a transistor the collector current is, in fact, controlled by the *voltage* applied across the base/emitter junction but, because a very wide range of collector current is controlled by a very tightly confined sweep of bias voltage (around 0.7 V for a silicon transistor), it is, as a rule, not practical to regard a transistor as a voltage-controlled device. This circuit is the exception to that rule. In a current mirror the input current is applied to both collector and base of the first transistor. This has the effect of making that transistor automatically adjust its base/emitter voltage so that the collector current *just* sinks the available input current, less the negligible base bias current. Now, if we connect the base/emitter junction of a second *identical* transistor in parallel with that of the first transistor, since it receives the same input voltage as the first, it will sink the same collector current. That is to say, output current equals input current. In this application, the second transistor of the current mirror, together with its collector load resistor (R10), forms a potential divider. The control voltage from the controller's speed control or speed/inertia circuit is applied to the 'top' of R10 and the output is taken from the collector of the transistor. The effect of this is that the circuit attenuates (ie reduces) the control voltage by an amount proportional to the charge on C1. So, as C1 charges, the control voltage gradually falls until it is so close to zero that the train stops.

When the positive voltage is removed from the base of T1, this transistor ceases to conduct, as does T2. Capacitor C1 now discharges via VR1 and R6: R6 is negligible compared to most settings of VR1 and so generally has little effect on the delay. As

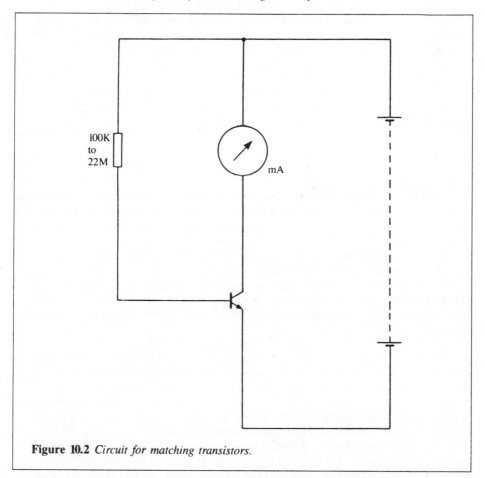

Figure 10.2 *Circuit for matching transistors.*

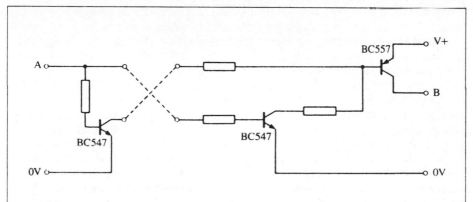

Figure 10.3 *Interface unit for linking two circuits having different 'ground' potentials. A positive-going input at A gives a positive-going output at B despite potential differences between the two 0 V rails. All resistors 33 K.*

C1 discharges, the current flowing into T3 gradually falls and so does the collector current of T4. Consequently, the control voltage applied to the input of the controller gradually rises and the train restarts and accelerates gently away.

Practical considerations

The unit as described is suitable only for controllers needing a positive-going input voltage, eg those in Chapters 3, 4 and 6 in this book and also Chapter 5, if the optional circuitry in Figure 5.4 is fitted.

This unit must have a *smoothed* power supply. If this is not available, add a 1N4001 rectifier diode between the unit's positive rail and the unsmoothed supply's positive terminal and add a 1000 μF 24 V electrolytic capacitor across the unit's supply rails.

You will need to match a pair of transistors for T3 and T4. Test the gains of a selection of individuals of the same type using the circuit shown in Figure 10.2. For various values of bias resistor between 100 K and 22 M choose the two transistors that give the closest values of collector current. The inclusion of R8 and R9 in the emitter circuits of T3 and T4 will compensate for minor mismatching.

The unit, as mentioned earlier, was originally intended for use in conjunction with the active interlock systems described in Chapter 26 of this book. Now, those circuits operate from the same power supply as the track circuit/signalling system, whereas this unit operates from the same power supply as the controller to which it is an appendage. Because of the controller's reversible output the 'ground' rails of the controller

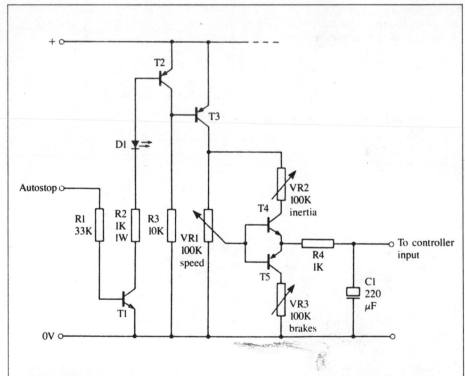

Figure 10.4 *A 'low cost' alternative 'autostop' system using the regular inertia and brake controls.*

and the signalling system may be at different potentials. If the controller has a positive-going output (before the reversing switch) you should find that a single-wire connection from the interlock output to the 'autostop' remote input socket works satisfactorily, but otherwise a relay, an opto-isolator, or the interface unit shown in Figure 10.3, should be used to maintain the potential difference between the two circuits.

A further application for this unit is in computerized control. A logical '1' from a computer output port applied to the remote input will stop the train. With a medium to high setting of the autostop inertia and a high setting of the speed control, a PWM computer output applied to the input can even be used to control speed, as well as stopping and starting.

Alternative 'autostop' unit

The unit described is, in many ways, a 'de-luxe' unit suitable for fitting to almost any controller and which can be used in conjunction with the bidirectional control system described in Chapter 9. Moreover, it has its own inertia or delay control quite independent of any inertia control that may be fitted to the 'main' controller.

Figure 10.4 shows how an 'autostop' facility can be fitted to a traditional inertia/brake voltage control circuit. With this arrangement 'autostop' does not have its own inertia control but shares the 'main' inertia and brake controls and, if these are set low, the 'autostop' will give sudden starts and stops. This unit is, however, fairly simple and inexpensive. In electronics, as in so many areas of life, 'you gets what you pays for'.

Components

All npn transistors BC547 (Maplin QQ14Q); all pnp transistors BC557 (Maplin QQ16S).

Chapter 11

Speedometer

A speedometer on a controller can give a lot of added interest to model railway operation. For instance, speed limits can be assigned to stretches of line and the operator must then use his skill to keep train on schedule but within the speed limits! Adding a current meter in series with the output will not, however, give an indication of speed. Current consumed, for instance, will *rise* when the train climbs a gradient, when its speed is liable to *fall*. Similarly, a voltmeter across the controller output, although it gives a more accurate indication of speed than the current meter, will indicate con-

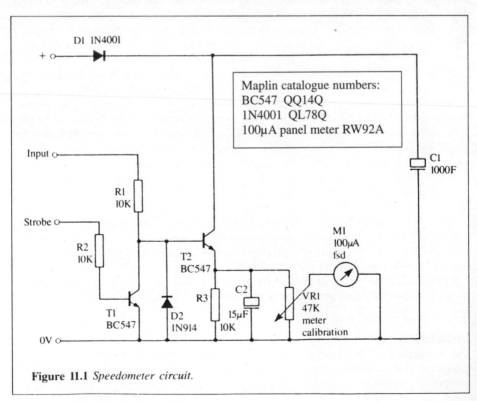

Figure 11.1 *Speedometer circuit.*

Thank You...

...for participating in this interview

You were interviewed today by our Interviewer:

Name: _Marilyn_ **Date:** _31/10_

ABA Research is one of the fastest-growing market research agencies in Britain. Now hugely experienced in retail research we are proud of the long standing relationships we have with some of Britain's biggest retailers.

It is crucially important that the interviewer conducting the survey does not influence your responses in any way. Therefore they must conduct it without altering any of the wording or expressing their own opinion.

How to ensure the best results

ABA Research observes the Code of Practice of the Market Research Society and qualitative recruitment best practice outlined by the Association of Qualitative Research. Copies of both can be found on the websites: **www.mrs.org.uk** and **www.aqr.org.uk**

In providing these services, we will comply with the Data Protection Act 2018. Your personal details are requested so that we can carry out satisfactory checks on interview authenticity. We will only use your information for research purposes. You can see our full privacy policy by visiting https://abaresearch.blob.core.windows.net/content/privacy/aba_privacy_policy.pdf

Like us on   **www.facebook.com/ABAFieldfirst**

Sign up to our panel - **www.sassieshop.com/2aba**

T: **01727 798 375** E: **fieldfirst@abaresearch.co.uk**

ABA Market Research Ltd, Hart House, 6 London Road, St Albans, Herts, AL1 1NG troller output voltage rather than train speed. For example, it will read the controller output voltage even when there is no train on the track.

The only way to obtain a tolerably accurate indication of the train speed is to add a voltmeter circuit across the output of the controllers *and to strobe it* so that it only functions during those brief occasions when the controller output transistor is *not* conducting. (Remember that most controllers deliver pulses of output, either by virtue of PWM or of an unsmoothed power supply.) In this way, what the meter indicates is the motor EMF, which is proportional to train speed. A practical problem is that the sampling time in a PWM controller is brief and becomes briefer as the speed control is advanced. So, the speedometer circuit must be a 'sample and hold' circuit in which a capacitor is charged up during the samples and holds its charge until replenished by the next sample. In certain PWM controllers there is an insurmountable difficulty; at a certain high setting of the speed control the pulses merge into a continuous full power output and this disables the speedometer circuit so that it registers zero. Another difficulty is that the speedometer needs separate calibration for each locomotive in use, but more of this later. Figure 11.1 shows the practical circuit diagram of a speedometer for a controller with positive-going output before the reversing switch.

How it works

The voltage at the output of a controller consists of three components when in normal use. During the power pulses there is the voltage that the controller itself is delivering. At the end of each pulse there is a spike of inductive overshoot from the locomotive motor, which, as measured by a voltmeter across the output terminals, is of opposite polarity to the controller output. Lastly, also only distinguishable between power pulses, is the motor EMF. This, as measured by a voltmeter across the output terminals, is of the same polarity as the controller output and, because it is proportional to motor speed, it is this which we wish to isolate and indicate on our speedometer.

The speedometer circuit input is taken from the controller output (before the reversing switch) and applied via resistor R1 to the base of T2. The strobe input is applied via current-limiting resistor R2 to the base of T1 which forms the lower limb of a potential divider with R1. The effect of this is that T2 only receives an input during the spaces between power pulses; during the pulses themselves T2's input is short circuited away by T1. Diode D2 is to kill inductive overshoot although it may be omitted if there is already an overshoot-killing diode across the controller output, as in Chapters 3 to 6.

Transistor T2 is used as an emitter follower and even brief pulses of input cause it to charge C2 up to the input voltage (less the offset of about 0.7 V). Resistor R3 allows C2 to discharge at a moderate rate; the values of C2 and R3 should be chosen to give a time constant of 0.15 seconds, equalling about 15 pulses, with recommended values of 10 µF and 15 K. Thus, a voltage is maintained across C2/R3 which is tolerably proportional to train speed. It is recommended that the meter be a 100 µA type for two reasons. Firstly, it enables the selection of a high value of calibration potentiometer, eg 47 K, which will have a minimal effect on the functioning of the circuit and secondly, it is easy to pretend that the units of calibration are not µA, but scale mph, with 100 mph as the full-scale reading.

Installation

The installation of this unit depends on the kind of controller to which it is being connected. If the controller is a closed-loop type, eg as in Chapter 4, both the strobe input and positive connection, shown in Figure 11.1 should be connected to the controller's positive rail. If the controller is a PWM type the strobe input should be connected to some point in the controller which goes positive in synchronization with the output pulses, but not the controller output itself (because of interference from other positive sources there, such as the back EMF that we are trying to measure). Some modification to the controller circuit may be needed in order to provide a suitable strobe input. If the controller has a *smoothed* power supply D1 and C1 may be omitted.

Calibration

Set a train running at a guessed scale speed of 50 mph. Now, adjust VR1 until the meter reads 50 (half scale) and try varying the train speed. You should find that the meter reading is indeed proportional to the train speed. Moreoever, if you lift the train off the track while it is still running, the speedometer should drop to zero, or nearly so. For more accurate calibration, you will need a stop watch and a known length of track, say 1 yard (0.91 m), over which to measure train time. The Table below shows how the time taken in seconds to cover 1 yard (915 mm) relates to scale speed for some popular model railway scales.

Scale	Scale speed in mph (km/h)							
(mm/ft)	10 (16)	20 (32)	30 (48)	40 (64)	50 (80)	60 (96)	70 (112)	80 (128)
2.00 (N)	31	16	10	7.8	6.2	5.2	4.4	3.9
3.50 (HO)	18	8.8	5.9	4.4	3.6	3.0	2.5	2.2
4.00 (OO/EM)	16	7.8	5.2	3.9	3.1	2.6	2.2	1.9
7.00 (O)	8.9	4.4	3.0	2.2	1.8	1.5	1.3	1.1

VR1 should be calibrated, eg, 1 to 10, and each locomotive in use tested, referring to the Table, and the correct setting of VR1 recorded for it. Calibration varies from loco to loco because it is dependent upon such variables as gearing, driving wheel size and motor characteristics. Keep a list of your locos with the appropriate VR1 setting for each by your controller.

Use with other electronic systems

The speedometer circuit described may be used on layouts fitted with track circuits (see Part 4), but a few words of warning are in order. Provided that the loco is making good contact with the track, the track circuit voltage will be short-circuited harmlessly away so cannot interfere with the speedometer reading. However, if the loco fails to make proper contact with the track, the track circuit voltage will be applied across the speedometer input. In practice, when a loco is making only intermittent contact with the track, each interruption leads to a momentary peak of speed reading or a momentary zero reading, depending on the setting of the controller's direction switch. If there is no loco in any section connected to the controller the speedometer will, of course, register a permanent high speed or a permanent zero, depending again on the setting of the direction switch.

The use of a high-frequency coach lighting system (Chapter 31) will cause spurious readings on the speedometer but this cannot be avoided. I have made many experiments with capacitors inserted all over the speedometer circuit to find an arrangement that filters out the high-frequency AC, but although it is easy to kill the high-frequency the desirable back EMF always vanishes as well! The same applies to through-the-rails sound (Chapter 36).

Part 4: Train detection

Preamble

There are many operations on model railways in which it is useful, or even essential, to know where trains are. Automatic signalling is an obvious example: we need to know which sections are occupied and which are vacant. And there are many accessories such as lifting barrier level crossings ('grade crossings' in North America) which need to come into action when a train approaches.

There are two kinds of train detector: *point detectors* give an indication if a train is passing the detector itself and *section detectors* indicate if a train is present in a certain section of line (which may be very long).

Examples of point detectors include reed switches which close momentarily under the influence of a magnet on a passing train; light dependent resistors which give a signal when shaded by a passing train; and check rails, short lengths of rail just inside the running rail which are short-circuited to the running rail potential by the conductive wheel flanges of passing trains.

In general point detectors are less useful than section detectors, but they can be converted to section detectors if two or more are used in conjunction with an electronic circuit that has a memory such as a bistable: as the train enters the section it activates a point detector which sets the bistable into its 'occupied state'; as the train leaves the section it triggers another point detector which resets the bistable to its 'vacant state'.

Chapter 12 considers the use of magnets and reed switches, the most popular kind of point detection system, and various sorts of bistable.

The most obvious example of a section detector is a *track circuit*. As on prototype railways these detect the presence of trains by monitoring the electrical continuity of the section of track; all model locomotives of necessity are conductive, as are vehicles fitted with lighting and other electrical equipment powered from the track. Many designs of track circuit have been developed for use with model railways; Chapter 13 considers some basic types and Chapter 14 more sophisticated ones. These provide reliable, versatile and economical train detection and are ideally suited for use with signalling systems.

Chapter 12

Train detection by magnet-operated reed switches

A favourite among railway modellers, this system's great virtue is complete electrical isolation from the track. *A reed switch* consists of a pair of gold-plated soft-iron contacts in a vacuum in a glass envelope (see Figure 12.1). Normally the contacts are apart, so the switch is 'off'. In the presence of a suitable magnetic field, however, the contacts become mutually attracted and they close. For this sort of application the reed switch is fixed on or beneath the sleepers (ties) and its contacts close momentarily under the influence of a magnet mounted beneath a passing vehicle.

Fitting the reed switches

There are two ways of installing the reed switches and you must decide at the outset which you are going to use as they are not compatible. You can lay them longitudinally along the track half-way between the rails — this is the easiest way to install them on an existing layout. You can later disguise them, eg as ATC ramps. Alternatively — and this the author considers preferable — lay them transversely just beneath the rails. Most miniature reed switches wedge neatly between the sleepers (ties) of OO or HO track and can be hidden by scattering additional ballast over them.

Fitting the magnets

Much will depend on the sort of magnet you use. Those used by the author are cylindrical, 25 mm long and 6 mm diameter. If you are fitting your reed switches longitu-

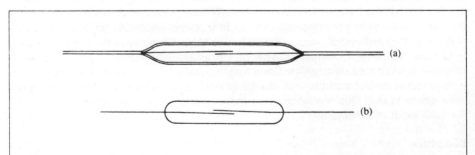

(a)

(b)

Figure 12.1 *Reed switches: (a) appearance of typical reed switch; (b) graphic symbol for a reed switch.*

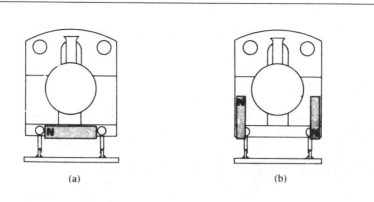

(a)   (b)

Figure 12.2 *Two methods of fixing magnets for use with transverse reed switches.*

dinally, your magnets too must be mounted beneath the vehicles longitudinally and centrally. On many locomotives, especially small tank locos, this poses problems. On tender locos in which the loco itself is powered (and not the tender) the most suitable location will be the tender.

If you are using your reed switches transversely, fitting the magnets will prove far easier. Indeed some locos will not need magnets at all. Some Hornby locomotives are fitted with magnets integral to their chassis to improve adhesion on steel-railed track. Often, but not always, these locos activate transversely-fitted reed switches perfectly satisfactorily without modification. Even locomotives not fitted with adhesion magnets will sometimes activate transverse reed switches. For instance, the author's Lima 'Crab' will — provided it is moving slowly — as the massive magnet in its tender-mounted ring-field motor passes the switch.

Most locos, however, will need to have magnets fitted. There are two methods for use with transverse reed switches. Either one magnet is fitted transversely across the loco at some suitable point on its (or its tender's) frames (Figure 12.2a) or two magnets are fitted vertically, one on each side with their poles in opposite directions (Figure 12.2b). The latter is especially useful in small tank locos, since the magnets can often be fitted just inside the steps to the cab entries. Diesel- and electric-outline models generally present no problems, there being ample space in the battery boxes or elsewhere between the bogies (trucks). If all else fails and you have a loco that seems to offer no suitable location (the Wrenn 2-6-4T is notorious from this point of view), the last resort is to fix the magnet(s) to a van or truck permanently coupled to the loco.

Because the reed switch contacts are only closed momentarily as the magnet carried by a train passes by, its output consists of a brief pulse (three brief pulses in quick succession when reed switches are fitted longitudinally). For most purposes this pulse is required to initiate a continuous change of state, eg to change a colour-light signal from green to red. One way to use this pulse to effect a change of state is to apply it to the input of a *bistable*.

Bistables

Bistables are circuits widely used in electronics, especially in computers, because they have *memory*. As the name suggests, it is a circuit that has two stable states. All bistables have two inputs, generally called the *set* and the *reset* input. Applying a pulse

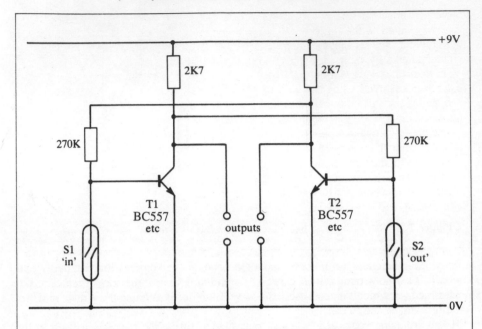

Figure 12.3 *A bistable composed of two transistors and four resistors, actuated by two reed switches S1 and S2. As a train enters the section it triggers S1 driving the collector voltages of T1 and T2 high and low respectively. As it leaves the section it triggers S2 whereupon the output states are reversed.*

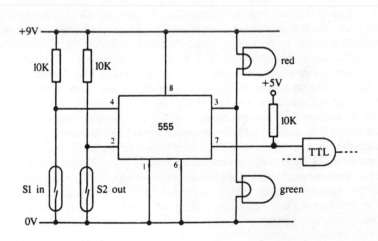

Figure 12.4 *A reed switch/bistable system that emulates track circuiting: the number of reed switches is doubled if bidirectional running is to be supported.*

to the set input puts the bistable into its active state; it remains in this state until a pulse is applied to the reset input, when it returns to its passive state. It remains in this state until the set input is again activated. Bistables may have one or more outputs which indicate by their voltage the current state of the bistable.

There are many ways in which bistables can be made. A simple and quite effective bistable can be made using two transistors and a handful of resistors. An example using reed switch inputs is shown in Figure 12.3. This is a symmetrical circuit in which one transistor or the other is conducting and short-circuiting the other's base bias.

Bistables can also be constructed using TTL ICs (see, for example, Figure A13.10); bistables using TTL are not recommended for train detection purposes since they are very prone to spurious changes of state caused by electrical interference, picked up from the trains by the long leads to the reed switches.

There is, however, an IC-based bistable circuit which is ideally suited for model railway applications. This uses our old friend the 555 timer IC. In Chapters 5 and 6 we saw the timer used as a *monostable*, ie a circuit having two states, only one of which was stable. When set it held its active state only until a capacitor in the timing circuit reached a certain critical level of charge and then it reset itself — in other words it was being used as an interval timer. If we make the capacitor infinitely large (ie a short circuit to ground which will take for ever to charge up), the 555 has become a bistable — obligingly the manufacturer provides a reset input on pin 2. The resulting circuit is shown in Figure 12.4. The 555 can operate from any supply voltage from 5 V to 18 V, the higher the voltage the greater the immunity to interference. On a 9 V supply as shown it can drive two-aspect signals using 'grain-of-wheat' bulbs direct. And pin 7 provides a TTL-compatible output (low when a train is present).

Section occupation

For many applications — and especially in signalling — we need to know whether there is a train in a given section of line. This can be achieved quite simply by the circuits shown in Figure 12.3 and 12.4. We position reed switch 1 at the beginning of our section and reed switch 2 at the end of it. As a train enters the section it activates reed switch 1, driving the bistable into what we shall call the 'occupied' state. As the train leaves the section, it activates reed switch 2 and the bistable resets to its original or 'vacant' state.

It all sounds too simple — and, sure enough, it is, because it only works if all the trains travel in the same direction. If our train were now to reverse back on to the section, it would pass reed switch 2 first, leaving the bistable in its 'vacant' state. If it kept on going, reversing out of the section over reed switch 1, the bistable would now go to its 'occupied' state, even though the section is vacant. However on a double-track line, with wrong-line working absolutely prohibited, this very simple system would be feasible.

Happily this system can be modified to cope with a bi-directional traffic. *Two* reed switches are now positioned at each end of the section. The two switches of each pair should be spaced at least 75 mm apart or there is a danger that both switches may be activated at once, causing a malfunction. The two *outer* switches are wired in parallel and both initiate the 'vacant' state; the two *inner* switches similarly are wired in parallel and both initiate the 'occupied' state. Now imagine that the section is empty and the bistable correctly in its 'vacant' state. A train entering the section at *either end* will trip first an outer switch, having no effect on the state of the bistable, and then an inner switch, correctly initiating the 'occupied' state. The train may now leave the section *at either end*, since it will trip first an inner switch, having no effect, and then

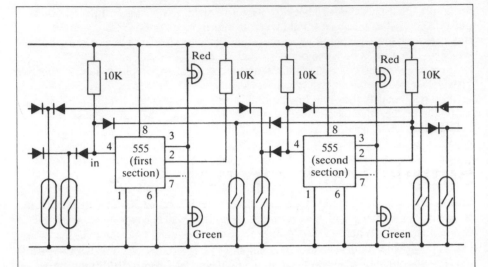

Figure 12.5 *Complete circuit for two adjacent section bistables with reed switches dupli-cated for bidirectional running and shared between adjacent sections. All diodes should be 1N914 or similar.*

an outer switch, correctly turning the bistable back to its 'vacant' state.

This system may at first appear extravagant in reed switches, since each section needs four. But this is only true of an isolated track section; for most purposes sections are not isolated – where one section ends, the next begins. If each section has its own bistable, the reed switch pairs may be shared between adjacent sections, but the 'outer' switch of one section will be the 'inner' switch of the next. For this reason a diode must be inserted between each switch and each bistable input to which it needs to be connected (Figure 12.5). Reference to the figure will show that these diodes prevent switch pulses from being passed down the line to other section bistables where they are not wanted. Figure 12.5 gives the circuit for two adjacent section bistables using 555s with three pairs of reed switches.

A piece of string has only two ends, but a track section may have more than two. Sidings and passing loops provide means by which a train may clear the main-line section with-out activating the reed switches at the section ends Therefore, additional reed switches must be positioned in the sidings passing loops. As these reed switches are not shared with other sections, they are connected direct to the bistable without diodes.

When a bistable-based system is first switched on, the bistables may latch in either of their stable states. For this reason it is essential before each operating session begins to send a 'dummy' train round the layout to correctly trigger each bistable and leave the system in order.

Maplin catalogue numbers
BC557 QQ16S, 555 QH66W, 1N914 QL71N, reed switch FX70M, magnet FX72P.

Chapter 13

Simple track circuits

Track circuiting is, in my opinion, the simplest, the most versatile, the most realiable and, not least, the most prototypical method of train detection. Its advantages so outweigh those of other train detection systems that these are not worthy of serious consideration except on certain existing layouts where the provision of the rail breaks essential for track circuiting may be precluded by problems of access.

Track circuiting demands no modification whatever to locomotives and the only modification to the track is its division into track-circuited sections by means of rail breaks or insulating fishplates. These may be in one rail or both, depending on track circuit type. Each track-circuited section must, of necessity, have its own feed from the controller(s) and the track circuit unit is wired into this feed. Sections may be long, eg blocks for signalling purposes, or short, eg for accessory operation, the lower limit being the electrical wheelbase of the longest locomotive (or other conductive vehicle) in use, since the section must be long enough to ensure that the locomotive (or other vehicle) draws current in it. Either rail, or even both, may be track-circuited. There are, however, subtle differences between live-rail and return-rail track circuits, which must be taken into account in layout planning.

Track circuit units need not be complicated. This chapter introduces a unidirectional live-rail unit using only two transistors and a handful of other components.

Chapter 14 is concerned with fully bidirectional track circuits. All the track circuits described in this book share the layout common return. Consequently, any number of units, of the same type or of mixed types, on the same layout may share the same power supply irrespective of the number of controllers in use.

Output and other considerations

Before embarking on any track circuiting project, a number of matters must be settled. Obviously, you must decide which rail is to be monitored and whether you need a unidirectional or bidirectional unit. These matters will be determined largely by the geography of your layout and by the kind of operations that you expect to take place in the sections which you are track circuiting. Ideally you should read through Parts 4, 5 and 6 of this book and then choose the track circuit type that is most appropriate to your needs. However, one other variable must be settled before you get out your soldering iron and that is the output facility required, which again will depend on the application that you have in mind for your track circuits.

Recently, amidst the largely uncharted sea of model railway electronics, a conven-

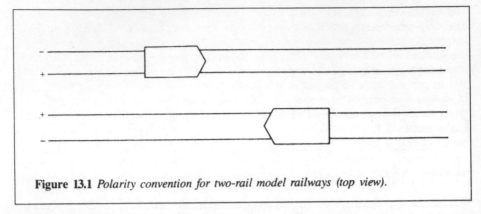

Figure 13.1 *Polarity convention for two-rail model railways (top view).*

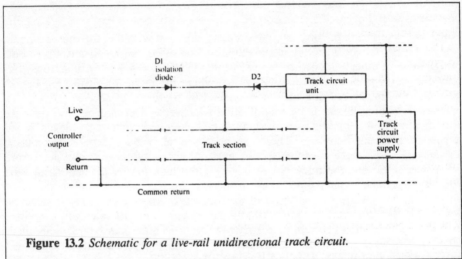

Figure 13.2 *Schematic for a live-rail unidirectional track circuit.*

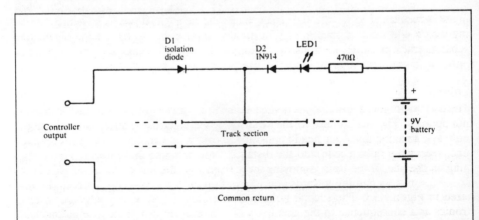

Figure 13.3 *Simple 'train-in-section' indicator. Its performance is likely to be disappointing for reasons discussed in the text.*

tion has emerged regarding track circuit (and other train detection system) outputs. This convention states that a unit generally has one output only and this gives a TTL-compatible logical '0' when a train is detected. (For an explanation of these terms see Appendix 13). This convention arises from the increasing use of TTL (transistor/transistor logic) in signalling circuits and automatic train control circuits. The easiest way to provide such an output is to take the track circuit output from the collector of an npn transistor, whose emitter is grounded and which is biased into saturation when a train is detected. The TTL system being driven will, of course, share the track circuit common return, although not necessarily its power supply. It is desirable, but not essential, to connect a pull-up resistor (1 K to 10 K) between the collector and the TTL positive supply. This 'pulls up' the TTL input to supply positive potential when the transistor is 'off'. You can kill two birds with one stone by making this resistor lower (180 R to 560 R) and putting in series with it an LED as a 'section occupied' indicator. All of the track circuits described in this book have this kind of single output. All of the signalling systems described in Part 5 (which use TTL throughout) assume this kind of track circuit output, as do those circuits in Part 6 which require input from a track circuit.

The availability of versatile and reliable track circuits will, I am convinced, lead to greater advances in model railway operation than even 'command control' systems have done. The time is coming when every layout of exhibition standard will be track circuited throughout — some already are. The track circuits may operate an automatic signalling system, but, perhaps more importantly, will light LED displays in a mimic diagram of the layout so that concealed operators will know exactly where trains are and, possibly with even greater significance, the track circuits may provide the essential inputs to a progressive cab control system (Chapter 29) in which individual controllers are automatically switched from section to section as the trains move around the layout.

Live-rail unidirectional track circuit

The principles underlying this, the simplest of two-rail track circuits, were formulated by Paul Mallery in 1947, when he described what is now known as the NMRA track circuit which uses relays. This is a transistorized version of his circuit. It is said to be *unidirectional* because in normal use trains can run in only one direction when in track-circuited sections. Simple arrangements can be made, however, to permit reversing which will be described later. The first requirement is to divide the layout into separate track-circuited sections by means of rail breaks. These may be in one rail only, or if one system of reversing is used (see later), in both rails.

Polarity

The division of the layout into sections entails the adoption of two conventions regarding polarity. The first relates to the polarity of the electrification of two-rail model railways. Imagine that your head is positioned over a line and you are looking up the line, seeing the rails recede into the distance. Now imagine that there is a train running on the line. If the train is moving away from you, the rail on the *right* is *positive* and if the train is coming towards you, the rail on the *left* is positive. This is summarized in Figure 13.1. The second polarity convention is one widely adopted in electronics as a consequence of the chemistry of silicon from which most semiconductor devices are made. This makes the 'earth' or 'ground', or common-return rail of an electric circuit the most *negative* part of the circuit, ie, this rail is connected to the negative terminal of the power supply.

This type of track circuit is sometimes called a 'shunt' track circuit (no connection with railway shunting) because the track circuit is connected across the track (it *shunts* it in the electrical sense) while most other track circuits are *series* types. To prevent the controller output from interfering unduly with the track circuit's operation, a heavy-duty diode is included in the live feed from the controller to the isolated track section. Figure 13.2 shows how this diode effectively isolates the controller from the track circuit; electrically they cannot 'see' each other. In practice D2 in the Figure may not exist as a discrete component, it is simply drawn to indicate that the track circuit unit only responds to negative-going inputs. Diode D1 is known as the *isolation diode* and it also serves to isolate the track circuit from any other track circuits or track sections connected to the same controller. To get from one section to another would involve passing through two isolation diodes in series, anode to anode which, clearly, is impossible.

Now we can see why it is that polarity plays such an important part in the design of this kind of track circuit. For the system to work, the controller output (for normal forwards movement) and the track circuit power supply must have the *same* polarity relative to a common return. From the electronics convention, negative equals common return, so controller output 'live' is positive. So the live rail is always assumed to be positive for normal forward running. Thus, we can decide which rail is live and which is return for any section in the layout. If the section is isolated in one rail only, it is the *live* rail that must be isolated. The return rail may be continuous, but if there is a reverse loop or a triangular junction in the layout, a reversible section isolated in both rails will be needed.

How it works

When a train arrives in the track-circuited section it completes not one but *two* separate circuits — one through the isolating diode to the controller and the other through the 'shunt' track circuit. The track circuit could be very simple indeed. For instance, if we only wanted a visual indication that the track section was occupied, all we need do (at first thought) is to add an LED with a series resistor and a power supply, which could be simply a 9 V battery. We should also need a series diode to prevent the LED from being reverse biased when the controller output exceeds the track circuit supply voltage, as is likely on occasions.

The resulting simple track circuit is shown in Figure 13.3. If you try this circuit you will probably find its performance disappointing. The LED lights brightly enough when the train is stationary or moving slowly, but when it is at speed the LED will be dim and may even be extinguished altogether. This is because at speed a high voltage is raised across the locomotive motor and this opposes the LED's supply voltage, limiting the current that it can draw and perhaps even reverse biasing the series diode, so that no current can flow at all. This problem could be solved quite easily by using a track circuit supply voltage higher than any voltage that the controller is likely to deliver, eg 25 V, but is this convenient. There is, however, a way to obtain a more consistently accurate output from a undirectional track circuit, even when operating from supplies at 9 V or less. We replace the LED with the input circuit of a pnp Darlington pair, giving the practical circuit diagram shown in Figure 13.4.

Capacitor C2 is useful for, as has already been seen, when a train is at speed peaks of voltage across the track may exceed the track circuit voltage. As with the LED under these conditions the Darlington will cease conducting. Without the capacitor the LED would be extinguished momentarily and successions of these extinctions would cause it to appear dim. The capacitor acts as a reservoir being topped up whenever the Darlington conducts and discharging through the LED whenever the Darlington ceases to conduct. Thus it keeps the LED at full brightness. It follows that if you use a controller that delivers steady DC, this type of track circuit will not work. With this type of controller a return-rail track circuit is almost essential, but see Chapter 36. This also helps considerably when the track circuit is used as part of a signalling system. It is important that, when the section is occupied, the track circuit output be *continuous*. Any interruption of its output, however brief, may be interrupted as 'section vacant' and may cause a green or yellow aspect to light intermittently. So, repeated interruptions would cause signal aspects to alternate rapidly (to the confusion of the train driver!). The smoothing capacitor eliminates this difficulty.

With BC557s or similar, up to 200 mA may be drawn from the track circuit's output terminal while the section is occupied. This may be used to light the red aspect of a signal, or it may provide an input for another electronic unit of some kind or it may energize a relay coil if needed.

Reversing
There is a price to pay for the simplicity of this kind of track circuit. This is the effect of the all-important isolation diode, for, since it blocks reverse current from the controller, trains cannot be reversed unless special arrangements are made.

There are two ways in which a reversing facility may be provided. If the section is isolated in *both* rails a two-pole, two-way reversing switch may be introduced between

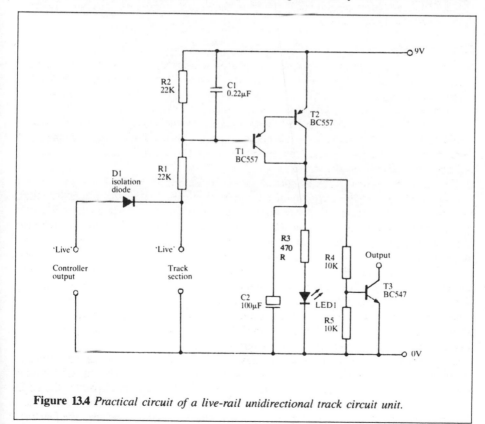

Figure 13.4 *Practical circuit of a live-rail unidirectional track circuit unit.*

the track circuit unit and the two rails of the section. To reverse, throw this switch and set the controller for *forwards* movement. The train will reverse and the track circuit will continue to function normally but care must be taken if the train reaches the end of the section, for, unless the next section is also set for reverse polarity, a short circuit may be caused if a metal-tyred wheel bridges the gap between the two sections.

If the section is isolated in one rail only, a simpler alternative is to add a switch to short-circuit the isolating diode. It is recommended that this switch be a non-locking push-button type with normally-open contacts. To reverse, hold the button down and set the controller to reverse. The train will reverse normally as long as the button is pressed and there will be no polarity problems when it reaches the next section. However, while the button is pressed the isolation from adjacent sections is lost and the track circuit will not function normally. It will give a 'section occupied' indication if there is a train in *any* section connected to the same controller, or if the controller output is negative or if the controller output presents a low resistance. Clearly, if the button is only pressed when the section is occupied, this anomalous behaviour will go unnoticed.

In sections where reversing is needed often it is preferable to use a more sophisticated type of track circuit. Unidirectional units, however, are quite useful on multiple-track main lines where most movements are forwards.

Components
Maplin catalogue numbers are as follows: 1N4001 diode QL73Q, BC547 QQ14Q, BC557 QQ16S.

Chapter 14

Bidirectional track circuits

Bidirectional track circuits, as their name suggests, permit full bidirectional movement of trains and under all normal conditions provide consistently accurate train detection. As with all track circuit types, rail breaks are essential and the track circuit unit is wired into a feed to the section which it guards.

Bidirectional track circuits function by monitoring the current flowing into the section. Often this is the power current from the controller but to provide for occasions when there is no output from the controller, eg when it is set to 'stop' or is off or disconnected, the track circuit power supply voltage is also applied to the section via the track circuit unit's current detector. The current available from this power supply to the section, called the *auxiliary* current, is limited by a resistor to a maximum of a few milliAmps to prevent unwanted movement of trains. However, this auxiliary current is sufficient to activate the current detector in the track circuit unit ensuring that trains are detected under all prevailing conditions.

You may wonder whether train detection is interrupted when the controller output is equal and of opposite polarity to the auxiliary current. Theoretically, of course, this is possible and indeed one authority (James Kyle) suggests for this very reason that the auxiliary current be AC! In practice, however, with most controllers and a DC auxiliary current no such interruption occurs. This is because most controllers deliver a pulsed output which cannot cancel a steady direct current! Between pulses, train detection continues and practical circuits include smoothing to convert intermittent detection into a continuous 'section occupied' indication. What *can* happen with certain electronic controllers is that auxiliary current enters the controller's feedback-loop, where it can cause a number of interesting phenomena, which are described in detail later.

The 'twin-T' detector

The heart of a bidirectional track circuit is its current detector. This poses a knotty design problem since it must both pass and detect current of either polarity, from a few milliAmps to over 1 A, without incurring a heavy voltage drop, which would adversely affect the performance of the trains. The easiest way to detect a current is to pass it through a resistor and to use the potential difference developed across this to bias a transistor into conduction. An ordinary resistor, however, could not cope with the wide range of currents encountered. For instance, to give the necessary minimum of 0.7 V at 10 mA (high for an auxiliary current) the resistor would need to be

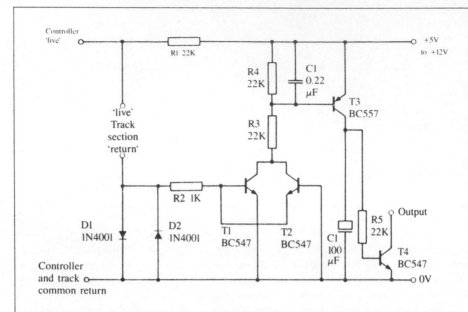

Figure 14.1 *A bidirectional return-rail track circuit, a modern example of the 'twin-T' type detector first described by Linn Westcott in the 1950s, a classic in model railway electronics. For use with O gauge and above, D1 and D2 should be uprated to type 1N5401.*

68 R, but then at 250 mA (typical for an OO/HO-scale loco at cruising speed) the voltage drop would be an intolerable, if not impossible, 17 V. So, we need a special resistor which will adjust its resistance to suit the prevailing conditions — ideally one whose resistance is inversely proportional to the current flowing through it, so that the voltage drop is constant at around 0.7 V. At once the mental bells should ring for we have just described our old friend, the (forward-biased) silicon diode. Because this conducts in only one direction while the controller output may be of either polarity, two such diodes must be used in reverse parallel, the so-called 'twin-T' arrangement.

One way to obtain a digital output, ie a two-state 'section occupied'/'section vacant' indication, from the voltage drop across the twin-T pair is to use this voltage as the input to a transistor amplifier. Since the voltage may be of either polarity, depending on the polarity of the current being detected, it is applied to the reverse-parallel base/emitter junctions of two transistors of the same polarity; their two collectors are bonded, so collector current from one transistor or the other (of uniform polarity of course) is stimulated by voltage drop of either polarity across the twin-T pair. Obviously, when the section is vacant, no current can flow into it, so there is no voltage drop across the twin-T pair and neither transistor conducts. A typical circuit of a practical twin-T unit is shown in Figure 14.1.

Since the twin-T track circuit was first described by the American model railway writer Linn Westcott in 1958, it has, together with a multitude of variant circuits, become the most widely used kind of track circuit unit on model railways. Nevertheless, until recently the system was not widely known in the UK and the author's own EDOTIS (Electronic Detection of Trains In Sections), which is a twin-T variant, was developed quite independently in connection with *Practical Electronics for Railway Modellers*.

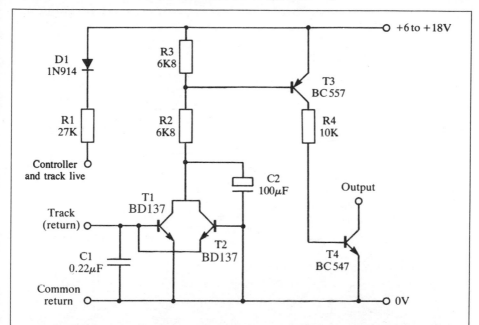

Figure 14.2 *A 'twin-T' variant, the author's own EDOTIS configured for return-rail operation and for a single output going low when a train is detected.*

In EDOTIS the twin-T pair itself is omitted, the entire traction current passing through the base/emitter junction (which behaves like a diode) of one or other of the front end transistor pair. Inevitably these transistors must be high-current types and both the BD137 and the 2N3055 have been used satisfactorily. A circuit diagram is given in Figure 14.2.

There is a choice of modes, live-rail and return-rail, in which a bidirectional track circuit may operate. But, as the live-rail mode poses certain difficulties, the current detector is generally positioned in the *return* feed to the section, ie return-rail operation. The section is normally isolated in both rails, the breaks in the return defining the limits of the section. The breaks in the live rail need not be opposite the others and in some circumstances, eg only one controller in use, may be omitted altogether. The live rail may be differently divided into zones capable of being fed from separate controllers. This is perfectly satisfactory, provided that each control zone, if at any point it is opposite a track-circuited section of return rail, is connected to the positive terminal of the track circuit power supply via a suitable resistor to provide a source of auxiliary current. Since return-rail track circuits share the layout common return, any number of them may share the same power supply.

Live-rail bidirectional track circuit

For many applications a bidirectional live-rail track circuit sharing the layout's common return would be invaluable and its design presented a challenge that I found irresistible! First, let us discover the reason for the 'live-rail problem'. Figure 14.3 shows a simplified EDOTIS front end reconfigured in an attempt at live-rail common-return operation. Under some conditions this unit performs satisfactorily, but the problem

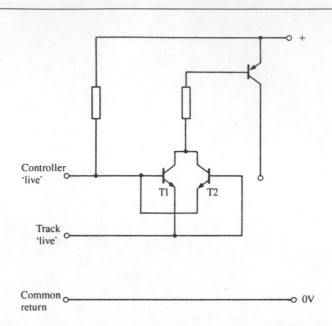

Figure 14.3 *Simplified front end of an EDOTIS-type track circuit reconfigured for live-rail common-return operation. Reasons for its unsatisfactory performance are given in the text.*

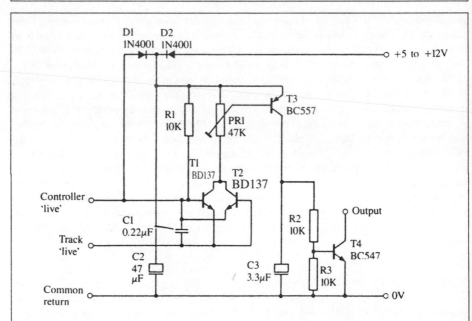

Figure 14.4 *Circuit of EDOTIS II (also called TEKTOR), a common-return, live-rail track circuit unit.*

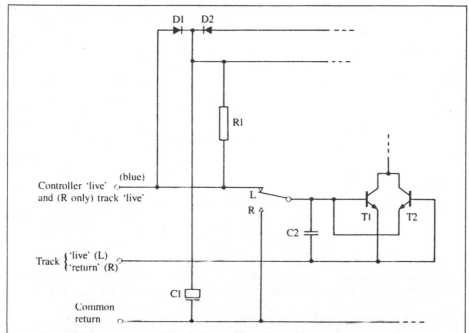

Figure 14.5 *The addition of an SPDT (single-pole double-throw) switch to the front end of TEKTOR provides the versatility of live-rail or return-rail operation.*

arises when the controller output is positive and at a higher voltage than the track circuit power supply. The controller output now *forward biases* the base/collector junction of T1 and *reverse biases* T3's base/emitter junction, preventing train detection. In practice train detection in this direction fails at all but the very lowest speeds.

One solution would be to operate this track circuit from a power supply at a voltage higher than the controller can deliver but this would need to be at least 25 V, which is inconvenient for a number of reasons. There is, however, a more subtle means of achieving the same effect, while still retaining a more convenient track circuit supply voltage (5 to 12 V).

Most controllers deliver an output that is pulsed. This output of necessity contains peaks of voltage higher than the mean. We can arrange quite simply for these peaks to charge up a capacitor which is then used as an alternative power supply for the track circuit's front end. Since this alternative supply voltage will approach the *peak* controller output voltage, it will be inevitably higher than the *mean* controller voltage, enabling train detection to continue. The front end's output will, on occasion, consist of pulses but later smoothing can convert this into a continuous 'section occupied' indication.

The complete circuit diagram of a track circuit unit which employs these principles is given in Figure 14.4. The juxtaposition of diodes D1 and D2 and capacitor C2 ensures that the front end takes as its power supply whichever of the track circuit power supply and the controller peak output offers the higher, ie more positive, output, since the higher voltage will forward bias the adjacent diode and reverse bias the other.

This track circuit functions satisfactorily under most normal operating conditions. Only if the controller delivers a steady DC more positive than the track circuit power supply, eg in a pure DC controller or when certain types of PWM controller are set to maximum speed, train detection may fail. The solution in a pure DC controller is to superimpose an audio frequency signal (Chapter 36) or in a PWM controller to reduce the controller setting until pulsing, and therefore train detection, is resumed. With controllers operating from unsmoothed power supplies there are no such problems.

Figure 14.5 shows a simple modification to EDOTIS II's front end to enable it to operate as either a live-rail or a return-rail track circuit, as selected on a single-pole double-throw switch which greatly enhances its usefulness. Note that in either mode the blue lead is connected to the live output terminal of the controller, the yellow lead to the track-circuited rail and the black lead to the layout common-return.

Capacitor C1 kills spurious detection caused by pulsed power charging and discharging the residual capacitance between the rails. The presence of a locomotive or other conductive vehicle in the section will always cause either T1 or T2 to become conductive, the combined collector currents in PR1 raising bias for T3. The setting of PR1 is critical. If too high, spurious detection may result, if too low detection by auxiliary current may fail, especially on low supply voltages. Capacitor C3 in the collector circuit of T3 provides smoothing of the 'section occupied' indication, which is essential for most applications, especially in signalling. Each pulse of output from the front end charges C3, which takes appreciable time (0.33 ms) to discharge via R2 and so has still retained most of its charge when it is replenished by the next pulse.

What track circuits detect

A track circuit could be defined as a system that provides an electrical indication when the continuity of a section of track is completed by the presence of rail vehicles. As mentioned earlier, most model rolling stock, being designed for use on two-rail track, is non-conductive and therefore has no effect on track circuits unless modified as described below. Model locomotives, however, generally are conductive by virtue of their motor windings and are detected by track circuits without needing any modification. You may find that detection of locomotives alone is sufficient for your needs, but read Chapter 19 on the problem of overlap.

One type of locomotive that may not be detected by a track circuit is an electric-outline loco drawing its power from an overhead catenary or a third rail. If your layout uses either of these systems of electrification, you must ensure that your track circuits are all return-rail types. If you use live-rail track circuits these will have to be duplicated in the overhead or third-rail feeds. Alternatively, you will need to modify the locomotive to ensure that it activates the live-rail track circuits, as described below.

Vehicles fitted with lights that operate from the controller output will also be detected by track circuits. Vehicles fitted with lights intended to operate only from a high-frequency lighting system (Chapter 31) and having blocking capacitors in series with the lamps will only be detected while the high-frequency generator is operating. Vehicles fitted with speakers for through-the-rails sound (Chapter 36) will be detected when the lighting or sound system is off and while the auxiliary current charges up the blocking capacitors. I have also seen HF-lit stock detected by EDOTIS II-type track circuits when the controller is on but the HF unit off. EDOTIS II is a very sensitive unit and will detect the charge/discharge of the blocking capacitors under pulsed power even at frequencies too low to light the lamps.

Any vehicle can be modified to activate track circuits by making it suitably conductive. The sensitivity of track circuits varies widely, depending on such factors as track circuit type, supply voltage and controller setting. If you wish to 'conductivize' a vehicle, I advise you to try placing various resistors across the track, testing at all settings of the controller, forwards and reverse, in order to determine the highest resistance that is detected under all conditions likely to be encountered. Start with 1 K.

There are three ways of 'conductivizing' stock and all demand that the vehicle be fitted with metal-tyred wheels. Firstly, solder a suitable resistor from a spoke on one wheel to the corresponding spoke on the opposite wheel or, alternatively, fit power pick-ups and connect these to a resistor mounted in or beneath the vehicle. The third alternative is to paint over the insulating bushes or spokes with electrically conductive silver paint (available from model shops) and, when dry, brush off the excess to raise the resistance to the required value. If, when using the first two methods, a 1 K resistor is used, it should be rated for 0.5 W. If a lower value is used it should be rated 1 W.

Fault finding

Track circuiting is very reliable and, in general, trouble free but it is advisable to be aware of the possible causes when they apparently do not work as they ought.

Spurious detection, ie a 'section occupied' indication in the *absence* of a train, is rare, but if observed, check the following: all wiring and pointwork (especially if you use live-frog turnouts); check for mains leads in proximity to the track and wiring, which can cause interference; check for damp in the ballast and, if suspected, spray the track with automotive water repellent; also check if some other electrical system is in use which may interfere with track circuits. For example, the RELCO track cleaning device and high-frequency coach lighting systems both cause spurious detection with EDOTIS II. If you use RELCO, have a track cleaning session first, then switch the RELCO off for your operating session. If you make your own track using copper-clad board for sleepers (ties), examine the gaps in the copper for stray particles of metal causing a partial short circuit; I have seen this cause spurious detection on a club layout.

Nil detection, ie absence of a 'section occupied' in the *presence* of a train is more common than the opposite fault and may be caused by many factors. Check the following: cleanliness of the track and loco wheels, power pickups, motor brushes and commutator. Check the track circuit power supply: short-circuit the track and see if this gives a 'section occupied' indication. The use of filament lamps as status indicators wired across the controller output should be avoided unless you use only unidirectional live-rail track circuits; these lamps when off have a very low resistance which short-circuits the auxiliary current. As status indicators use LEDs (with series resistors, of course) which cause no such adverse effects. The same effect occurs if a controller is connected to a number of zones, some of which are track-circuited and some not; a stationary locomotive in a non-track-circuited zone with short-circuit auxiliary current so that a conductive vehicle in a track-circuited zone will not be registered while the controller is at stop. Similarly a loco stopped so that it is partially in a track-circuited zone and partially in a non-track-circuited zone will not be detected, but, if it is parked so that it straddles two track-circuited zones, it will normally be registered in both.

Mutual interference is caused, unfortunately, when track circuits are used (but not any described in this book) with certain types of electronic controller because auxiliary current enters the controller's feedback loop. This causes a variety of fascinating phenomena such as nil detection, slowing of trains in track-circuited sections, speeding of trains in track-circuited sections and even inability to bring trains to a complete stop (in one direction). The cure for this is to modify the *controller* by the addition of a 4K7 resistor in parallel with the output transistor to provide a leakage current that 'swamps' the auxiliary current and is not itself controlled by the feedback loop.

Selection of track circuit type

Your choice of track circuit type will be influenced by three factors: (i) the kind of operations taking place in the section; (ii) the system of electrification; and (iii) expense. The following guide should help you choose the appropriate track circuit for your situation.

1 Does your section carry traffic in both directions or in one direction only? If both directions, go to (2) below; if one direction, go to (4) below.

2 Do you use (or intend to use) high-frequency train lighting? If so, use only return-rail bidirectional track circuits. Otherwise go to (3) below.

3 Does your controller deliver a steady or a pulsed output? If steady, do you use through-the-rails sound? If not, use only return-rail bidirectional track circuits. Otherwise use return-rail or live-rail bidirectional track circuits, as convenient.

4 Do you use (or intend to use) high-frequency train lighting? If not, proceed to (5) below. If so, use a return-rail *bidirectional* track circuit.

5 Is your controller output (relative to the common return) positive or negative? If positive proceed to (6) below. If negative, use a live-rail or return-rail *bidirectional* track circuit.

6 Does your controller deliver a steady or a pulsed output? If steady, do you use through-the-rails sound? If not, use a return rail *directional* track circuit. Otherwise, use a live-rail unidirectional track circuit.

Components

Maplin catalogue numbers of semiconductors are as follows: BC547 QQ14Q, BC557 QQ16S, BD137 VR09K, 2N3055 YH98G, 1N914 QL71N, 1N4001 QL73Q.

Part 5: Automatic signalling and turnout (points) control

Preamble

A working signalling system adds a lot to a layout. The sight of a colour-light signal changing automatically as a train passes, or as a loco is unprototypically placed on the track by an out-of-scale hand, gives a layout a feeling of 'life' that has to be seen to be believed. Now it's no longer just the trains that are doing things.

Much of Part 5 is devoted to the automatic operation of colour-light signals. For this the author makes no excuses. The book, after all, is on the applications of electronics to railway modelling and electronics can make a greater contribution to automatic colour-light signalling than it can to other forms of signalling or turnout control (although these are described). If excuses are needed, there is no shortage of them. Colour-light signals are far simpler to set up and use than semaphore types: moreover they are not — as some modellers mistakenly believe — a recent innovation only appropriate on modern-image layouts. The first installation of colour-light signals on a main line in the UK was in 1924 on the former Great Central line between Marylebone and Neasden in connection with special services operating to the Empire Exhibition at Wembley. The first four-aspect installations were on the Southern Railway in the late 1920s. All four pre-nationalization companies had some colour-light signals before the Second World War so they are not out of place in layouts depicting 'the Big Four' or British Railways steam era.

There are two sorts of colour-light signals.

Searchlight signals have a single colourless lens; the colour shown (the *aspect*) is changed by means of a slide between the lamp and the lens moved by solenoids. Some searchlight signals are fitted with repeaters below the main signal head. On the LNER main line near York at one time three-aspect searchlight signals were operated as four-aspect by the addition of a yellow light above the main signal head. Model searchlight signals generally operate on the light-transmission principle; coloured bulbs in the base of the signal send their light up a light guide in the post of the signal to the signal head.

Multiple-lens signals have a separate lens for each colour (aspect); generally the lenses are 8 inches (203 mm) in diameter and 1 foot (305 mm) apart. These are usually modelled using coloured 'grain-of-wheat' bulbs. Those in the excellent 'Eckon' range of signal kits for OO scale are 3.5 mm in diameter, slightly larger than scale although this is not very noticeable in the finished model.

The principles of signalling are essentially simple. To prevent collisions between trains the line is divided into *blocks* or *sections* in each of which normally no more than one train may be present. Each section is guarded by a signal which must display danger, of course, when the section is occupied.

A *two-aspect signal* displays two colours (aspects) only. Two-aspect colour-light signalling is sometimes a direct replacement for older semaphore units. A 'home' or 'stop' signal guarding a section or a junction displays green when the line is clear and red at other times. A 'distant' signal is a repeater, giving the train driver advance warning of the indication currently shown by the next home signal. Its aspects are amber (always called yellow by railwaymen) if repeating a red, and green if repeating a green. In three- or four-aspect areas the last signal on the approach to a terminus is a two-aspect type showing red if the approach is not clear and *yellow* if it is. This yellow is a 'distant' warning of the buffers at the end of the line, which are regarded as a permanently red signal. In two-aspect signals the most restrictive aspect is generally positioned below the other.

A *three-aspect signal* combines the functions of home and distant two-aspect types. Red, as on a home signal, means 'stop — the next section is not clear'. Yellow, as on a distant signal, means 'caution — the next signal is red'. Green means 'proceed — the next two sections are clear'.

Four-aspect signalling was first introduced on the Southern Railway on lines required to carry both intensive suburban passenger traffic and fast express services. To accommodate minimal-headway low-speed services the length of the sections must be kept short, but then an express train, passing a three-aspect signal showing yellow, would have only one short section length in which to stop, which would be insufficient (except by the application of emergency braking which would cause discomfort to passengers). Hence the introduction of the fourth aspect: double yellow which means 'caution — the next-but-one signal is red'. This gives the driver two sections in which to stop his train, which is adequate even for the fastest trains. Green on a four-aspect signal means 'proceed — the next three sections are clear'. Red and yellow, of course, have the same meanings as on two- and three-aspect signals. In a four-aspect area the last-but-one signal before a terminus is a three-aspect type which displays red, yellow or double yellow. Since the next-but-one signal is the 'permanently red' buffer stop, a green indication would be inappropriate. Sometimes a standard four-aspect signal head is used with a white blanking disc in place of the green.

Both searchlight and multiple-aspect signals can be modelled using LEDs. LEDs offer many advantages over miniature bulbs: (i) modern LEDs are much brighter and have stronger colour than is available from grain-of-wheat bulbs; (ii) the best LEDs are available in 'water clear' transparent epoxy resin encapsulations, which enhance the realism of non-illuminated aspects; (iii) LEDs run cold and so do not cause melting or distortion in plastics or white metal structures; (iv) LEDs are not prone to catastrophic failure provided they are used within their limits. Their brightness fades only very gradually. Modern types have a half-life (ie time for brightness to fall to 50 per cent) of 100 operating years! (v) T1¾-size LEDs are 5 mm in diameter, ideal for use in 7 mm scale models. T1-size LEDs are 3 mm in diameter, ideal for use in 4 mm scale models. Smaller-sized LEDs are available, which may suit those modelling in even smaller scales; (vi) LEDs consume little power — I have read a newspaper by the light of a T1-size extra-bright red LED drawing less than 10 mA (and my night vision is said to be worse than average!) and (vii) LEDs can be driven direct from TTL outputs.

TTL, standing for 'Transistor/Transistor Logic', is a series of integrated circuits which perform simple logical operations. Since signalling is essentially a logical discipline, the 74 series of TTL ICs will be used extensively in this and later sections of the book.

Readers unfamiliar with TTL are recommended to read Appendix 13.

Throughout Parts 5 and 6 the vocabulary prototype signalling is employed in regard to the positions of trains relative to signals. This may take a little understanding. Imagine that you are a train driver looking out of your cab at the line in front of you. Everything in front of you is said to be in *advance* of you. Everything behind you is in *rear*. So far so good. If your train has just passed a signal, that signal is now in *rear* but if we are standing beside the signal watching the train disappear into the distance, we say that the train is *in advance* of the signal or inside the signal. A second train approaching the signal is said to be *in rear* of it. So, *in advance* always means further on in the normal direction of travel, while *in rear* always means further back, contrary to the normal direction of travel. Readers wanting a detailed account of UK signalling practice (which is not greatly different from much North American practice) are recommended to read *Two Centuries of Railway Signalling* by Geoffrey Kichenside and Alan Williams (OPC).

Chapter 15

Basic colour-light signalling systems

Once your layout has track circuiting or a train detector/bistable system that emulates track circuiting (Part 4), automatic colour-light signalling is quite easy to install. You will need to decide whether to use LEDs or 'grain-of-wheat' bulbs as your aspects. LEDs, as mentioned in the preamble, have many advantages, but circuits using bulbs are also possible. All the circuits included require inputs from the track circuits or section bistables which go *low* when a train is detected.

Two-aspect signalling

Two-aspect signalling is easiest. Indeed, two-aspect signals using bulbs were shown in Figure 12.4 and 12.5 being driven direct from the outputs of the 555 IC used as a bistable. A repeater signal could be wired in parallel with the stop signal shown.

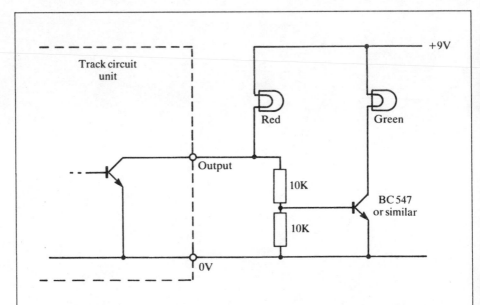

Figure 15.1 *Driving a two-aspect signal using bulbs from the output of a track circuit.*

If you are using track circuits having an open-collector output that goes low when a train is detected (eg, in Figures 13.4, 14.1, 14.2 or 14.4) you could wire a red bulb (and a yellow bulb in parallel if you want a repeater) between the output terminal and a suitable positive supply; a little extra circuitry would be needed to drive the green aspect(s). A possible circuit is shown in Figure 15.1.

If you wish to use LEDs in place of bulbs in this circuit, you may simply substitute each bulb by an LED of the appropriate colour, ensuring, of course, that each LED is the right way round (anode to the positive supply rail) and that each LED has a resistor in series with it to limit the current. There is a simple formula to find the resistor value required for 10 mA:

$$R = \frac{Vcc-2}{10}$$

where R is the resistor value in Kilohms and Vcc is the supply voltage. So, for a 5 V supply, R = (5-2)/10 = 0.3 K. Either 270 R or 330 R would be acceptable. The resulting circuit is shown in Figure 15.2.

There is, however, a slight problem with LEDs. Using the circuit of Figure 15.2 you may find that the red aspect glows dimly but nevertheless visibly when it is supposed to be off. Careful study of Figure 15.2 shows the reason. When the track circuit output transistor is off, 'sneak current' flows through the base/emitter junction of the second transistor, through R2 and R1 and into the LED. The current is only about 250 μA, but that is enough to make an LED glow. The solution is simple — connect a resistor in *parallel* with the LED. The value required will depend on the supply voltage. You want a value that forms a potential divider with R1 to give about 1 V across the LED, since this is not enough to light it. In this example a 1 K resistor would be ideal.

The examples of two-aspect signalling considered above have the advantages of simplicity. They also have the disadvantages, the principal one being that the signal aspect

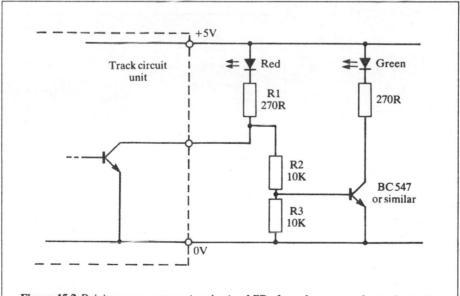

Figure 15.2 *Driving a two-aspect signal using LEDs from the output of a track circuit.*

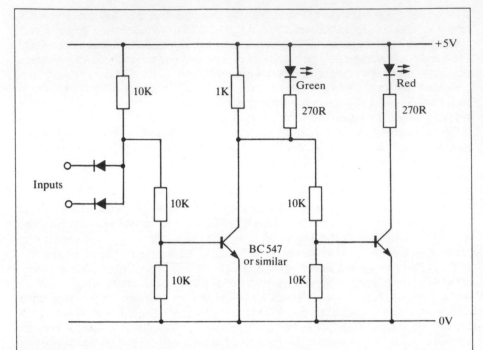

Figure 15.3 *A two-aspect signal circuit using LEDs. Its two outputs allow the easy addition of a manual override or incorporation into junction signalling.*

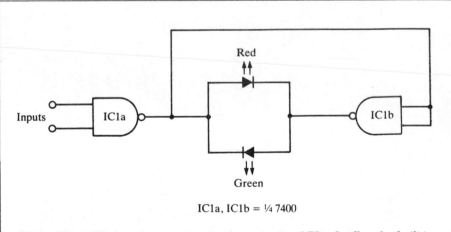

Figure 15.4 *A TTL-based two-aspect signal circuit using LEDs. It offers the facilities of Figure 15.3 with far fewer components.*

is linked inexorably with the bistable or track circuit status. There is no way, for example, in which you could override the signal to danger when the section is vacant. For this reason you certainly could not use this circuitry at a junction where the signal aspect must also take account of the setting of turnouts (points). And you cannot easily extend such a system to give three- or four-aspect operation. For these reasons a separate *signal driver* circuit is to be preferred.

Figure 15.3 shows one possible driver circuit for a two-aspect signal using LEDs. The LEDs and their series resistors could be replaced by bulbs. Two identical inputs are shown, although any number could be provided. One could be fed from the track circuit and another from a manual override switch or a microswitch linked to a turn-out tiebar. A low voltage on either input sets the signal to danger. If both (or all) inputs are high the signal will clear.

The facilities of the circuit of Figure 15.3, however, can be implemented far more neatly using TTL as shown in Figure 15.4. The driver uses two of the four NAND gates on a 7400 (or 74LS00) IC, the two LEDs and no other components, so two signal drivers could be built from one IC. Each LED protects its partner against inverse voltages; internal resistors inside the IC limit the current through the LEDs and each signal requires only a two-wire connection. Note, however, that TTL ICs (with the exception of a few highly specialized types) cannot handle the voltages and currents needed to light grain-of-wheat bulbs.

Three- and four-aspect signalling

Three- and four-aspect signalling is complicated by the need for the signal driver to take into account the occupancy of the next two or three sections in advance. Separate driver circuits are essential. Using bulbs the simplest circuits make use of an ingenious IC, the 74145 (or 74LS145) decoder with high-voltage buffer outputs. An exceptional TTL IC in that it can drive grain-of-wheat bulbs direct, it is described in detail in Appendix 13. It has 10 output terminals numbered 0 to 9, only one of which is active (low) at a time depending on the binary code applied to its four input terminals. Figures 15.5 and 15.6 show the circuits for three- and four-aspect signal drivers respectively.

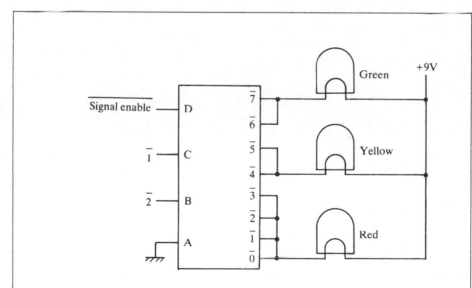

Figure 15.5 *A three-aspect signal driver using bulbs based on the 74145 BCD-to-decimal decoder IC. The decoder IC needs a 5 V TTL supply while the lamps will need a separate higher voltage (typically 9 V) supply.*

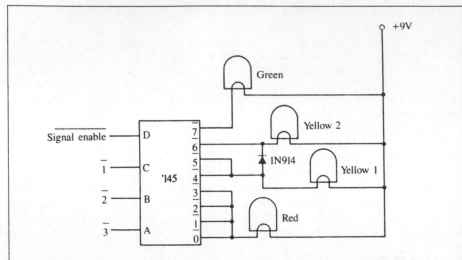

Figure 15.6 *A four-aspect signal driver using bulbs based on the 74145 BCD-to-decimal decoder IC. See the caption to Figure 15.5.*

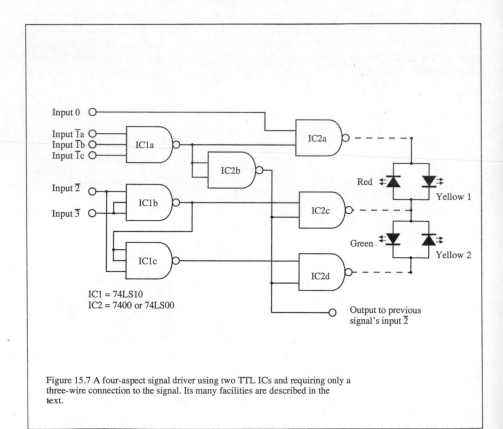

Figure 15.7 A four-aspect signal driver using two TTL ICs and requiring only a three-wire connection to the signal. Its many facilities are described in the text.

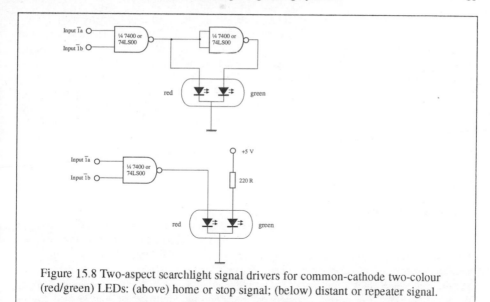

Figure 15.8 Two-aspect searchlight signal drivers for common-cathode two-colour (red/green) LEDs: (above) home or stop signal; (below) distant or repeater signal.

In each of these input D must be kept low to enable the signal; if it goes high the only outputs that can be activated are 8 and 9 which are not used. This facility could be used to provide flashing aspects.

For three- and four-aspect signals using LEDs the circuit shown in Figure 15.7 is strongly recommended. Although designed for four-aspect installations its advantages make it a worthwhile proposition for three-aspect signalling. The signals require only

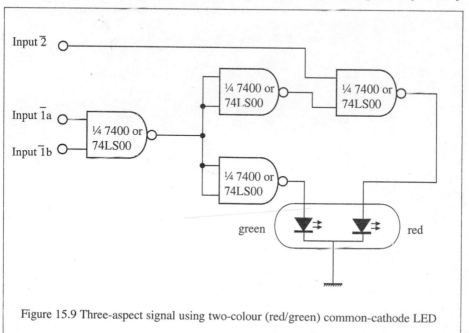

Figure 15.9 Three-aspect signal using two-colour (red/green) common-cathode LED

a three-wire connection and each LED is protected against reverse polarity by its 'partner'. The three identical input 1s provide for manual override and turnout switches as well as section occupation. Moreover, if one input 1 is paralleled with input 0 the resultant input provides a blanking facility, a low input extinguishing the signal; use is made of this in the flashing yellow aspect system described in Chapter 22. The additional output provides correct output (the product of the three input 1s) for the previous section's input 2.

For three-aspect operation keep input 3 high (leave it disconnected or, better, tie it to supply positive via a 10 K resistor) so that the double-yellow aspect is impossible and omit the LED yellow 2.

The circuit's only disadvantage is that sneak current can cause the red aspect to glow while the green is on and *vice-versa*. If this happens connect a resistor (start with 1 K) in parallel with each LED pair.

Searchlight signals

Multicolour LEDs make the modelling of two- and three-aspect searchlight signals very simple, there being no need to employ separate coloured light sources for mixing in a light pipe. Unfortunately the huge diversity of multicolour LED types including three-lead common anode, three-lead common cathode, four-lead independent and two-lead reverse-parallel types is further complicated by the availability of types having red and green and red and amber LED junctions. Space does not permit the inclusion of diagrams for all the possible permutations, so circuits for three-lead common-cathode red/green types are shown — circuits for the other types can be deduced quite easily. Figures 15.8 and 15.9 show circuits for two- and three-aspect signals respectively.

Components

Maplin catalogue numbers are as follows: BC547 QQ14Q, 7400 QX37S, 74LS00 YF00A, 74LS04 YF04E, 74LS05 YF05F, 74LS138 YF53H, 74LS139 YF54J.

The 74LS145 is not available from Maplin, but is stocked by some other suppliers; see advertisements in the electronics press.

Tri-colour common-cathode LEDs: 3mm GW62S, 5 mm YH75S.

Chapter 16

Semaphore signalling and turnout (points) operation

There are two ways by which a semaphore signal can be operated from the output of an electrical circuit. The simplest method, only possible when the entire signal mechanism is very free-moving, is to provide a mechanical link between the mechanism (the counter-balance is a suitable part of it) and the armature of a low-voltage relay. The relay coil may then be connected to the output of a section bistable or track circuit unit. If the relay contacts are left in place, they may be used to operate other signals or in interlock systems. The relay may be replaced by a home-made solenoid consisting of a coil wound on such a former as a section of ballpoint refill using a steel pin as armature, but you will need some means, eg a counterbalance weight, to return the signal arm when the coil is not energized. The coil will need a large number of turns, eg 2,000, if it is to be operated by the output of a bistable or track circuit unit, ie current in the region 10 to 50 mA.

The alternative method of driving a semaphore signal — and the only method of operating turnouts (formerly called points in the UK and switches in the USA) — is to use a turnout motor (switch machine). This consists of a pair of solenoids enclosing a common armature, which is free to slide between them. Usual practice is to energize briefly one of the solenoids using ac or dc so that the armature is drawn into its core. It then remains in that position until the other solenoid is similarly energized, when it is drawn back again. A spigot on the armature provides for the mechanical link to the turnout blade or signal mechanism. Since only a brief burst of power (say ¼ second) is needed to operate the motor, current is normally switched using a passing-contact switch or an 'electric pencil'.

A turnout motor draws a substantial current. The dc resistance of each solenoid is typically about 5 R so that a 12 V dc supply could drive up to 2.4 A through it. Appreciable power is needed to draw a turnout blade against the spring. Semaphore signals for this kind of operation do not need to be so free moving! Obviously it is not possible to operate a turnout motor direct from the output of a section bistable or track circuit.

It is possible, however, to drive a turnout motor electronically and the driver circuit may itself be operated direct from a bistable or track circuit unit or from an ordinary two-way slide or toggle switch. A suitable circuit is shown in Figure 16.1.

Figure 16.1 shows a suitable circuit. In its simplest form it consists of SPDT switch S1, capacitor C1, the two solenoids and a 22 V *smoothed* power supply. When S1 is set to the upper position, capacitor C1 charges up via solenoid L2. As long as the switch is kept in this position, the capacitor will be kept fully charged, which is use-

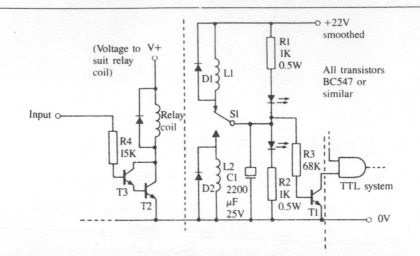

Figure 16.1 *Capacitor charge/discharge system for turnout motors and semaphore signals. The turnout motor solenoids are represented by L1 and L2. S1 may be a switch (SPDT) or relay contacts driven by circuitry to the left of the dotted line. R3/T1 provides a TTL-compatible output.*

ful. When the switch is moved to the lower position, the capacitor discharges through solenoid L2 and, as long as the switch is kept in that position, the capacitor will be short-circuited and therefore kept discharged. A useful feature is that this eliminates the need for those awkward passing-contact switches. Any good-quality SPDT switch will do. For automatic operation, which we shall discuss later, the switch may be replaced by relay contacts. Another convenient feature of this circuit is that a digital indication of the setting of the turnout (or signal) can be obtained from the 'top' of the capacitor. When the capacitor is charged, the voltage will equal the supply voltage. When the capacitor is discharged, the voltage will be zero.

So, we can fit a pair of LEDs, shown in Figure 16.1, to indicate the setting of the turnout in a mimic diagram perhaps. If we want a TTL-compatible output, eg as an input to a junction signalling system (Chapter 20), it is essential to use a transistor as a 'buffer' between the 22 V 'high' and the TTL's 5 V 'high'. This, too, is shown in Figure 16.1. Note that when the switch is in the 'upper' position and the capacitor is charged, the output obtainable from the collector of the transistor will be a logical '0'.

The diodes D1 and D2 protect the electronic circuitry against the effects of inductive overshoot when the solenoids are de-energized. These diodes may be omitted if the basic circuit (no LEDs and no transistor) is being used.

Automatic operation

For automatic operation SPDT switch S1 is replaced by SPDT relay contacts and again any good quality relay will do. The contacts are never required to *break* current, which is the more demanding operation.

The relay may be driven by transistor circuitry such as that shown in Figure 16.1 and much depends on the rating of the relay coil, although you may not need a Darlington. The input of this circuit is TTL-compatible. A logical '1' applied to the input will energize the relay coil and use is made of this facility in the route-setting system described in Chapter 23.

Chapter 17

Manual override

In prototype automatic signalling systems — as in the model signalling systems described in Chapter 15 — the signals clear automatically as the trains vacate the blocks being guarded. On prototype railways, however, there are occasions when the signalman needs to stop a train even though the line is clear. For example, there may be a fallen tree, a subsidence, or even — as I discovered once on a visit to Rugby Power Box — damage by vandals to the signalling system itself. For this reason UK legislation demands that a certain proportion of automatic signals be fitted with *manual override*, that is, a system whereby the signalman can override the automatic system and set the designated signal to danger and, of course, the one or two signals in rear of it to caution aspects as appropriate.

On a model railway manual override is similarly invaluable on certain signals, and not simply with the aim of emulating prototype practice, worthy though that may be. A facility to set a signal to danger forms the basis of simulated manual signalling (Chapter 18), signalling at junctions (Chapter 20) and some forms of overlap (Chapter 19).

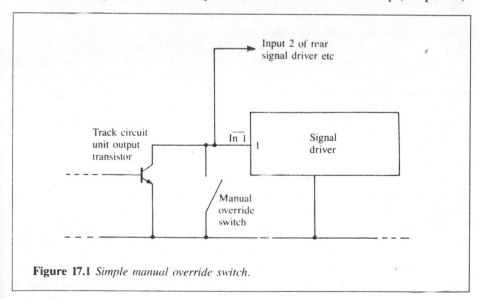

Figure 17.1 *Simple manual override switch.*

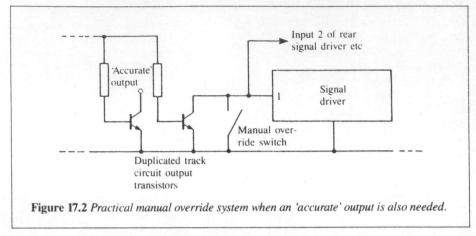

Figure 17.2 *Practical manual override system when an 'accurate' output is also needed.*

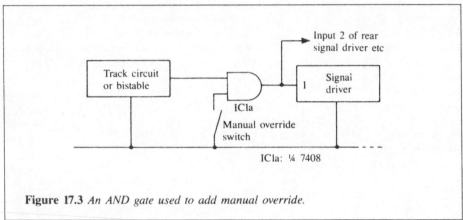

Figure 17.3 *An AND gate used to add manual override.*

The signal driver circuit — and this applies equally to all the circuits described in Chapter 15 — sets the signal to danger when a logical '0' is applied to input 1. Normally this '0' comes from the track circuit unit or block bistable. In manual override we 'trick' the signal driver into thinking that block 1 is occupied, even though it is not. The easiest way to do this is to connect a single-pole single-throw switch in parallel with the track circuit unit's output transistor, as shown in Figure 17.1. Closing the switch short-circuits this transistor, giving the same effect as if a train were detected. So, a logical '0' is presented to the signal driver input and the signal goes to danger.

But, and it's a big but, there are many circumstances in which you cannot use this simple arrangement. For instance, (i) you cannot use it if the train detector involves a bistable using NAND gates. You should avoid short-circuiting to ground the output of any TTL device, unless it has open-collector outputs. Even if your bistables use the 7401 or 7403 ICs which have open-collector outputs, your manual override switch will interfere with the bistable action, so that the signal will not necessarily clear when the manual override is removed and (ii) you cannot use it on a track circuit output if that output is also required to feed some other system which demands consistently accurate block occupation information, such as a 'block occupied' indicator LED or a progressive cab control (Chapter 29) unit. Closing the switch would, of course, light the LED although the block is vacant and might trick the progressive cab control (PCC) unit into connecting a controller to a vacant block. What you must do is to distinguish between the 'accurate' track circuit output needed by the indicator and the PCC unit and the 'vulnerable' input to the signal driver. Also, you must keep these two signal paths separate, so the latter cannot interfere with the former.

There are two ways in which this can be done:

(a) If the track circuit unit is easily accessible and if there is room on its circuit board, give it a second output transistor in parallel with the first. You will need to duplicate its bias resistor as well (see Figure 17.2). Now you have two identical and separate track circuit outputs, one of which may be dedicated to 'accurate' indications and the other for the 'vulnerable' feed to the signal driver, complete with manual override switch.

(b) If the above is not feasible, or even if it is, consider instead inserting an AND gate between the 'accurate' track circuit (or bistable) output and the signal driver input. Connect the manual override switch between the other input of the AND gate and ground, as in Figure 17.3. Closing the switch will put a '0' on that input of the gate, ensuring that it delivers a '0' to the signal driver, whatever the state of the other input. When the switch is open, of course, the track circuit (or bistable) will drive the signal driver normally.

Note that for many reasons (b) is preferable. For instance, we could use a three-input AND gate. This gives us a spare input on which the application of a logical '0' will set the signal to danger. If our signal were at a trailing junction this third input might be related to the setting of the turnout (points) receiving a '0' when the turnout is set against the approaching train. See Chapter 20 for further information. For another system of manual override applicable to signals at running junctions see Chapter 20.

You may well wonder what is wrong with the simple system shown in Figure 17.4, in which a single-pole double-throw switch applies a '0' to the signal drive input without affecting the track circuit or bistable output. It's fine in theory, but you may find that in practice it is less than satisfactory, especially with bistables. The reason is that this arrangement is liable to introduce more noise into the system but try it by all means if you wish.

If your signals are three- or four-aspect types, the input 2 to the signal driver in rear of that being overridden *must* be taken directly from input 1 of the overridden signal driver, so that the override will set the signal in rear to yellow. So, too, if your signals are four-aspect types, the input 3 to the signal driver next-but-one in rear must be similarly derived. The connection to signal drivers in rear is shown in Figures 17.1, 17.2 and 17.3.

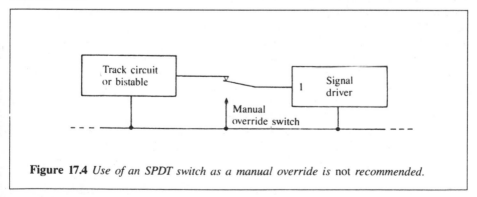

Figure 17.4 *Use of an SPDT switch as a manual override is* not *recommended.*

Chapter 18

Simulated manual signalling

Even to a casual observer of prototype railways there is a fundamental difference between the behaviour of automatic signals and manually operated ones. Automatic signals, as we noted in Chapter 17, clear automatically to green as the trains vacate the blocks being guarded. Consequently, even on intensely trafficked lines, automatic signals generally spend most of the time at green. Manually operated signals, on the other hand, spend most of the time at danger (or caution if two-aspect repeaters). They are only cleared by the signalman when he is expecting a train (assuming of course that the line is clear).

We could simulate a manual signalling system by giving every signal a manual override (Chapter 17) and releasing the override switches by hand whenever a train approaches a signal. However, that would be tedious and it is quite easy to arrange for the track circuits in *rear* of a signal to pull off an otherwise permanent 'manual override'. The signal now *behaves* like a manual signal, although its operation is in fact automatic; this is why I call this 'simulated manual signalling'. Figure 18.1 shows the unit which must be added between the track circuit unit (or bistable) for the block being guarded and the signal driver, which may be any of the driver's circuits in Chapter 15. The unit uses the three-input NAND gates in the 7410 IC, although IC1c is used

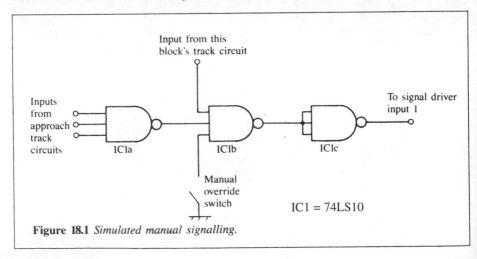

Figure 18.1 *Simulated manual signalling.*

as an inverter only. Indeed IC1b and IC1c together behave like a three-input AND gate. As shown in the Figure, the unit clears the signal when there is a train in any of the *three* track circuits on the approach to the signal. If you wish to modify this to the *two* or even *one* block in rear of the signal, simply connect the spare inputs of IC1a to the supply *positive* rail via a 10 K resistor. A manual override is shown on one input to IC1b.

Components
The Maplin catalogue number of the 74LS10 is YF08J.

Chapter 19

Overlapping of blocks

In model railway signalling there is a very cogent reason for incorporating some form of *overlap*. Often a model train will consist of a locomotive, which, of course, is detected by track circuits, pulling unmodified rolling stock which remains undetected. Without overlap a train whose locomotive has just entered a block will trail into the previous block in which it is not detected and therefore unprotected. If the blocks are short, as they often are on model railways, spectators will be presented with the sight of coaches or wagons inside a signal showing a proceed aspect — and that just does not look right. An *overlap* system ensures that, when needed, there are at least two danger signals protecting the train. This makes signal operation more authentic and, if you use interlock (Chapter 26), the protection is more complete.

There are three ways in which overlap may be provided.

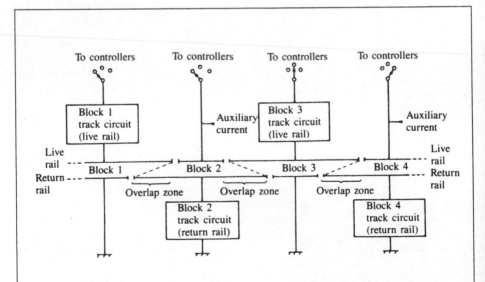

Figure 19.1 *Alternate-rail track circuiting. By staggering the rail breaks blocks can be made to overlap giving prototypical protection even when locomotives only are detected.*

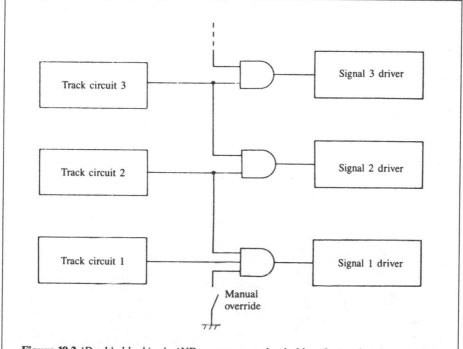

Figure 19.2 *'Double blocking': AND gates are used to hold each signal at danger while the train is in either of two blocks. A manual override has been fitted to signal 1, demanding the use of a three-input AND gate.*

Alternate-rail track circuting

In Part 4 we saw that there are two modes, live-rail and return-rail, in which track circuits operate and that the limits of a live-rail track-circuited section are defined by rail breaks in the live-rail and those of a return-rail track-circuited section by rail breaks in the return rail. If, therefore, successive blocks use live-rail and return-rail track circuits alternately, by careful staggering of the rail breaks as shown in Figure 19.1 it is possible to make adjacent blocks overlap; when in an overlap zone a train will be detected by *both* circuits.

A consequence of this is that, while in an overlap zone, a loco will suffer two 0.7 V drops, one from each track circuit. In practice this generally makes little difference to the performance of trains, especially with PWM controllers. With closed-loop controllers, however, a slight loss of speed, especially at low speed control settings, may be noticeable. One other problem arises if track circuits overlap in a zone connected to a controller having a diode across its output terminals, as in Chapters 3 to 6. When the controller is at 'stop', or is off, this diode is either forward biased or reverse biased by the source of auxiliary current, depending on the setting of the direction-change switch. If the diode is reverse biased, it will, of course, have no effect on the track circuit but if forward biased it will limit the track circuit voltage to about 0.7 V which is insufficient to activate the two track circuits in series. So, if a train is stopped in an overlap zone, on one setting of the direction control, train detection will fail. The solution is to modify the controller by adding a second diode in series with the first.

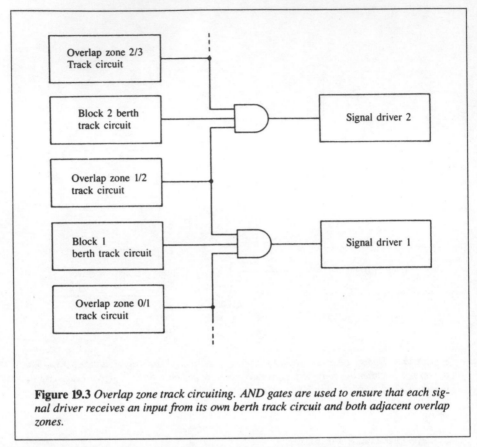

Figure 19.3 *Overlap zone track circuiting. AND gates are used to ensure that each signal driver receives an input from its own berth track circuit and both adjacent overlap zones.*

This diode, which serves to protect the controller against the effects of inductive overshoot, has no effect on the operation of track circuits used singly. It is in parallel with the twin-T pair or the base/emitter junctions of the front-end pair of transistors.

Double blocking

This term was originally applied in prototype signalling to the practice of giving additional protection to high-speed trains by clearing the signals only when there were at least *two* clear blocks in advance. The model version, however, works retrospectively by ensuring that there are always at least *two* signals at danger behind the locomotive. The simplest way to provide double blocking is to feed each signal driver's input 1 from the outputs of *two* track circuits — the one guarding the block being signalled and the other guarding the next block in advance. Use AND gates to parallel the feeds; this will prevent interference between the track circut outputs; see Figure 19.2.

Overlap-zone track circuiting

Each block is given two track circuits: one immediately inside the signal, which separately guards the overlap zone, and one, called the *berth* track circuit, which is specific to its block. Electrically this system is similar to double blocking, the output of the overlap-zone track circuit being added to that of the two adjacent berth track circuits by means of AND gates as shown in Figure 19.3.

Chapter 20

Junction signalling

The signalling systems considered so far have all related primarily to *running signals*, ie signals guarding blocks without the complications of junctions. These signals, when functioning automatically, are operated simply by the movements of trains through the block sections. At junctions, however, the signals must also take into consideration the setting of the turnouts (formerly called 'points' in the UK and 'switches' in the USA). For this reason it is necessary to feed into any junction signalling system information about the setting of the turnouts. There are several ways in which electrical outputs for feeding into the signalling system may be derived:

1 Some turnouts, eg the long obsolete (but still obtainable) Hornby Dublo live-frog OO/HO types, incorporate built-in SPDT contacts linked mechanically to the turnout tiebar.

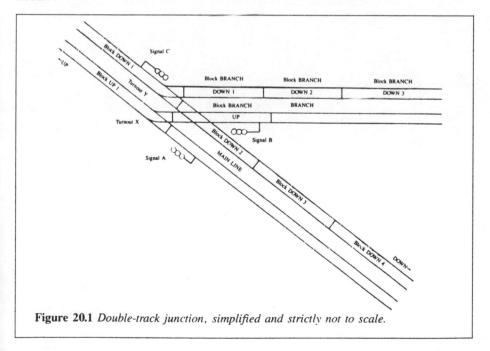

Figure 20.1 *Double-track junction, simplified and strictly not to scale.*

2 Peco manufactures a SPDT switch which may be fitted to the Peco turnout motor.

3 If the turnout is electrically operated by an electronic system, eg as in Chapter 16 of this book, a suitable output can be obtained from the driver circuit.

4 Some passing-contact switches intended for the electric operation of turnout motors also include SPDT contacts from which a suitable output can be derived.

5 On some parts of my own layout I have tackled the problem the other way round. These turnouts are operated mechanically by a spring-and-cable mechanism from the toggles of a bank of drawstop-type switches whose electrical contacts provide the inputs to the signalling system.

6 If all else fails, it should not be beyond the ingenuity of the average model railway enthusiast to fashion some means of linking the turnout tiebar to a microswitch.

Junction signals are of two types: at a *trailing junction* lines converge and at a *facing junction* lines diverge, so the trains have a choice of routes. Some signals at facing junctions have a separate head for each route, while in others a single head shows the appropriate aspect for whichever route is set up, the route being identified by some sort of indicator. Any junction is, of course, both trailing and facing depending on the direction of a train approaching it. At a double-track running junction, one route will send the train across the path of oncoming traffic, which can add further complications.

Trailing junctions

Figure 20.1 shows a typical double-track junction. You will notice that there are two trailing-junction signals, A and B, and one facing junction signal, C, with the two trailing junction signals requiring quite different inputs. Signal A is simplest as all that is needed is a simple manual override type circuit; the type shown in Figure 17.3 is recommended. When turnout X is set for the branch, a '0' must be applied to one input of the AND gate, so that input 1 of the signal driver receives a '0' setting the signal to danger.

Signal B is more complicated. A similar override to that on signal A must be incor-

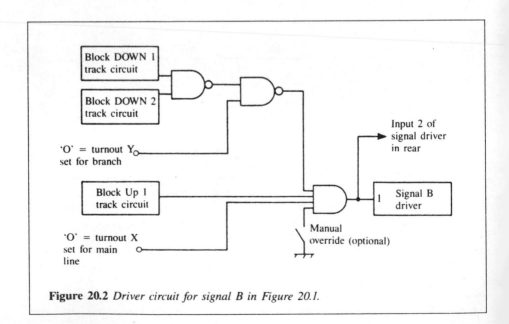

Figure 20.2 *Driver circuit for signal B in Figure 20.1.*

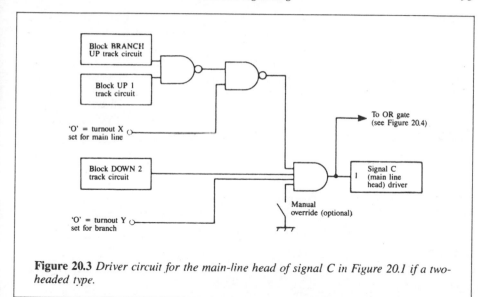

Figure 20.3 *Driver circuit for the main-line head of signal C in Figure 20.1 if a two-headed type.*

porated, but this time, of course, it is when turnout X is set for the main line that a '0' must be applied to the AND gate. However, the crossing introduces further complications. Clearly we must also override signal B to danger when turnout Y is set for the down main line and a train is approaching the junction or crossing it. Figure 20.2 shows a suitable scheme for feeding input 1 of signal B's driver. The drivers themselves for signals A and B may, of course, be any of the driver circuits described in Chapter 15.

Facing junctions

The facing junction signal C in Figure 20.1 could be either of two types. It could employ separate heads for the main line and the branch or it could use a single head with a route indicator. In the UK the commonest types of route indicator are the 'feather' of three or five 'lunar' lights illuminated when the line is cleared for a diverging route and the 'theatre'-type alphanumeric indicator which is separately treated in Chapter 21. Electrically, the two-headed version may be regarded as two separate signals, one for each route, the head for the unselected route being overridden to danger by the setting for turnout Y.

For the branch head the circuitry is simple, resembling that of signal A. All that is needed is a simple override to set this head to danger when turnout Y is set for the main line. For the main-line head the circuitry is exactly like that for signal B. The head must be overridden to danger when turnout Y is set for the branch or when turnout X is set for the branch and there is a train on the up with a circuit like that in Figure 20.3. Unfortunately our difficulties do not end here. If the signalling is three- or four-aspect, we need to set the signal in rear of C to yellow if *both* heads of C are at danger. To do this we need an OR gate or its equivalent as shown in Figure 20.4.

If signal C is a single-head type with route indicator, life gets really interesting. To make sure that all eventualities are covered, let's assume the worst by making signal C a four-aspect type with a 'feather'-type route indicator. 'Feathers' are available in 4 mm scale in the 'ECKON' range of products from CCH Models and they are

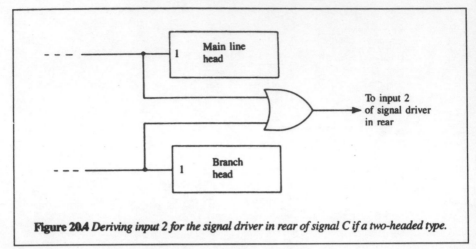

Figure 20.4 *Deriving input 2 for the signal driver in rear of signal C if a two-headed type.*

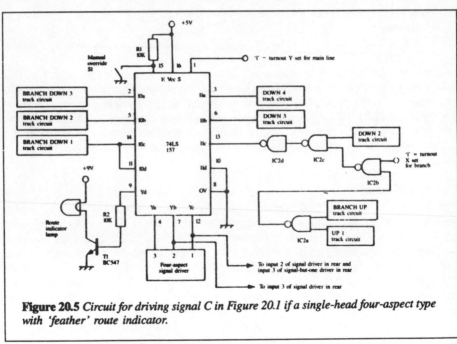

Figure 20.5 *Circuit for driving signal C in Figure 20.1 if a single-head four-aspect type with 'feather' route indicator.*

illuminated by a 'grain-of-rice' subminiature filament lamp which operates well from a 9 V supply. The difficulty is that the three inputs to the standard four-aspect signal driver (see Chapter 15) must all be simultaneously switched between the three main-line block track circuit outputs in advance (Down 2, Down 3 and Down 4) and the three branch line block track circuit outputs (Branch down 1, Branch down 2 and Branch down 3) in advance. This looks like a candidate for a three-pole, double-throw switch ganged to the turnout switch. However, although we could use a switch or a relay to perform this function, their use is not recommended for reasons of expense, convenience and reliability for all mechanical switches are prone to wear. The good news is that those responsible for the design of TTL have anticipated our problem and produced a 'chip' which seems to have this very application in mind: the 74157 (or the 74LS157). This is called a 'quad two-input data selector' or 'multiplexer'. It is, effectively, a four-pole two-way logic switch and it selects one set of four inputs out of two sets. (See Appendix 13 for more detailed information.)

Figure 20.5 shows the resulting circuit. Three of the four 'selects' in the '157 switch the inputs to the conventional four-aspect signal driver. Note that the Down 2 input includes the now familiar arrangements to override the signals to danger if a train from the branch should be crossing its path. Only a two-input AND gate is needed and this is provided by a pair of NANDs which neatly uses all four gates on a 74LS00. One 'select' has been used to derive bias for a transistor switching the 'feather' route indicator. This correctly only illuminates the 'feather' when the turnout is set for the branch and the first block (at least) in the branch is available.

An interesting feature of the '157 is its 'enable' input (pin 15). As long as this is kept at '0' the device functions normally but if a '1' is applied to it, the four outputs all go to '0'. This provides us with a useful manual override. If S1 is switched to the 'high' position, '0's will be applied to all inputs of the signal driver, setting it to danger, and the route indicator will be extinguished.

If signal C is a three-aspect signal, the same arrangements will apply, but one 'select' of the '157 will not be used.

Components
The Maplin catalogue number of the 74LS157 is YF61R.

Chapter 21

'Theatre' indicator

Theatre indicators are widely used on British Rail in conjunction with ordinary multiple-aspect signals to indicate to train drivers approaching facing junctions which route has been set up. Often they are used at the approach to major stations to show the platform number into which the train is being routed. In general they consist of a 7 × 7 matrix of white lights, but when single-digit numbers are displayed only the centre five columns are used, so that a 7 × 5 matrix may be used to represent this. When the signal is at danger, the theatre is extinguished.

The circuit described here displays either an F (for Fast) or an S (for Slow), a typical application where a train has access to fast or slow tracks on a multiple-track main line, eg when leaving London (Euston). There are also constructional reasons for this choice — see later under 'Anode Drive Circuit'. Figure 21.1 shows the dot formation generated by the circuit described here.

LED dot matrix
The Kingbright small dot matrix is a full 7 × 5 dot matrix. But the connections to its total of 36 LED junctions are *not* straightforward. If each junction had been given, say, its own

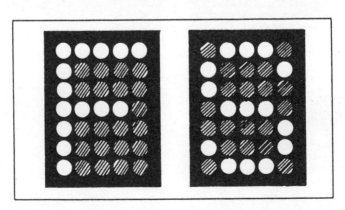

Figure 21.1 *Dot configurations for the characters generated by this circuit.*

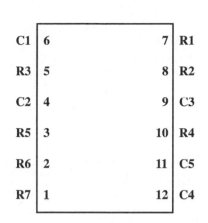

Figure 21.2 *Pin-out of the Kingbright dot matrix.*

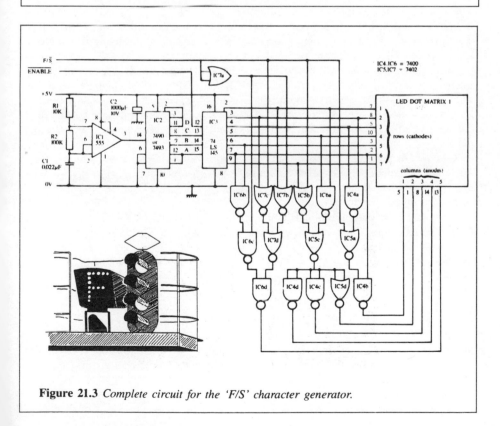

Figure 21.3 *Complete circuit for the 'F/S' character generator.*

dedicated anode connection while all shared a common cathode, the device would have required 36 pins, impractical in a package measuring only 18×13 mm. So instead, in each (vertical) column the *anodes* are commoned and in each (horizontal) row the *cathodes* are commoned. This reduces the number of pins to a manageable 12. Pin-out of the device is given in Figure 21.2.

To display most alphanumeric characters, however, it is necessary to use a strobing system. The most convenient way of doing this is to energize each row of cathodes in sequence and, while a row is energized, only those columns of anodes are energized whose dots at the points of intersection are required to be illuminated.

Although no more than one row of dots can be illuminated at once, if the complete cycle of rows is repeated at a frequency of 25 Hz or higher, it will *appear* that the whole character is illuminated. A bonus from this technique is that each dot lit in this (flashing) manner will seem brighter than it would if it were continuously lit and drawing the same average current.

Cathode drive circuit

The part of the circuit that is concerned with driving the cathodes is in principle the same no matter which characters are to be displayed. This circuitry is that surrounding IC1, IC2 and IC3 in Figure 21.3.

IC1 is a 555 timer set up as a free-running multivibrator at about 500 Hz, although the exact frequency is not critical. The 555 runs continuously, even while the display is disabled.

The output of IC1 is applied to input A of binary counter IC2. This could be a '90 or '93 in the 74 or 74LS series; in our prototype it was a 7493 hexadecimal binary counter, but we also tried a 7490 BCD counter (readily available from ex-equipment panels) and found it worked satisfactorily. These two ICs are pin-for-pin equivalents in this application provided the connections shown in Figure 21.3 are followed exactly. We returned output Q_C to reset 0, not strictly necessary with the '93, but essential with the '90. If you use the '90 you must ground the reset 9 inputs (pins 6 and 7) or the counter will be disabled and held with a constant 1001 (= 9) output. If you use the '93 these pins are not internally connected so the connections may be omitted, but it does not matter if they are left in place.

IC2 converts the train of pulses from the 555 to a four-bit binary count which resets at 1000 (= 8). Output Q_D is not used (except to reset the count); outputs Q_C, Q_B and Q_A are applied to inputs C, B and A respectively of IC3, a '145 (74LS145 in our prototype) BCD to decimal decoder with driver outputs.

The '145 has 10 output terminals numbered 0 to 9 each of which is energized, ie goes *low*, when its unique binary equivalent is applied to the inputs. The open-collector outputs are capable of sinking 80 mA and they may need to in this application because they drive the cathode-rows direct and may need to light five LED dots in parallel, eg in the top row of the F.

As the count proceeds, each output of the '145 from 0 to 7 is energized in turn. In our prototype output 0 was not used, while outputs 1 to 7 drive the cathodes of rows 1 to 7 respectively, row 1 being the top row and row 7 the bottom row.

Input D of the '145 is used as an $\overline{\text{ENABLE}}$ input. The decoder functions normally as long as this input is kept low. But if this input is allowed to go high, the '145 can only energize outputs 8 and 9 which are not used. Consequently no cathodes are driven and the display is blanked.

The prototype incorporated some additional features concerned with research and development. One was a 4.7 µF capacitor which could be switched in parallel with C1 which slowed the pulse rate to about 1 Hz. An LED (with series resistor) was connected in the output circuit of IC1 and three more in the Q_C, Q_B and Q_A outputs of IC2. These facilities made it possible to run the circuit in 'slow motion' and see exactly what was happening at each stage of the count. This proved invaluable in debugging the system.

Anode drive circuit

This circuitry, unlike the cathode drive circuitry, is determined by the characters to be displayed. F and S are ideal characters for a simple circuit since, as reference to Figure 21.1 will show, in both the three centre columns are identical, so the driving devices for these three columns can receive their inputs from the same logic circuitry. Because in each column of anodes only one LED junction at a time may be illuminated, ordinary TTL totem-pole outputs source sufficient current, the internal series resistor providing suitable limiting.

Each column's logic circuit requires inputs from the cathode drives and the character selector circuit. The latter in our application is a one-bit switch providing an F/S function, ie a high for the F and a low for the S. The anode drive circuitry of our prototype is shown as the circuitry around IC4 to IC7 in Figure 21.3. It neatly uses all the gates in twos '00s and two '02s.

Column 1 (the left-hand column) is simplest. In either F or S we want the anode on at counts 2, 3 and 6. And for the F we want the anode on permanently. NAND IC4a delivers a '1' at counts 2 and 3, which is applied to one input of NOR IC5a. The F/S control signal is applied direct to the other input of IC5a. So the output of IC5s will be a '0' if the count is at 2 or 3 or if the character selected is F. This is fed to one input of NAND IC4b, the other input of which is taken from the row 6 cathode drive. Consideration of this will show that the anode of column 1, driven from the output of IC4b, goes high when the application demands it.

Columns 2, 3 and 4 are driven by the three spare gates (IC5d, IC4c and IC4d) used as inverters and all controlled from the output of IC5c. For both F and S we want these anodes on at counts 1 and 4. IC6a's output delivers '1' at these counts. For S only we want these anodes on additionally at count 7; IC5b provides a '1' only when the count is at 7 *and* S is selected. IC5c NORs these '1's to feed the drivers.

Column 5 (the right hand column) is the most complex. For F we want the anode on at count 1 only. For S we want it on at counts 2, 5 and 6. IC7a and IC7b select 1 for F; IC7c selects 2 for S and IC7a, IC6b and IC6c select 5 and 6 for S. IC7d and IC6d combine these outputs and drive column 5.

Construction

The prototype was assembled on a Veroboard measuring 7¾ × 3¾ in (197 × 95 mm). This was larger than this circuit strictly demands, but in order to test the circuit we mounted the dot matrix in a socket on the circuit board itself. The plans were later to remove it and install it in another socket in a signal assembly connected by a bundle of 12 wires to yet another socket used as plug and plugged into the original socket on the circuit board. The scenic problem is to conceal the 12 wires. If the signal is on a gantry, it may be possible to conceal the bundle of wires inside the truss and perhaps take the wires away through a hole in a trackside retaining wall.

Control

The circuit has two controls: $\overline{\text{ENABLE}}$ and F/S. A '1' on $\overline{\text{ENABLE}}$ blanks the display. A '1' on F/S gives F and a '0' gives S, in either case provided there is a '0' on $\overline{\text{ENABLE}}$. On our prototype these control functions were both provided by single-pole slide switches to ground with 10 K pull-up resistors to the positive rail but they could be provided automatically from other parts of a TTL-based signalling system.

Power supply and other considerations

Like all TTL-based circuits, this one requires a smoothed, regulated 5 V supply. Mine consumed a steady 90 mA, but this will vary depending on the TTL families (74 or 74LS) used.

It is essential if this circuit is to be used in close proximity to a working model railway, as is likely, that a hefty smoothing capacitor (I used 1000 μF) be connected across the supply lines on the circuit board). Without this, electrical interference from the trains wreaks havoc with the operation of this circuit.

Components

The Kingbright small LED dot matrix is available from Maplin (catalogue number FE25C). Maplin catalogue numbers for other ICs are: 555 QH66W, 7490 QX66W, 74LS90 YF38R, 7493 YF40T, 7400 QX37S, 74LS00 YF00A, 7402 QX39N, 74LS02 YF02C.

The 74145 is not available from Maplin, but is supplied by some other stockists.

Chapter 22

Flashing yellow aspects

The introduction of the Inter-City 125 high-speed trains (HSTs) on British Rail caused an interesting problem regarding junction signalling. HSTs have superior braking which enables the drivers to delay the application of the brakes. For example, the drivers learned by experience that they could pass a signal at double yellow and only apply the brakes on passing the next signal at yellow as there was still adequate braking distance.

Difficulties arose because in UK practice multiple-aspect signalling is also used to regulate the speed of trains approaching junctions. In Figure 22.1a the diverging route at the junction is speed restricted to, say 40 mph. Standard practice to slow down trains taking this diverging route is to manually override signal 5 to danger. When the turnout is set for the diverging route, therefore, signal 4 would display single yellow plus the diverging route indication, signal 3 would display double yellow and signals 2 and 1 green. As a train approaches signal 4, the manual override on signal 5 is automatically removed, so that signals 5 and 4 change to less restrictive aspects. Now, there was a danger that HST drivers might ignore the double-yellow aspect of signal 3, believing that at signal 4 they would still have adequate braking distance, and approach signal 4 at 100 mph, almost at once entering the diverging route dangerously above its 40 mph restriction. The problem was overcome by the introduction of two new aspects, which advise train drivers that they are routed for a restricted divergence and must adjust their speed accordingly. Manual override is applied to signal 5 as before, and signal 4 shows single yellow plus divergence as before. Signal 3, however, shows a *flashing* single yellow aspect and signal 2 a flashing double-yellow aspect. Signal 1, as before, shows green. As before, when the train approaches signal 4, the manual override is removed from signal 5. (This is shown in Figure 22.1b.) The flashing aspects flash at 70 cycles per minute (1.2 Hz), 50 per cent duty cycle. In the flashing double-yellow aspect, the aspects flash in unison, not alternately.

Modelling the system
If you are a modern-image modeller and if your layout is sufficiently large to justify four-aspect signalling, you can add interest and variety to your layout by modelling a flashing yellow-aspect system. Alternatively, you may be able to adapt the following to simulate the flashing yellow aspects seen on some continental railways. What follows is a description of one way of reproducing the British Rail system. We shall start by considering the signals in reverse numerical order.

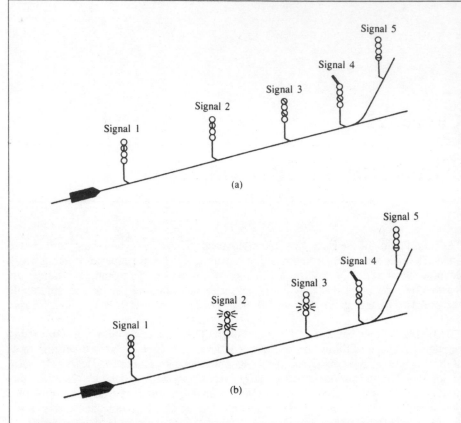

Figure 22.1 *Four-aspect signalling on the approach to a running junction: (a) the 'traditional' system; (b) the system recently introduced on parts of British Rail — signals 2 and 3 show flashing yellow aspects.*

Signal 5: Any four-aspect signal driver (Figures 15.6 or 15.7) is suitable provided it is fitted with a manual override (Chapter 17) whose free input is taken from $\overline{F}$ — I'll explain what this means later.

Signal 4: Any four-aspect signal driver with diverging route indicator and two-way input selector (Figure 20.5) is suitable.

Signal 3: This signal is required on occasions to display the flashing single yellow aspect. Only the signal driver circuit of Figure 15.7 is suitable and it must be connected as shown in Figure 20.2. A manual override from $\overline{F}$ is applied via NAND gates IC1a and IC1b to input 2, when this is activated, the single yellow aspect is displayed (overriding the double yellow or green aspects) unless, of course, input 1 is also activated whereupon the signal will go to danger.

The signal's blanking input (inputs 1a and 0 paralleled) is taken from the output of IC1c. One input of IC1c is fed from the output of IC2, a 555 timer set up as a free running multivibrator at 1.2 Hz and about 50 per cent duty cycle. The other input of IC1b is taken from input F (the inverse of input $\overline{F}$). We shall see shortly how inputs F and $\overline{F}$ are derived.

When the flashing system is on, a '1' from input F is applied to one input of IC1c and the pulses from the 555 are applied to the other. The output therefore consists of the pulses derived from 555 and these are applied to the signal's blanking input so that aspect yellow 1 is made to flash at 1.2 Hz. When the flashing system is off, F is at '0', so a '0' is applied to one input of IC1c. This holds its high output regardless

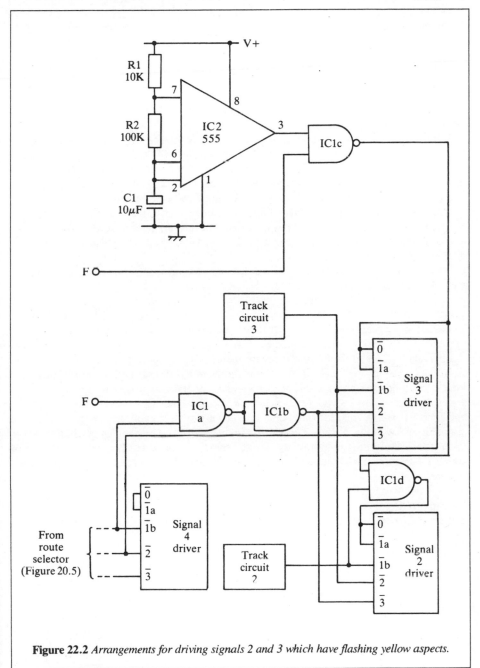

Figure 22.2 *Arrangements for driving signals 2 and 3 which have flashing yellow aspects.*

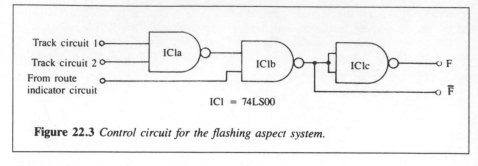

Figure 22.3 *Control circuit for the flashing aspect system.*

of the pulses from the 555 which are still being applied to the other input, so that the signal behaves normally.

Signal 2: This signal is required on occasion to display the flashing double-yellow aspect. It is driven in a manner generally similar to signal 3, as Figure 22.2 shows. Only the driver circuit of Figure 15.7 is suitable. The manual override is applied to input 3 of the signal driver to activate the double-yellow aspect. Pulses from IC1c are applied to its blanking input, so that the two aspects flash in unison when required.

You may wonder why there is also a feed from input 1b of signal 2's driver to IC1d. The reason is as follows. When a train passes signal 2 at flashing double-yellow, signal 2 goes to danger but it is still receiving blanking pulses. IC1d overrides the pulse so that a steady danger aspect is given.

Signal 1: Signal 1 is not affected by the flashing system, so may be driven in the normal way. Any four-aspect driver circuit may be used.

Control

The flashing system is controlled as follows: the flashing system is on when a train is in section 1 (that is, the section guarded by signal 1 and approaching signal 2) *or* in section 2 (approaching 3) *and* the turnout is set for the diverging route, the first section (at least) of which is vacant, so that the 'feather' route indicator is illuminated. It helps if there is a long overlap beyond signal 3 so that it is not until the train is, prototypically, approaching signal 4 that it vacates section 2, clearing the system. The two complementary outputs F and F̄ are '1' and '0' respectively when the flashing system is on. Figure 22.3 shows the simplicity of the control circuit. Note the input from the route-indicator circuit; this is taken straight from the output of the fourth 'select' of the data selector on the input of signal 4's driver circuit (Figure 20.5). This input goes high when the route indicator is illuminated.

Components

Maplin catalogue numbers are as follows: 555 QH66W, 7400 QX37S, 74LS00 YF00A.

Chapter 23

Route setting

In old-fashioned signal boxes (or 'towers' as they are called in North America) each turnout ('point' or 'switch') and each signal was operated by its own individual lever. As a train entered the area covered by the box, the signalman ('towerman') had to set up its route which might involve the operation of a dozen or so levers. On many model railways a similar practice was observed. In modern power boxes, however, the task is greatly simplified. A huge mimic diagram shows at once all that is happening in the area controlled. In order to set up a route the signalman has only to pull a drawstop for the starting point and another for the destination and the whole route is set up automatically, all the turnouts and signals being changed as necessary. The route set up is indicated on the mimic diagram by white lights and these are replaced by red lights as the train enters the area and activates its track circuits. The aspect of the signals is indicated in a simplified manner, a red lamp alongside the track representing a danger signal and a green lamp a signal showing any proceed aspect, which may be a yellow or double yellow.

Interest in modern practice is growing apace among railway modellers and several have satisfactorily installed this kind of route setting panel. Obviously each panel must be tailor-made for the layout or part of a layout that it represents, which means that only general guidance can be given here. It is assumed that track circuiting is installed throughout and that each turnout is controlled by the automatic turnout system described in Chapter 16. Only one route at a time can be set on the system to be described, but it is surprisingly simple.

Electronics of the panel
Figure 23.1 shows part of a route-setting control panel. Routes can be set from A or B via N to X, Y or Z, X, Y and Z may represent sidings. A and B may represent parts of a main line, A' and B' representing one end of the next section of that main line.

There are five drawstops that we shall consider: A, B, X, Y and Z. Each drawstop, when pulled, breaks a contact and allows a number of logic inputs to rise from logical '0' to '1'. Figure 23.2 shows the electronics behind the panel. The inputs from the drawstops and the relevant track circuits are applied to an array of NAND gates (IC1 and IC2). When a route is selected and its track circuit shows the line as available, a gate receives two '1's on its inputs *and* so its output goes to '0'. The lamps are replaced by LEDs with current limiting resistors from gate output to the +5V supply. A suitable resistor value is 330R.

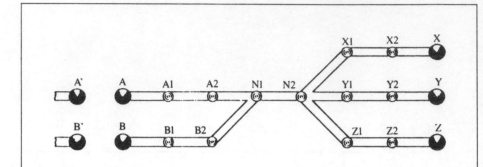

Figure 23.1 *Part of a modern-image but freelance route-setting panel. The black blobs are drawstops; the smaller white circles are lamp bezels.*

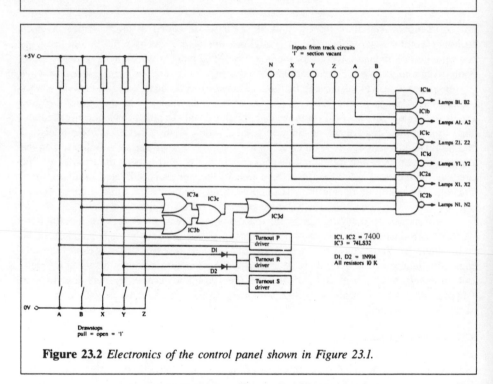

Figure 23.2 *Electronics of the control panel shown in Figure 23.1.*

The central section of the route, N, has its lights illuminated if it is vacant and if *any* route is set. So the four OR gates (IC3) are used to combine the outputs from the five drawstops for application to IC2b. The three turnout drivers (see Chapter 16 for a suitable circuit) are driven direct from the drawstop contacts, turnout R via diode matrix, since it must be actuated for routes to X or Y. (We could use an OR gate, but two diodes are cheaper and the turnout driver, unlike TTL, will respond to positive-going inputs).

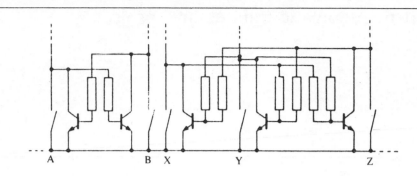

Figure 23.3 *An optional protection circuit for the drawstops shown in Figures 23.1 and 23.2: all transistors are BC547 or similar; all resistors 10 K.*

An optional extra for the drawstops is shown in Figure 23.3. Unless you can find or fabricate mechanically linked drawstops, in which the pulling of one cancels the adjacent one (eg pulling B causes A to return), there is the danger of two conflicting routes being set simultaneously (eg A *and* B). We can eliminate this ambiguity quite simply by connecting an npn transistor across each pair of contacts and arranging that this receives bias when any conflicting route is set. So, if you pull A (B not being pulled), B's transistor is turned on (although for the time being it is of course short-circuited by the B drawstop contacts) and if you now inadvertently pull B, its transistor holds the circuit closed so that route A remains set. The route set up will be displayed by the lights on the panel irrespective of the drawstop pulled.

Part 6: Automatic train control projects

Preamble

In this section a varied assortment of circuits are gathered together which all, in some way, control the train — or, at least, relieve the operator of some of the more tedious aspects of train control.

The first two are 'passive' in that they need no power supply of their own. Chapter 24 describes a circuit which enables a train to run round a reversing loop without stopping, while Chapter 25 is about a unit which provides gentle slowdowns and stops, but cannot restart a train.

Chapter 26 describes an interlock to stop trains automatically at danger signals and restart them when the signal clears with Chapter 27 extending this idea to timed station stops. In both of these projects it is assumed that the 'autostop' unit of Chapter 10 is fitted to the controller in use. The last two Chapters in this section are devoted to that age-old quest of railway modellers — multiple train control — but both avoid the complications of 'command control' systems, eg the need for 'modules' in the locos. Chapter 27 considers the idea of giving every section its own controller, a scheme that is not as bizarre as it sounds. Chapter 29 takes the idea a stage further — progressive cab control is neither as complicated nor as expensive as it sounds and permits different trains to run successively over the same section, each powered by a different controller, without operator intervention. The system does the 'thinking' and 'switching' and will even bring a train to a gentle halt when it reckons it's on a collision course.

Chapter 24

Automatic reversing loop

Reversing loops have always caused difficulties on two-rail model railways. The problem is, as Figure 24.1 shows, that the outer rail of the loop is continuous with the live rail at one end of the loop and with the return rail at the other end, causing a permanent short circuit. Standard practice has been to isolate a length of the outer rail in the loop and to arrange for it to be switched to the live or return side of the power circuit as necessary.* As a train runs around the loop, it must be stopped in the isolated section and, while it is stopped, the polarity of the section is changed, the turn-out is reset and the direction-change switch on the controller is operated. The train can now resume its journey round the loop and back on to the main line, where it is now running, of course, in the opposite direction. This stopping of the train and the three switching operations are clearly inelegant, although whatever improvements may be possible in convenience, it is inevitable that the turnout is changed and the direction switch operated while the train is in the loop. It is possible and, indeed, quite simple to arrange for trains to run around the loop *without stopping*. To do this it is necessary to isolate as much as possible of both outer and inner rails in the loop. Their power supply is derived from that of the main line via a bridge rectifier, as shown in Figure 24.2. You must decide whether you want your trains to run clockwise or anti-clockwise around the loop, since this depends upon the polarity of the connections to the bridge rectifier output (Figure 24.2 shows connections for clockwise running) and if you wish to vary the direction of running in the loop, you must fit a reversing switch between the bridge and the loop. The procedure now is to run the train into the loop (ensuring that the turnout is correctly set, of course) and, at any time while the train is wholly in the loop, change the turnout and the direction setting on the controller. It is not necessary to stop the train unless your controller has a combined speed and direction control like the one described in Chapter 9.

However, there is one disadvantage in the system just described, which is a property of the characteristics of the bridge rectifier. The voltage drop across this is about 2 V, and sufficient to cause a noticeable loss of speed as a train enters the loop. If this is unacceptable, consider replacing the bridge rectifier with the arrangement shown in Figure 24.3. This 'transistor bridge rectifier' behaves like its diode counterpart but

---

* The standard reference books on model railway electrification say that it is necessary to isolate and switch the inner rail of the loop as well. In fact this is only necessary if the turnout used is a live-frog type. If it is an insulated-frog type, the turnout action itself will correctly switch the supply to the inner rail of the loop.

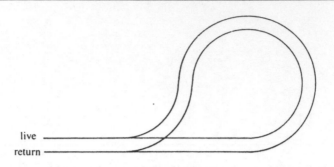

Figure 24.1 *Simplified drawing of a reverse loop. Note that the outer rail of the loop is continuous with both live and return rails, causing a permanent short circuit.*

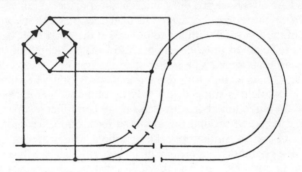

Figure 24.2 *Automatic reversing loop with connections for clockwise running.*

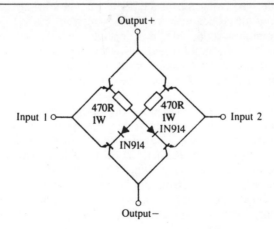

Figure 24.3 *Transistor bridge rectifier. The transistors need to be matched complementary power types.*

has a much lower voltage drop of about 0.4 V total. This is because the voltage drop across a saturated transistor is rather less than that across a forward-biased diode. The circuit is more expensive, of course, since it demands four power transistors — but then in this life there is always a price to pay for any improvement in performance!

Components

Maplin catalogue numbers are as follows: Power rectifier (1N4001) QL73Q, NPN power transistor (TIP3055) QH56L, PNP power transistor (TIP2955) QH55K, small-signal diode (1N914) QL71N.

Chapter 25

'Autoslow'

Project 3 in *Practical Electronics for Railway Modellers* described a capacitor slow-down unit for siding ends. As a loco approaches the end of a siding, it crosses a rail break, whereafter its supply is via a high-value electrolytic capacitor. As this charges up, its charge current — which is the loco's traction current — falls, giving a gradual slow-down. The trouble is that the effectiveness of this circuit varies widely according to the locomotive's characteristics. With a small light loco, such as the Mainline J72, the effect is impressive, whereas with my elderly Hornby Dublo 8F, which draws 1A, the charge-up is almost instantaneous and the slow-down unprototypically abrupt.

The 'autoslow' unit was designed as an improved version of my earlier capacitor slow-down system and in it the rate of slow-down is independent of the loco type and, usefully, adjustable. The device is 'passive', that is to say, it does not need an external power supply as it draws its power from the track.

How it works

Here it is necessary to refer to the circuit diagram in Figure 25.1. As a train approaching the siding end crosses the rail break, its power feed is diverted via Darlington pair T1/T2. The train now completes the charge-up circuit for C1, which also includes R3, VR1 and the base/emitter junctions of the Darlington. The proportion of the charge-up time during which the Darlington conducts depends on the setting of VR1. With the components shown the slow-down time is adjustable from zero to about 10 seconds.

At first, C1's charge current is high, biasing the Darlington into saturation, so that there is little effect on the speed of the train. As the charge rises, the Darlington's bias current and, therefore, its collector current falls, slowing the train until eventually it stops. As the voltage across the Darlington rises, LED1 lights up and even after the train stops remains illuminated as long as the controller remains set 'into the siding'. Therefore the LED provides a useful 'train stopped but power still on' indication which is extinguished as soon as the controller is turned to stop or to the 'out of siding' direction (or if the train is removed from the siding).

Although this unit gives gentle *stops*, it cannot by itself give a gentle *start* (if you want automatic stop *and* starts, you need the 'auto*stop*' unit described in Chapter 10. As soon as the controller is set for the 'out of siding' direction, the power circuit is completed via D1 and T3's base/emitter junction and the train will give a normal controlled start, except that it will be subjected to two 'diode drops' across the two junctions (about 1.5V). Transistor T3 now conducts removing any remaining charge on C1.

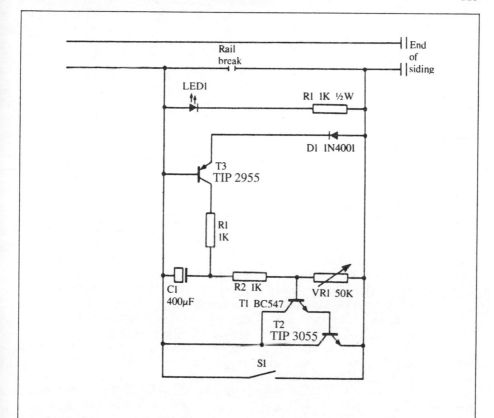

Figure 25.1 *'Autoslow' unit: the rail break is in the rail which is positive when the train is going in the direction in which it is to be slowed down.*

Optional switch S1 provides another interesting possibility for this unit as it may be used to give automatic gentle station stops in a through station. S1 is normally left open so that the unit functions in the normal way. To restart the train (in the same direction) *first* set the controller to 'stop' then close S1 so the train can now be started manually in the normal way. Cl will gradually discharge via VR1 and R2, but there will be no indication from LED1 and S1 must be reopened before the unit can stop another train. If it is left closed, trains will run through the station without stopping.

Components
Maplin catalogue numbers are as follows:
    TIP2955 QH55K, TIP3055 QH56L, BC547 QQ14Q, 1N4001 QL73Q.

Chapter 26

Active interlock

Within this book, as in *Practical Electronics for Railway Modellers*, an 'active inter-lock' is a system which automatically causes a train to gradually slow down and stop as it approaches a signal at danger and to gently restart when the signal clears. There are many ways in which this could be achieved, but nearly all present savage compli-cations. For instance, we could use a simple logic circuit like the one in Figure 26.1. This circuit activates the 'autostop unit' (Chapter 10) when there is a train in block 1 *and* in block 2. So, undoubtedly, it *would* activate the autostop unit when a train enters the block approaching a signal at danger guarding the next block in advance which is also occupied.

There are, however, many other circumstances in which adjacent track circuits are simultaneously activated. For example, when a train passes from one block to the next, for a short while, both track circuits are activated. If you use overlap (Chapter 19), this 'short while' may well last several seconds — long enough to stop the train. We could build a timing circuit (Chapter 27) to delay the activation of the autostop system in order to allow for long overlaps.

There are still other occasions when trains may legitimately occupy adjacent blocks. For example, on a single-track line, train 1 may be in a passing loop and train 2 pass-ing it on the main line and proceeding on to the block in rear of train 1. The system in Figure 26.1 cannot distinguish between approaching trains and trains drawing apart. Clearly an efficient interlock system must do so. Hence the system described in this Chapter.

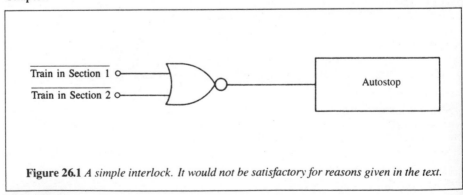

Figure 26.1 *A simple interlock. It would not be satisfactory for reasons given in the text.*

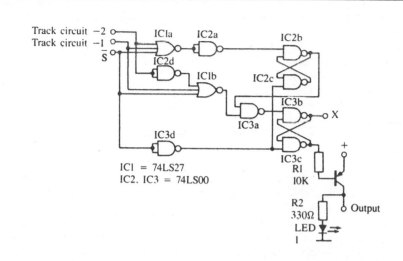

Figure 26.2 *A 'sequence-controlled' interlock. Output X is used in the timed station stop application (Chapter 27).*

How it works

The circuit shown in Figure 26.2 is 'sequence controlled'. It needs three inputs: (i) input S is taken from input 1 of the driver circuit of the signal being interlocked, so that the system 'knows' when this signal is at danger; (ii) from the track circuit of the block (called block -1) on the approach to the interlocked signal, ie in rear of it and (iii) from the track circuit on the block (called block -2) in rear of block -1. All these inputs are negative true, ie activated by a logical '0'.

The interlock unit is activated by the passage of a train from block -2 to block -1 while the signal is at danger. When the train passes from block -2 to block -1, for a few moments (at least) both track circuits are activated simultaneously. If, at the same time, the signal is at danger IC1a receives three '0' inputs and delivers a '1' output, inverted back to '0' by IC2a. This sets the bistable IC2b/IC2c to what we call the 'standby' condition. As the train approaches the signal, it clears block -2 and activates only the track circuit for block -1. Now, NOR gate IC1b, which receives the same inputs as IC1a except that the output from track circuit -2 is inverted by IC3a, delivers a '1' output. The first bistable is now in its 'standby' condition and thus IC2d receives '1's on *both* inputs and delivers a '0' output, which sets a second bistable, IC3c/IC3d, to what we call the *activated* state. Output from this bistable, when activated, drives the interlock output. The two bistables can only be reset by the clearing of the signal. When the S input goes to '1', inverter IC3d converts this to a '0' which is fed to the reset inputs of both bistables.

If your controller has positive-going output before its reversing switch (as in Chapters 3 to 6), you can connect the interlock output direct to the controller's autostop remote input. Otherwise, you will need the interface unit shown in Figure 10.3.

Although this interlock comes into operation at the right moment and clears when it should do, it nevertheless poses one problem. If two or more controllers are in use on the layout (and presumably this is so if an interlock is needed), how does the interlock unit know which controller's autostop unit to activate? The answer is that, as described, it does not but there are a number of ways in which it can make itself useful. These are as follows;

(i) If you are using cab control, you could arrange for an additional pole of each section's controller selector switch to be used to connect the interlock's output to the appropriate controller's autostop input.

(ii) If you use 'block section control' (Chapter 28), there is no problem. Each block section has its own controller, so there is no ambiguity.

(iii) If neither (i) nor (ii) is applicable, the following may be helpful. Using blocking diodes arrange for *every* interlock output to activate *every* controller's autostop unit. It may be useful if you can arrange for an alarm to sound as well. Put an LED in the output circuit of each interlock unit, so that you can see at a glance *which* interlock is operating. Then set the autostop switches on the other controllers to the 'Cancel' position to allow the other trains to proceed. (Remember to restore these switches to 'Remote' when the interlock clears.)

If you are considering the use of progressive cab control (Chapter 29), the system described in this book incorporates a comprehensive interlock system that 'knows' which controller's autostop input to address, so, the system described in this Chapter is not needed.

Problems

This circuit poses a number of problems for the unwary. It uses bistable latches which, in close proximity to a working model railway, may be subject to spurious setting and resetting as a consequence of electrical interference from the trains. If you find yourself in such difficulties try the following modifications individually or in any combination:

(i) Replace the '00s with '132s, which are pin-for-pin equivalents, but have harsher switching characteristics;

(ii) Connect a massive (470µF) electrolytic capacitor between the positive and negative supply lines *on the circuit board*;

(iii) Connect 0.1µF capacitors between all inputs and the supply negative rail.

Components

Maplin order codes are as follows:

74LS00 YF00A, 74LS27 YF18U, 74LS132 YF51F.

Chapter 27

Automatic station stops

Chapter 26 showed how we can arrange for trains to stop automatically (but gradually) at danger signals and to restart automatically (and again gradually) when the signal clears. This Chapter extends that facility to stop trains automatically at stations for a timed period.

Often there is a signal (at one time known in UK practice as the starter signal) at the locomotive end of each platform of a through station. We shall assume the presence of this signal at the station where we want our train to stop automatically. If to this signal we were to apply the active interlock considered in Chapter 26 and the manual override considered in Chapter 17, by overriding the signal to danger, we could make the train stop automatically in the station. Releasing the manual override would clear the signal and allow the train to restart. However, that would not be prototype practice. The aspect of the signal should not depend (at least not normally) on the intention of the railway to stop the train in the station; normally, it should depend only on the availability of the road in advance of the train. What we can do, however, is to apply a separate manual override to input S of the interlock unit via an AND gate, as shown in Figure 27.1. Closing the switch will not affect the signal aspect — if clear,

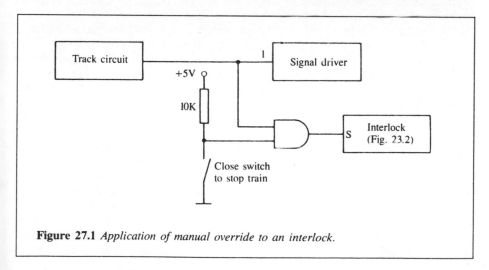

Figure 27.1 *Application of manual override to an interlock.*

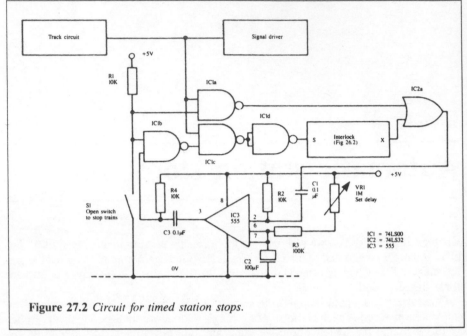

Figure 27.2 *Circuit for timed station stops.*

it will remain clear — but the interlock will now behave as though the signal were at danger and will stop the train in the station. Opening the switch will allow the train to proceed. Leaving the switch open will allow trains to pass through the station without stopping, providing of course that the signal is clear. If the signal is at danger, the train will be stopped by the interlock until the signal clears.

Timed station stops

The arrangement described above is not *fully* automatic. It stops the train in the station well enough, but you have to operate a switch to clear the interlock and restart the train. With a little more technology, however, we can arrange for the train to restart automatically after a timed interval.

The timing is carried out by the 555 timer IC which we met in Chapter 5. Again it is used as an interval timer, but this time the period timed is much longer. With the component values shown in Figure 27.2 the period is (approximately) 10 to 100 seconds. This period, incidentally, is the time from the *activation* of the interlock, when the train begins to slow down, until the *release* of the interlock, when the train will restart. In setting the delay, you must allow for the 'autostop' inertia time; the difference will represent the length of the station stop. For this application switch S1 must be *open* if automatic station stops are required. When this switch is open and when the signal is clear, input S of the interlock is activated bringing the interlock into action as a train enters the station and approaches the signal. As the interlock comes into action, a negative-going pulse is applied via C1 to the trigger input of the timer, which starts its timing cycle. During this timed period the interlock remains 'engaged' so that the train slows and stops. At the end of the timed period, the output of the timer goes 'low' and a negative-going pulse is applied via C3 to IC1b, where it causes a positive-going pulse of output which is applied via IC1c and IC1d (together acting as an AND gate) to input S of the interlock. This momentary '1' on input S resets the two bistables in the interlock, so that it clears and permits the train to restart. It is also ready immediately to stop the next train that approaches the signal.

If, at any stage during the timing cycle, switch S1 is closed, the interlock will clear and the train will restart. If the switch is left closed trains will run through the station without stopping, provided, of course, that the signal is clear. If at any time the signal goes to danger, the interlock will be activated by an approaching train, whatever the setting of the switch, and the train will be stopped until the signal clears. If this should happen during the timer's cycle, the timed period will not be affected but the ending of the period will not release the interlock. The interlock will remain engaged until the signal clears. In this way the system retains full security and follows prototype practice.

Note that this circuit, like the interlock itself in Chapter 26, is liable to be affected by electrical interference from the trains. Ensure that there is a decoupling capacitor (100 µF at least) between the positive and negative supply lines; if still troubled try 0.1 µF capacitors between inputs and supply negative.

Components
Maplin order codes for ICs are as follows: 555 QH66W, 74LS00 QX37S, 784LS32 YF21X.

Chapter 28

Block section control

The philosopher's stone, as far as railway modellers are concerned, is a system enabling the independent control of a number of trains on the same layout. Recently a number of 'command control' systems have appeared on the market which meet this need.

These systems work by making the track permanently live and by using a 'module' inside each locomotive, which is, in effect, a controller. This controller responds to 'commands' superimposed on the traction power by the master control unit. Some systems use pulse position modulation and others a 'radio-type' carrier frequency system to ensure that individual 'modules' respond only to those unique signals intended for them. 'Command control', however, does pose certain problems, which is why no detailed description of such a system is included in this book. One reason for this is its sheer complication and expense. Another more immediately practical problem is *compatibility* for a loco cannot be run on a 'command-controlled' layout unless it has been fitted with the appropriate 'module'. So, your friend cannot run his newly acquired loco on your layout unless you temporarily fit a spare 'module'. Furthermore, the 'modules' occupy precious on-loco space, so it can be difficult, or even impossible, to fit them in smaller OO/HO locos. Command control for this reason is not at present practical for gauges smaller than HO.

If you do decide to change to command control, you must modify your entire layout all at once. You cannot do it by stages and the best results, I am reliably informed, are obtained from purpose-built layouts designed with command control in mind.

An alternative approach

There are, however, alternative approaches to multiple train operation, some of which overcome the problems associated with command control. Two such approaches are considered in this book: block section control and progressive cab control (Chapter 29). Both simulate prototype practice by dividing the layout into block sections, in each of which normally no more than one train is allowed at one time. In block section control each section has its own controller, dedicated to that block whereas in progressive cab control only a limited number of controllers are used as a vacant section is not connected to any controller, but when a train arrives its section is automatically connected to the same controller that the train had in the previous section.

Economically there is not much to choose between these. For a comparable layout, having n sections, block section control will cost $£n$ for output transistors (for all the controllers) while progressive cab control will cost £n/3 in output transistors, £n/3 in TTL ICs and £n/3 in relays. 'You pays your money and you takes your choice'.

Block section control

I must confess at this stage that I have not built block section control, nor do I know anyone else who has done so, but it was an option that I seriously considered. Only as a result of certain considerations did I opt for progressive cab control, but I am happy to share with you the thoughts that I had about block section control.

Let us imagine that you have a layout divided into 10 block sections. You will now need 10 of everything. In fact, what you have is virtually 10 layouts, end to end, so that the trains can run between them. In view of this you will probably want the simplest of everything, initially at least (not that this involves any compromise of quality or interest). Each block section needs a controller. The ideal types are those described in Chapters 3 to 5 and you should be able to make several in an evening although you might find the one in Chapter 5 preferable because heat sinks (which are bulky and expensive) are not needed.

Each block section may have its own track circuit unit. Since each section has its own controller, and therefore its own reversing switch, further economies can be made here by using a unidirectional track circuit unit *before* the reversing switch. A return-rail circuit is suitable with a DPDT switch to the two rails of the section. (See Figure 28.1.) All your controllers may share the same unsmoothed power supply and all the track circuits the same smoothed supply, which may be derived from the unsmoothed controller supply.

If you install a signalling system, this too may be run from the track circuit smoothed supply via a 7805 or similar 5 V regulator IC. Interlocks (Chapter 26) are especially easy to add since there is no ambiguity as to which controller is addressed, but you will need to give each controller (or at least each interlocked controller) an 'autostop' unit (Chapter 10). Obviously you must ensure that your transformer can deliver all the power that the system will need. With, say, 10 sections you may have as many

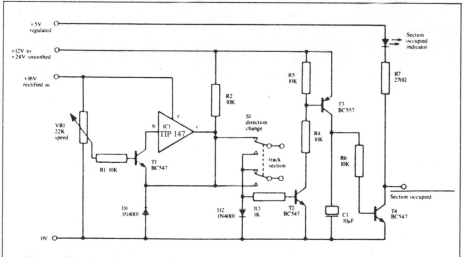

Figure 28.1 *Combined controller/track circuit for one section of a block section control system.*

as five trains running simultaneously, plus peripheral systems (signalling etc) in action, too.

Operating the system

To operate the system you have to cultivate a 'block' mentality rather than a 'cab' mentality. In other words, you must think like an old-style signalman rather than like a train driver. You have an array of controllers in front of you, but they relate to sections, not to trains, and the trains keep moving from block to block in a most disconcerting manner. For instance, suppose you want to stop a train at a station in a certain block. Before the train enters the block you must set the speed control and direction switch as appropriate for that train when it enters the block. (The skill in operating block section control is to keep the train speed steady as trains pass from block to block, which is to say, from controller to controller). You will see when the train enters the block by the illumination of the track circuit LED. As soon as the track circuit LED for the train's *previous* block is extinguished, your block has 'captured' the train and you can begin to reduce speed for the station stop. The situation to avoid is reversing a train into a block whose controller is set for forwards movement or *vice versa*. That causes very nasty short circuits.

Try to keep at least one vacant block between trains. So, if you have n sections, the maximum realistic number of trains in 'steam' is $n/2$. Even so, every train is going to be checked by signals at caution unless you reduce your traffic density to $n/3$. This system is ideally suited to automatic and semi-automatic operation making use of interlocks (Chapter 26) and timed station stops (Chapter 27). Once you've started a train on its journey, provided you set all the controllers to the appropriate speeds, you can leave your train to pursue its journey. You can leave the interlocks to stop it if it catches up with the train in front or to stop the train at some wayside station.

You may be different from me, but I find there's something therapeutic in just sitting back and watching the trains go by.

Components

Maplin order codes are as follows: TIP147 UJ31J, BC547 QQ14Q, BC557 QQ16S.

Chapter 29

Progressive cab control

Progressive cab control (PCC) is an alternative approach to multiple train operation. Unlike block section control (Chapter 28) trains keep their own controllers throughout their journey. It is less expensive than command control and offers the advantage that locos need no modification. Also conventional wiring is maintained, so you can install PCC step by step as time and money permit. Track circuiting (or some other reliable train detection system which gives an indication of block occupancy) is not only possible but an essential prerequisite.

PCC is based on 'cab control', a popular conventional system of model railway electrification. In cab control the layout is divided into control zones, each of which may be connected to any of several controllers by means of switches on the control panel. As the trains move from zone to zone, the operators throw the switches so that each train always keeps the same controller (or 'cab'). In PCC the principles are the same, but the switching is automatic, so that as a train enters a zone, that zone is automatically connected to the same controller the train had used in the previous zone.

It has been asserted that each PCC system must be tailor-made for its particular layout. This is true, of course, since it will inevitably depend on the number of zones or sections, the positions of the junctions and termini etc, as well as on the secondary functions that the system is required to serve. It is possible, however, to adopt a *modular* approach, each zone or section being serviced by an essentially similar unit. The number of units required and the way in which they are inter-connected will depend on the nature of the layout.

The unit described in this Chapter is very versatile, offering an interesting range of facilities, including a sophisticated interlock system. The 'standard' unit is for two-controller operation only, but the circuit for a three-controller version is also given. Units for use with any number of controllers can be deduced, but the complexity of the units increases dramatically as the number of controllers is raised. For most purposes the two- and three-controller versions are adequate, as will be seen later.

Prerequisites
To use the complete PCC system described in this Chapter, a number of conditions must be met. Various simplifications are possible and are discussed briefly later on. These may lead to the waiving of some of these prerequisites.

Firstly, your layout must be divided into cab control sections by rail breaks in the live rail and, secondly, your layout must be track-circuited or fitted with some other system for indicating the presence of trains in block sections. For convenience, this system will be called 'track circuiting' throughout this chapter. Each track circuit must give TTL-compatible logical '0' when its block is occupied. It simplifies matters if your cab control sections correspond to your track circuit sections, so you have one track circuit per cab control section. If you have more the track circuit outputs must be paralleled using AND gates (see Chapter 19). Track circuits may be live-rail or return-rail and may overlap (Chapter 19) if you wish. Thirdly, all controllers used must have their own fully independent power supplies. Also they must have positive-going output before the reversing switch (or relay contacts) and should be fitted with the 'autostop' facility described in Chapter 10. Fourthly, there is an extra feature that must be fitted to controllers for use with this PCC system. This is an additional output terminal that is negative-going whenever the controller is set to reverse. There are several ways in which this may be provided. If the controller uses a reversing switch or relay having spare contacts, choose a pair of contacts that 'make' when reverse is selected, wire one to the controller's negative supply line and the other to the new output. If the controller uses a reversing relay and spare contacts are *not* available, insert an additional npn transistor with its emitter grounded to the supply negative line and its collector to the new socket. Arrange for it to receive base bias only when reverse is selected and resist the temptation to wire the output direct to any existing point in the circuit that happens to go negative when reverse is selected.

Note that this circuit, like that in Chapter 26, depends on bistable latches and is liable to interference from the trains. See the notes at the end of that chapter, which apply equally to this.

Function of the unit

Each unit (we are considering the two-controller version) has a front panel with three controls and six indicator LEDs. The controls are an SPDT 'isolate' switch and two push-button (push-to-make) switches labelled 'advise A' and 'advise B'. (A and B are the two controllers.) The six LEDs are labelled 'section isolated', 'unconnected train', 'A connected', 'B connected', 'A autostop' and 'B autostop'. Normally the unit will be used in conjunction with other similar units and you will have an array of these front panels as part of your control console.

The unit also has no fewer than 19 connections, as follows:

1 Supply positive (+ 5 V DC, smoothed, regulated).
2 Supply negative and layout common return.
3 $\overline{\text{Input}}$ from this section's track circuit ('0' — 'section occupied').
4 'Section unavailable' output (to adjacent units).
5 '$\overline{\text{Advise A}}$' input (from all adjacent units).
6 'Advise B' input (from all adjacent units).
7 Selected controller live output to track (via track circuit if live-rail type).
8 'Previous section unavailable' input (from previous section's unit).
9 '$\overline{\text{Advise A}}$' output (to previous section's unit).
10 'Advise B' output (to previous section's unit).
11 'Next section unavailable' input (from next section's unit).
12 '$\overline{\text{Advise A}}$' output (to next section's unit).
13 '$\overline{\text{Advise B}}$' output (to next section's unit).
14 $\overline{\text{Live output}}$ of controller A.
15 $\overline{\text{Reverse selected}}$ input (from controller A).

16 Output to 'autostop' (of controller A).
17 Live output of controller B.
18 Reverse selected input (from controller B).
19 Output to 'autostop' (of controller B).

(Throughout this Chapter *the next section* refers to the new section entered by a train travelling *forwards* and the *previous section* to the next section entered by a train travelling in *reverse*.)

As a train approaches the section under consideration, the unit for the section which the train currently occupies applies a logical '0' to our unit's 'advise A' or 'advise B' input. This 'advises' our section's unit that a train is approaching and tells it which controller is in use. Our unit, however, takes no further action until the train arrives in its section, whereupon it automatically connects the section to the controller that has been 'advised' (unless the section is isolated). The 'A connected' or 'B connected' LED lights up as appropriate.

The unit 'knows' whether or not the connected controller is set for reverse, so it now activates the appropriate 'advise' input of the unit for the section which the train will enter next. We'll look at the complications caused by termini and junctions later. If, however, the destination section is occupied or isolated, the unit will activate the 'autostop' circuit of the connected controller and will light the appropriate 'autostop' LED. The 'autostop inertia' control on each controller should be set so that a train stops in just under an average section length. When the train leaves the section, the controller is disconnected. Under this system a controller cannot be connected to a vacant section.

The 'isolate' switch may be operated at any time. When the switch is thrown to the 'isolated' position any controller attached to the section is disconnected. While the switch remains in the 'isolated' position, no controller can be connected to the section and the 'section isolated' LED is illuminated.

Under certain circumstances a train may enter the section without the 'advise' input being activated, for example, at the start of an operating session, or if a train has been in the section while it was isolated but the switch is now restored to 'normal', or if a train is placed in the section by hand or is in a normally isolated siding now switched into the section. In any of these circumstances as well as whenever a train is isolated in the section, the 'unconnected train' LED will light. Under these circumstances the unit will not connect the section to either controller, for the simple reason that it does not 'know' which controller to connect. The 'advise A' or 'advise B' button must be pressed momentarily to enable the unit to connect the desired controller.

It is possible to change a train from one controller to another while in a section.* The train must be stopped and the 'isolate' switch operated for a moment and then restored to normal. The appropriate 'advise' button is now pressed for a moment to connect the selected controller. A unit cannot be 'advised' of more than one controller at a time. For example, if a unit is being advised of controller A on an approaching train, a subsequent '0' on the 'advise B' input will not change the 'advice' 'seen' by the unit. The unit will, however, interpret this as a hazard situation with trains on a collision course and will activate the 'autostop' system on controller B to bring that train to a halt. The train on controller A will be allowed to proceed. When the train on controller A has cleared the section, that on controller B will be 'released' and

---

*There is a way in which a train can be switched from one controller to another at the border between sections without stopping the train. This will be considered later.

allowed into the section. Normally,* a unit cannot connect more than one controller to the same section (which would cause spectacular results), but the same controller may be connected to several sections, provided that each contains a train.

Description of the unit

Figure 29.1 gives the circuit diagram for the two-controller versions. Readers without experience of TTL should refer to Appendix 12 for an introduction.

(i) *Controller selection circuit*. The 'advise' input (a logical '0') is applied to one of the two NOR gates, IC1a and IC1c. The function of these gates in their 'near bistable' configuration is to accept only the first input applied, if two inputs should be applied simultaneously, since the output of each gate inhibits the other. If both inputs are activated simultaneously, NOR gate IC1b applies a '1' to one input of the NAND gates IC2a and IC2b. The one of these whose other input is derived from the *selected* advise line will activate the 'autostop' output transistor, T4 or T5, for the *other*, ie non-selected, controller. The selected advise input, now a logical '1' is applied to a three-input NAND gate, IC3a or IC3b. These gates only give a '0' output when, besides having the advise input, the section is occupied and not isolated, and the other controller is not connected to it. A logical '0' from the output of IC3a or IC3b trips one of the two SR bistables made up from the four NAND gates in IC4. The tripped bistable provides bias for one or other of the relay-drive transistors T1 and T2. These energize the relay coil and the 'A connected' or 'B connected' LED. T1 and T2 may need to be Darlington pairs. The relay coils may be driven from a separate power supply if it is inconvenient for them to share the 5 V TTL supply.

The relays need a minimum of DPST contacts which 'make' when the coil is energized. The contacts should be capable of carrying 1 A for use with OO/HO and smaller gauges. However, very rarely are the contacts called upon to switch such high current.

From the foregoing, a relay coil becomes energized only when (i) the appropriate 'advise' input is activated, and (ii) the section is occupied and not isolated and (iii) the other relay is not energized. These conditions are met briefly when a train enters the section from an adjacent section having a similar unit.

Once tripped, the bistable can only be reset by the vacating of the section or the throwing of the 'isolate' switch to the 'isolate' position.

(ii) *Occupation/isolation circuitry*. This is a group of related functions served by the circuitry around IC1d, IC3c, IC5a, IC5b and IC6a.

When the section is occupied, a logical '0' from the track circuit is applied to the input of IC5a, which is used as an inverter to apply a '1' to IC3a and IC3b in the controller selector circuit. An open-collector output is essential for IC5a, as the closing of the 'isolate' switch short-circuits the output of this gate. When the 'isolate' switch is in the 'isolate' position, the input of IC5b goes 'high' and its output 'low' lighting the 'section isolated' LED and also applying a '0' to one input of IC6a. The occupation of the section applies a '0' to the other input of IC6a. So, if the section is isolated or occupied (or both), IC6a delivers a '1' output which feeds the 'section unavailable' output.

The spare NOR gate IC1d is used as an inverter to apply a '1' when the section is occupied to one input of IC3c. This gate only delivers a 'low' output, lighting the 'unconnected train LED', when the section is occupied and neither controller connected to it.

---

*At the start of an operating session, when the unit's power supply is first switched on, there is a possibility that the bistables controlling the relay drive circuitry may both latch in the 'engaged' state. If so, both 'A connected' and 'B connected' LEDs will light. The system *must* be cleared using the 'isolate' switch.

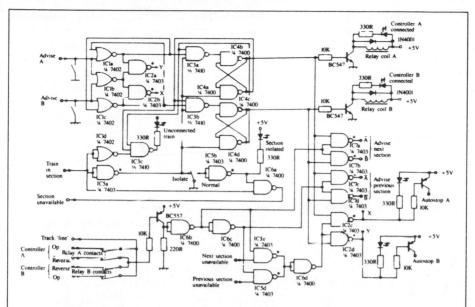

Figure 29.1 *Circuit of a section 'module' for progressive cab control; this version is for use with two controllers only.*

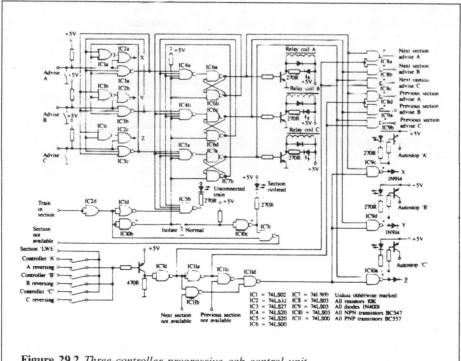

Figure 29.2 *Three-controller progressive cab control unit.*

(iii) *Direction-sensing circuitry*. To simplify the electronics, spare relay contacts are used to select the 'reverse-engaged' output of the connected controller. Provided that the controller has positive-going output before the reversing switch (or relay contacts), its negative supply will always be negative relative to the PCC system's *positive* supply (work it out for yourself if you don't believe me). So, a connection to the controller's negative line via the relay contacts will bias T3 into conduction applying a '1' to the input of IC6b, used as an inverter. Thus, a '1' from its output means 'forward selected'. Its output is applied to the inputs of IC6c, used as a further inverter, so a '1' from the output of this means 'reverse selected'.

(iv) *Output arrangements*. The four NAND gates in IC7 service the four 'advise' outputs drawing their inputs from the controller-selection bistables and the direction-sensing circuitry. Open-collector gates are used as these outputs often find themselves paralleled and short-circuited by the 'advise' switches of adjacent units.

Besides the interlock facility described earlier, which operates when both 'advise' inputs are activated simultaneously, another system is provided by IC5c, IC5d, IC6d, IC2c and IC2d. If the next section towards which a train is heading is isolated or occupied, the appropriate autostop will be activated. Transistors T4 and T5 are essential in the 'autostop' output circuit as they feed into a controller circuit which may be at a potential more negative than that of the PCC negative supply.

Three-controller version

Figure 29.2 shows the circuit of a three-controller version offering the same facilities. Note that this circuit uses 11 ICs in contrast with the seven for the two-controller version.

Simplifications

The unit described is emphatically a deluxe, full feature unit. Many simplifications are possible if you are willing to sacrifice some of the facilities. Ultimately, only the controller selector circuitry and most of the occupation/isolation circuitry are essential. For example, if you do not want the 'autostop' facilities, you can dispense with IC1b, IC2, IC5c, IC5d, IC6a, IC6d, T4, T5 and associated components. You can also remove the direction-sensing circuitry if your trains run consistently in the same direction, eg on a multiple-track main line. The second pair of relay contacts and the circuitry around T3, IC6b and IC6c now disappear. In its simplest form you can eliminate IC7 as well. You take your 'advise' outputs from the outputs of IC4b and IC4c and apply these direct to the inputs of the next section's unit only. The system will work as long as trains run forward and you will be able to reverse normally *within a section* but trains will not be able to reverse from one section to another unless you fit open-collector buffers into the 'advise' lines and activate the 'advise' buttons manually as the train crosses the 'borders'.

With an intermediate level of sophistication you can arrange for each unit to apply its 'advise' outputs to the units both in advance and in rear to permit bidirectional running but you will need to introduce AND gates or buffers between the outputs and inputs or otherwise the 'advise' signals will be passed on down the line to other units where they are not wanted. With TTL you cannot use blocking diodes.

Main line running

I am now assuming once more that you are using the full-feature unit. Installation is simplest in main-line blocks, but even here you must be careful about inter-connecting your units. The 'advise A' input, for instance, must be connected to *both* the 'next block advise A' output of the previous block's unit *and* the 'previous block advise A' output of the *next* block's unit. The same will apply to the corresponding B outputs and input (and C, if applicable).

Termini

If our section is in a terminus, one set of 'advise' outputs will not be needed and either the 'next section unavailable' or the 'previous section unavailable' input should be wired to supply positive via a pull-up resistor to give a permanent 'section unavailable' input. Thus, a train entering the section will automatically have its controller's 'autostop' activated. If the train stops short of its destination, the controller's 'autostop cancel' switch should be used to override the interlock and get the train home.

Junctions

Junctions pose many complications in the installation of PCC. The simplest way to handle them is as follows. Outputs, eg 'next section advise A' or 'this section unavailable', may be fanned out to many other units, the limit being the fan out of TTL (see Appendix 12). Thus, if our section ends in a facing junction, giving a choice of two possible 'next sections', we apply our 'advise input' to *both* but we may do some selecting on the inputs of the units of those two next sections. Where a section has a choice of inputs, eg if there is a trailing junction at one end, so that trains may enter our section from two different lines, the unit's inputs should be selected using, for instance, the 74LS157 quad two-input data selector which we met in Chapter 20. Its select input is derived, as before, from the setting of the turnout. In this way only the relevant data will be fed into the unit.

Using the units

The unit described in detail is for two controllers only; we called them A and B. We also looked at the circuit for a three-controller version; we called the controllers A, B and C.

It may seem that the restriction of a complex layout to two or three controllers only is rather limiting but remember that it is only those *sections* of the layout that were restricted to two or three controllers; the total layout may have many more controllers. Indeed, with a little ingenuity this PCC system permits endless combinations and permutations.

Consider the layout shown in simplified form in Figure 29.3. Basically it is a double-track oval, each track being divided into four sections. In E1 and W1, which represent the site of a main station, the tracks included passing loops, crossovers and sidings. It would be very easy to organize this layout using PCC for operation with *five* controllers, A, B, C, D and X. We should need six two-controller units and two three-controller units. Controllers A and B are dedicated to running on the westbound (clockwise) line (W1 to W4) and controllers C and D to the eastbound line (E1 to E4). Controller X is only used for movements within the main station area (E1 and W1). So, the three-controller units are for section E1 and W1; the other six sections have the two-controller units. Thus, we could easily have four trains running simultaneously on the main lines and still have controller X in reserve while there could be other trains or pilot locos waiting isolated in the loops and sidings in the main station area.

Controller X is used when we want to pass a train from the eastbound to the westbound lines and *vice versa*. Imagine a train drawing into the station (W1) from W4 and powered by controller A. As soon as it is stopped, the PCC unit for W1 is isolated, restored and controller X selected. The loco can now run round its train and be coupled up at the other end. The crossover turnouts are set for E2 and the train

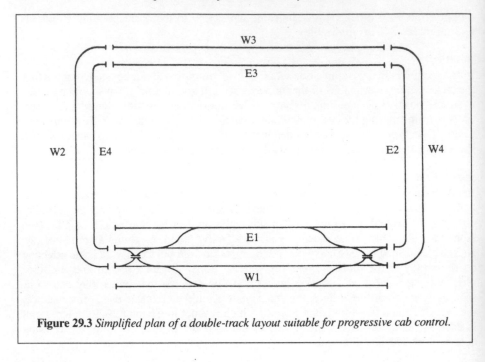

Figure 29.3 *Simplified plan of a double-track layout suitable for progressive cab control.*

is restarted for E2. The train can pass from W1 into E1 using controller X without diffi-culty, but cannot proceed into E2, since controller X is not on E2's 'menu'. So, as the train crosses the rail breaks at the intersection you will need to press the 'advise C' or 'advise D' button on E2's PCC unit. The train will now be able to run indefinitely on the eastbound line with the selected controller. Alternatively, you could arrange for X-controlled trains entering E2 always to 'pick up' controller C (or controller D), simply by making connec-tions between the appropriate 'advise' output and inputs,

On a very large layout — too large for any one operator to oversee — there may be several operators located at strategic points. Each operator looks after a limited area of the layout, say, ten sections. Each has two (or three) controllers selected by the PCC system described. At the intersections of areas, trains pass not only from one section to another but also from one controller to another. In this way between 8 and 12 trains may be running simultaneously — but the PCC units are all two- or three-controller units.

So, as you can see, the system is very versatile indeed and probably a whole book could be written on the ways it could be used, but I'll leave that for another time!

Components

Maplin order codes are as follows: 7400 QX37S, 74LS00 YF00A, 7402 QX39N, 74LS02 YF02C, 74LS03 YF03D, 74LS10 YF08J, 74LS20 YF14Q, 74LS27 YF18U, 74LS32 YF21X, BC547 QQ14Q, BC557 QQ16S, 1N4001 QL73Q, 5V relay DC39N.

Part 7: Train lighting

Preamble

That the romance of railways is enhanced by the night is evidenced in the work of many railway artists. On main lines traffic continues through the night and includes types of train rarely seen in daytime, such as sleeping-car expresses, mail trains and maintenance trains. In the dark, signal lamps, train headlamps and coach lighting become more conspicuous, adding extra drama to the atmosphere.

Many railway modellers enjoy simulating night-time scenes. Station lights, street lighting and lights in lineside buildings are scenic and electrical matters outside the scope of this book, but train lighting is a different matter. Effective constant-brightness headlights, tail lights and coach lighting can only be achieved using electronic circuitry, all of which, compared with many of the earlier projects, are surprisingly simple. The first high-frequency generator for coach lighting in Chapter 31, for instance, uses only 13 components (apart from those in its power supply), none of which is expensive.

If you have not tried night-scene modelling, you have missed a thoroughly worthwhile railway modelling experience. If your scenic capabilities — like the author's — are weak, the dark will conceal a multitude of sins of omission and commission. In addition, the sight of a fully lit model express train thundering past an illuminated signal and disappearing into the dark, its tail lamp gradually fading into the distance, gives a thrill that words cannot describe.

Chapter 30

Head and tail lamps using LEDs

Some proprietary model locomotives are fitted with headlamps or route indicators which light up when the train is running; these employ miniature 12 V bulbs connected in parallel with the motor. Sometimes the illumination is directionally controlled, eg the headlamps only light when the loco is running forward, or, on a double-ended diesel-outline model only the headboard at the end that is facing forwards is illuminated. Similarly some proprietary guard's vans have a red tail lamp that only lights up when the train is running forwards. Directional control is obtained by including a suitable diode in series with the lamp(s).

Effective though such lighting is, it has two drawbacks. Firstly, the lighting is extinguished altogether when the controller is at zero. Secondly, the brightness varies with the setting of the controller. Both problems can be mitigated to some extent by the simple LED system described below, although the lights will, of course, be extinguished when the controller is off or at 'stop'. Systems for running headlamps and tail lamps quite independently of the controller are described in Chapter 31.

How it works
The brightness of LED illumination is much less dependent on supply voltage than that of tungsten lamps. So if a headlamp assembly consisting of a diode (for direc-

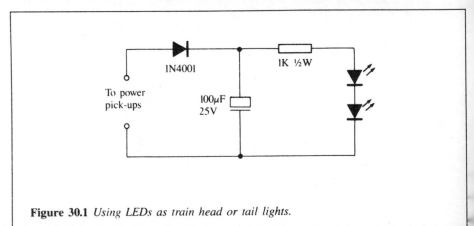

Figure 30.1 *Using LEDs as train head or tail lights.*

tional control) and two miniature lamp bulbs were replaced by the circuit shown in Figure 30.1 *omitting for the time being capacity C1*, one result should be improved consistently of brightness. Yellow LEDs are a fair substitute for the colour of old-style oil-burning train headlamps. White LEDs are expected by the end of 1997. They are likely to be expensive at first, but should become cheaper in time and will be useful as headlamps.

If, however, you use a PWM controller, you can go a stage better. Since each pulse is theoretically a pulse of *full power*, you can use a capacitor to store that power, acting as a 'reservoir' to keep the LEDs at constant brightness. The result is very effective, giving headlamps (or tail lamps if you use red LEDs) whose brightness is apparently constant at all settings of the controller, except, of course, at zero. But you may find that just above zero there is a setting on your controller where the pulses are too brief to set (or keep) the train moving, but where nevertheless there is sufficient power to light the lights. By skilful manipulation of the speed control, then, you may be able to achieve constant brightness lighting even with the train stopped,

The presence of diode D1 means that these headlights and tail lamps will be directionally controlled — be sure to connect the circuit to the power pick-ups the right way round! The diode also protects the LED(s) against inverse voltages. If you wish to run your train with your lights off, you will need to include a switch in series with D1.

Construction
The circuit is simple and the components small. Mounted on a small piece of Veroboard or similar, it should be possible to miniaturize the circuit sufficiently to fit in the smallest OO/HO gauge locos.

An afterthought
In a steam-outline loco, add an amber LED in the firebox doors to simulate the glow of the fire.

Chapter 31

High-frequency coach lighting

Many years ago some coaches in the Trix Twin range incorporated lighting; more recently lighting units have been available for the Hornby range of OO-scale coaches. The lamps are lit direct from the controller output, so, of course, brightness varies with controller setting and they cannot be left on while the train is stationary (unless you use 'Zero-1' or some other command-control system). This section of the book describes three systems for constant train lighting which are independent of the traction power. This chapter details two systems using high frequency ac, while Chapter 32 is concerned with a scheme using rechargeable batteries. Both systems present their own individual problems, but all train lighting projects share certain difficulties.

The principal difficulty is the nature of the light source itself. One day LED technology will greatly simplify train lighting and, indeed, I recently heard of a modeller who lit a train, apparently quite effectively, using *green* LEDs. The trouble is that white-light LEDs are not yet available and the high-brightness yellow types which offer the most realistic alternative are expensive. You would need a great many, ideally at least one per compartment, but the wealthy amongst us might like to try it. However, until the day of cheap, bright, white-light LEDs dawns, we shall be compelled to rely on tungsten lamps for train lighting. These posed few problems in the tinplate-constructed Trix coaches mentioned earlier, but tales abound among modellers of those who have filled modern coaches with tungsten lamps and sent the train off in a dazzling blaze of light only to find a few minutes later that the loco is pulling a sticky mass of molten polystyrene. Never forget that tungsten lamps run *hot*; indeed they only emit light as a product of their heat.

It is important to limit the number of lamps, so I impose an arbitrary limit of two per coach. These I position as far as possible from any plastic structures and use foil reflectors to direct the light *upwards*. Also I paint the underside of the coach roof matt white so that the light is reflected downwards fairly evenly along the length of the coach. The result is quite effective.

It also helps to under-run the lamps, ie to use a voltage lower than that specified. This does, admittedly, make the lamps less bright and more yellowish, but it also keeps them cooler and, for that reason, prolongs their life. Moreover, I have never suffered any melted coaches! If in doubt about the heating effects of any proposed lighting system try out a 'mock up' on an old discarded coach body. Remember that a system which apparently stays cool in free air in a draughty attic may not stay cool in the cramped confines of an air-tight polystyrene coach!

HF lighting – system 1

A separate generating circuit injects high-frequency (hf) alternating current (ac) into the track via the same wires as the power from the controller. This ac is the power for the coach lighting. Since capacitors conduct ac but not dc, these are used both at the output of the hf generator and at the input to the coach lights to prevent the dc from the controller interfering with the lighting system. (Actually a very feeble glow may be seen from the coach lights when the hf generator is off and the train is running slowly under pulsed control. This is because at the end of each pulse from the controller the locomotive motor generates a pulse of inductive overshoot. These pulses are of opposite polarity and therefore behave as ac, passing through the capacitors and lighting the lamps. The glow is so feeble that it is barely visible even in the dark.)

A suitable hf generator circuit is shown in Figure 31.1. It consists of a multivibrator (T1 and E2) which generates ac at a frequency of about 30 kHz, ie, 30,000 cycles per second. T3 amplifies its output and drives the complementary-symmetrical output pair T4/T5, which delivers the output to the track via capacitor C3.

There are three reasons for the use of such a high frequency, as opposed to, say, the 100 Hz used for the PWM controller in Chapter 5. Firstly, low-frequency ac would interfere with the running of locomotives, especially when PWM controllers are used. Secondly, lower frequencies set the armatures of loco motors vibrating, giving an objectionable noise. However, 30 kHz is outside the audible spectrum of sound and therefore silent. Thirdly, the resistance of capacitors to ac (known as their *reactance*) falls as the frequency of the ac rises. At 30 kHz 1 μF corresponds to 5.3 R so small and inexpensive mica and polyester capacitors can be used for coupling; at lower frequencies ac electrolytic types would be needed; these are bulky and expensive.

How it works

The multivibrator (T1 and T2 in Figure 31.1) resembles the symmetrical bistable that we met in Chapter 12, but the coupling between the two transistors is via capacitors. As in the bistable, as one transistor conducts it cuts the other one off — but only for

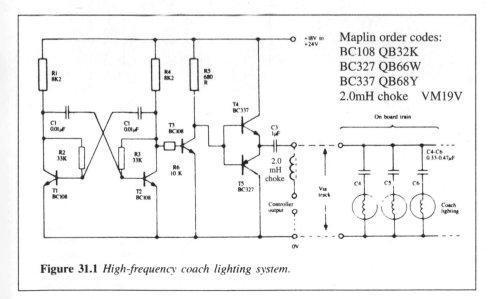

Figure 31.1 *High-frequency coach lighting system.*

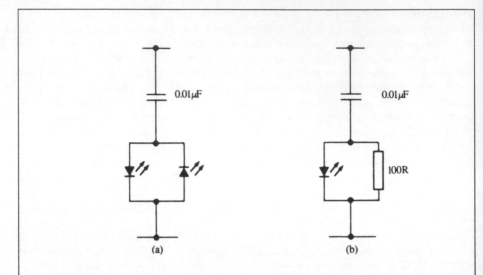

Figure 31.2 *Circuits for running (a) two and (b) one LED from the high-frequency lighting system.*

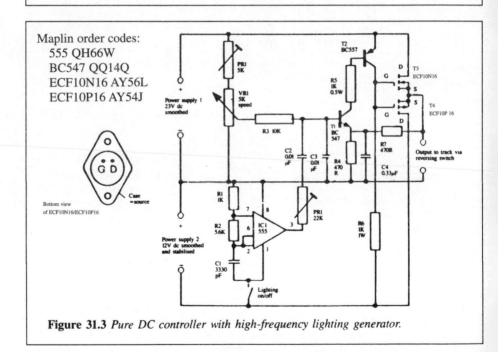

Figure 31.3 *Pure DC controller with high-frequency lighting generator.*

as long as it takes for the coupling capacitor to charge up. When this happens the transistors automatically reverse their roles. So in the multivibrator the transistors repeatedly change from one state to the other at a frequency fixed by the values of the coupling capacitors (C1, C2), bias resistors (R2, R3) and supply voltage. The voltage on either collector will alternate between near zero when the transistor is 'on' and near supply voltage when the transistor is 'off'. This output is amplified and applied to a capacitor (C3) whose charge and discharge currents form an ac power output.

Strictly a 24 V dc smoothed power supply is needed for the 12 V ac output necessary for full brightness; lower supply voltages give lower output and dimmer lighting; 18 V is probably the lower limit of acceptability. 'Grain-of-wheat' 12 V bulbs are the traditional type used in coach lighting, but the author prefers the slightly larger bulbs used in slot racing cars which are cheaper and far brighter. Consumption is about 20 to 30 mA per bulb and the hf generator should drive 12 or more.

The bulbs

Installing the bulbs is a constructional rather than an electronic matter and therefore strictly beyond the scope of this book. As many pick-ups as possible should be used to ensure continuity over turnouts, crossovers, 'dead' sections (if used) and dirty or twisted tracks. If a train of permanently coupled stock is being lit, it is worthwhile fitting wires between coaches so that all lights receive power from all pick-ups. It is recommended that each bulb have a 0.33 μF or 0.47 μF capacitor fitted in series. Without this the lamp will also be lit by the controller output and the facility will be lost for running trains with the lights off. All conventionally fitted loco headlamps (with or without direction-sensing diodes) will be lit by the hf system as well as by the controller.

Lighting LEDs from the hf system

LEDs for loco headlamps or for loco, guard's van or brake end tail lamps can also be driven from the hf supply, if required, but they will not be directionally controlled as they were in Chapter 30; they will light up whenever the hf generator (and therefore the coach lighting) is working. To ensure isolation from the controller's dc output, capacitor coupling is recommended; Figure 31.2 suggests circuits for twin-LED and single-LED applications. No current-limiting resistor is needed in the twin-LED application; the capacitor itself limits the current, 0.01 μF (corresponding to 530 R at 30 kHz) being a suitable value for most applications.

Use of the hf generator in connection with other equipment

The output coupling capacitor C3 in Figure 31.1 prevents dc or pulsed dc from the controller from entering the hf generator and interfering with it directly. Certain types of controller, when delivering full power, effectively short-circuit the coach lighting, turning it out and causing very heavy current consumption on the part of the hf generator. The output of the hf generator, while unable to interfere with locomotives directly, can affect the function of controllers having a feedback loop, into which the ac penetrates.

Both difficulties can be eliminated by fitting a 2.0 mH (milliHenry) choke in series with the output of the controller. This is a coil which presents a low resistance to the dc output from the controller (if possible use one having a dc resistance no greater than 2 R), but which has an effective resistance of 500 R at 30 kHz. This, then, prevents the controller from short circuiting the power for the lighting. The further addition of a 0.1 μF capacitor across the output terminals of the controller will prevent ac from the hf generator from entering the controller's feedback loop.

HF lighting – system 2

The high-frequency (hf) train lighting system just described, used a separate hf ac generator whose output connected in parallel with that of the controller to put hf power on to the track. Two difficulties attend this arrangement. Firstly, there is the danger that the controller itself, especially at high speed settings, will short-circuit the hf generator's output. This was remedied by inserting a choke coil in series with the controller output, but this can cause appreciable traction voltage loss when the load is heavy. Secondly, to light a long train or several trains, considerable hf power is needed and the hf generator described may not be able to deliver the power needed. There is, as often, a single solution to both problems. We generate the hf pulses in the heart of the controller itself, so that the same output stage handles both sets of pulses simultaneously. All of its power handling capacity (subject to the controller's overload cut-out threshold) is available to handle lighting or traction current according to load.

Practical problems

The idea was to modify a closed-loop controller, resembling that of Chapter 2, by adding a hf generator consisting of a 555 timer IC set up as a free-running multivibrator at 30 kHz. The complete circuit is shown in Figure 31.3. The feedback loop (R7/R4) is decoupled to ac by C4 so that the *mean* output voltage is determined by the control voltage set by the speed control VR1, while the instantaneous output voltage is free to make the temporary excursions associated with delivering the hf ac output.

Unfortunately, although the scheme sounds simple enough, it is fraught with complications. To begin with, if we are to deliver ac while the dc output is nil, ie if we want to stop a train but keep its lights on, the output must be capable of delivering negative-going as well as positive-going excursions of power, so that the mean output remains nil. This demands that we use a split power supply or, as in my prototype, two power supplies in series. Furthermore, to deliver true ac which is capable of alternately charging and discharging a capacitive load demands push-pull output but this causes the reappearance in a different guise of the short-circuiting problem associated with the earlier type of high-frequency lighting system. All attempts at making heavy-duty bipolar power transistors deliver a steady 30 kHz failed. Even though theoretically impossible, both transistors of the pair insisted on becoming conductive simultaneously, leading to a very heavy current drain from both power supplies and considerable heating of the transistors. The process then became regenerative, the heating making the transistors more conductive and *vice versa*, a well known effect called *thermal runaway*. To protect the transistors it was essential that the circuit be operated for no longer than two minutes at a time. Clearly such a circuit was of no practical use.

The problem was solved by replacing the bipolar output transistors with power MOSFETs. These are expensive (I paid £7.50 for the complementary pair) but are ideally suited to hf work and quite free from thermal runaway.

Power MOSFETs

The ECF10P16 is a p-channel enhancement-mode device. It behaves like a pnp power transistor except that it presents infinite input resistance on its gate and, when conductive, will conduct drain current in either direction. The ECF10N16 is an n-channel enhancement-mode device, which behaves like an npn power transistor with the same exceptions as before. Both are rated for drain currents up to 8 A.

Care should be taken in handling these devices. They are not nearly so susceptible to damage by static charges as are small-signal MOSFETs and CMOS ICs but even so it is best to avoid handling them in hot, dry environments. Fingers or soldering irons should always be touched to an earth point before contact with the gate or drain terminals. The sources of these devices are connected to the metal can, which is convenient, since both devices may be bolted direct to the same heat sink. *In this circuit it is essential that both devices he mounted on a heat sink.*

The two devices are used as source followers only and so give no voltage gain. T2 replaces the output Darlington of Chapter 4 and T3/T4 act as buffers to ensure that ample current is available at any output voltage. Resistor R6 provides pull-down to the level of the negative terminal of the power supply, to facilitate negative-going excursions of output.

Performance of the circuit

It must be stated that this circuit did not work as well as was intended. The prototype suffered a leakage current of 25 mA, which, at least, was steady and negligible compared to that experienced with bipolar output transistors. In general, while the circuit did permit the independent operation of train lights and running of locomotives, there was some interference. The lights were brightest with the train stopped and they dimmed perceptibly as the train ran and gained speed. At full speed they were extinguished altogether, but with this controller full speed is unprototypically high and R3 should be chosen for a reasonable compromise of maximum speed and acceptable minimum brightness. Switching the lights on while the train is is running causes a noticeable slowing of the train.

Nearly all tests were carried out using 12 V lamps for lighting and the brightness was adequate but not dazzling. A few tests were carried out using 6 V miniature bulbs, which were far brighter and less susceptible to variation of brightness. It is recommended that train lighting for use with this system use 6 V bulbs. If they show evidence of being overrun, ie of having a short operating life, the value of the series capacitors should be reduced, eg to 0.047 µF. In general the circuit poses few other problems. C3 appears redundant and yet *is* essential. Without it the controller is prone to burst into supersonic oscillation so that lights come on even with the light switch off. PR1 provides some adjustment of brightness to prevent hf overloading of the output which can cause trains to creep forward at 'stop' when the lights are on.

My prototype used two power supplies. The 'upper' supply concerned mainly with traction, used a standard model railway controller/full-wave rectifier unit delivering 16 V at up to 2 A. This was smoothed using a 2200 µF electrolytic capacitor to give a steady 23 V, hence the high speeds obtainable. The 'lower' power supply was an adjustable stabilized supply set to 12 V and capable of delivering up to about 750 mA. This is concerned mainly with the lighting power at lower settings of the speed control, when excursions of output fall below 0 V. On no account should trains be run with the 'lower' supply off.

Using the unit

When the hf system is on, *all* train lights (including *all* those with direction-sensing diodes) will be illuminated. As mentioned above, the lamps may be 6 V to 12 V types used singly or lower-voltage types, eg 3 V, could be connected as pairs in series. All lamps or pairs of lamps should have series capacitors which may be 0.1 µF or 0.047 µF. Lower values may be used if the lamps appear excessively bright. Alternatively, LEDs may be used. These should be connected as reverse-parallel pairs with a 0.01 µF series capacitor. No series resistor is needed, since current is limited by the reactance of the capacitor (530 R at 30 kHz).

Interference with other equipment

Hf systems do not normally interfere with return-rail track circuits but behave as a second controller so that a locomotive-less train of illuminated stock is detected as long as the hf system is on. They do, however, interfere with live-rail track circuits producing spurious 'section occupied' indications and also with speedometer circuits, causing wildly erratic readings. However, the controller itself cannot be used with either live-rail track circuits or speedometers, as it is a pure dc controller.

Radio interference is a concomitant of hf lighting systems. See the warning below! Indeed, the easiest way to check the frequency at which the system is operating is to place an AM radio receiver beside your layout while the hf system is on. Tune along the long- and medium-wave broadcast bands noting the frequencies (the tuning scale should be calibrated in kHz or MHz) at which interference from the unit is heard. This will sound like a hum, hiss or squeal from the receiver and you can easily check whether any particular noise originates from your HF system by momentarily switching it off and seeing if the interference disappears. When you have logged a number of interference frequencies, you should find that they are spaced at regular intervals along the waveband and that interval should be the 30 kHz or so fundamental frequency of your hf generator.

Warning! The Electromagnetic Compatibility Directives

The Electromagnetic Compatibility Directives (Ref 89/336/EEC) (as amended) and Regulations — which in the UK are Statutory Instrument 1992/2372 (as amended) — require apparatus put into use to be neither liable to cause electromagnetic disturbance nor liable to be affected by such.

For this reason, if you construct the high-frequency train lighting circuits described in this chapter, you should take steps (such as an earthed foil or wire screen around the room and an earthed metal sheet beneath the layout) to ensure that when these circuits are used, they do not cause electromagnetic interference outside the immediate environment. If you operate these circuits without taking proper precautions and you thereby cause interference with radio or television reception or other equipment, you could be prosecuted. You have been warned!

Furthermore, it is emphasised that these circuits are published for hobbyist purposes only. They should not be exploited commercially, for example as the basis of a kit or finished product offered for sale or apparatus operated as part of a business.

Chapter 32

Battery-based train lighting

The high-frequency lighting systems described in Chapter 31 suffer two major disadvantages: (i) the expense of the equipment and (ii) incompatibility with live-rail track circuits, speedometers and through-the-rails sound systems (Chapter 36). This prompted me to re-examine a train lighting system described by M.H. Babani in *Electronic Circuits for Railway Modellers* (published by Bernards, London, 1977, but now out of print).

Babani lit his lamps from the controller output when it was available, but provided an auxiliary lighting supply in the form of rechargeable nickel-cadmium (NiCad) cells for those occasions when the controller output was not available, eg when the train was stationary. The controller output, when available, was also used to recharge the NiCads. I have not tried Babani's circuit, because it uses NiCads and lamps of types not easily obtainable, but it looks sound enough. Instead I devised a system operating on similar principles but using six easily obtainable 'size AA' (14.3 mm diameter × 50 mm long) NiCad cells (developing 7 V to 9 V) to drive 6 V bulbs via a 6 V switching regulator. This keeps the lighting level absolutely steady under all circumstances. The circuit was designed to run up to 10 lamps (6 V 50 mA nominal) giving a total consumption of 0.5 A.

Maplin order codes: BC557 QQ16S, BC547 QQ14Q, 555 QH66W, BC461 QB72P, 1N4001 QL73Q.

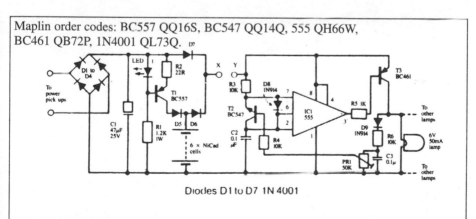

Diodes D1 to D7 1N4001

Figure 32.1 *Circuit for a battery-back-up train lighting system. Alternative switching systems, which go between X and Y, are shown in Figures 32.2 and 32.3.*

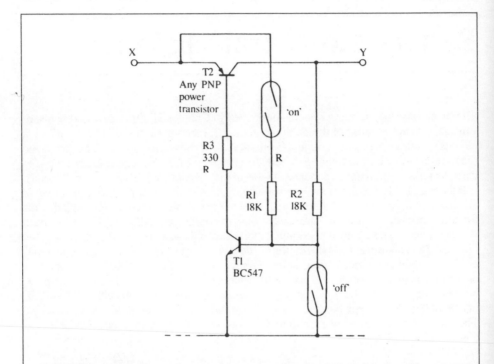

Figure 32.2 *Simplest option — a plain on/off switch on the coach.*

Figure 32.3 *Complementary bistable used to switch the train lighting by means of magnets and reed switches.*

The circuit

Figure 32.1 shows the basic circuit and Figures 32.2 and 32.3 two alternative types of on/off switching. Current from the power pick ups enters the bridge rectifier D1 to D4 making the circuit fully bidirectional while capacitor C1 smooths the input. LED 1 is used as a voltage regulator to hold the base of T1 at about — 1.6V over a wide range of input voltage. It only lights up when the NiCads are charging so cannot double as a tail lamp. Resistor R2 in the emitter circuit of T1 limits collector current to 50 mA, the maximum recommended charge current for the NiCads. Blocking diode D5 prevents the NiCads from discharging via T1's base/collector junction and R1. The circuit therefore provides for the NiCads to be charged and kept topped up by controller output of either polarity, provided of course that the voltage is sufficiently high. The juxtaposition of D6/D7 ensures that the lighting circuit uses as its supply whichever of the bridge rectifier output and the NiCads offers the higher voltage and consequently the circuit switches automatically between power supplies as the voltage on the track varies.

Voltage regulator

When the controller output is at a higher voltage than the NiCads (plus the drop across the bridge rectifier) the lamps run from the controller. Now, the voltage that the 6 V lamps 'see' may vary from 6 V to 16 V depending on the controller type and setting so, unless some form of voltage regulator is introduced between the lamps and their supply, the brightness of the lamps will vary with controller setting and, at higher settings, there will be a very real danger of burnout. It may seem that all that is needed is a 7806 or 7805 voltage regulator IC. Either can handle up to 0.5 A, but at higher loads even an input of 8 V causes the IC to get very hot and with an input of 15 V at a load of 0.5 A a 7805 would be called upon to dissipate an intolerable 5 W. In fact, the ICs contain in-built protection against such overloads and they simply shut down, but not before they get hot enough to melt polystyrene coaches! I did experiment using a 7805 with an array of 12 V lamps in parallel; these light up as the voltage across the regulator rises and thereby dissipate some of the waste power as light. Although this arrangement showed promise it also caused some loss of regulation with resultant fluctuations of brightness in the lighting lamps. Moreoever, as a circuit, it was clumsy.

More elegant is the circuit I finally adopted which employs a switching regulator circuit (around IC1, T2 and T3 in Figure 32.1). This is a voltage regulator which works by pulse width modulation and in which the output transistor does not get hot. IC1 is a 555 timer IC1 set up as a free-running multivibrator. The charge-up period of timing capacitor C2 is fixed at about 0.1 ms (R3 × C2, D8 being negligible) but the discharge period is variable, depending on the bias applied to T2. T2 really should be npn and apparently 'upside down' in this application. Remember that it is bypassed by D8 during charge-up periods while its emitter is shorted to ground via pin 7 during discharge periods. It is during discharges that T3 is enabled. Feedback loop D9/R6/C3 (chosen to have the same time constant as R3/D8/C2) provides efficient regulations of the output voltage, which is adjustable by means of VR1.

On/off switching

A facility is needed for switching the lighting off, otherwise the lighting will rapidly discharge the NiCads when the train is not in use. This must be connected between X and Y in Figure 32.1. The simplest alternative, shown in Figure 32.2, is to use a plain on/off switch somewhere on the coach in which the circuitry is installed. Probably the best places for the switch are underneath or tucked inside a gangway connection. The alternative is to replace the switch by the complementary bistable shown in Figure 32.3. This is activated by a pair of normally open reed switches, one for the 'on' function and one for the 'off'. It is suggested that the 'on' switch be mounted just beneath the roof centre line and the 'off' switch vertically on one side of the coach. The lighting can now be turned on by placing a permanent magnet on a bridge or signal gantry beneath which the train is to pass. Better still an electromagnet in the same position may be energized from the control panel if it is desired to run the lighting. To turn the lighting off, the train must pass a permanent magnet or an energized electromagnet in some structure alongside the track. Do ensure that the correct side of the vehicle is presented to the magnet or, alternatively, use parallel reed switches, one on each side of the vehicle.

Practical considerations

The main problem is finding accommodation in the train for the NiCads. Babani used smaller cells and managed to conceal them in the kitchen section of a restaurant car (OO scale). Mine were contained in a battery box from Maplin Electronic Supplies Ltd (no longer available) which measures $158 \times 28 \times 16$ mm (empty). The only OO-scale passenger vehicle in which this could be easily concealed is the Lima BR Mk I full brake and then only after the removal of the partitions around the guard's compartment. Fortunately this vehicle has few windows so that its unprototypical load is not obvious. Maplin and other suppliers offer a range of battery boxes.

The electronics can easily be installed on pieces of Veroboard but try to keep the voltage regulator output transistor away from any plastic structures. If you wish to recharge the NiCads — and this may well be necessary after continuous slow running — switch the lighting off before placing the battery coach on permanently live track.

Another problem is concerned with electrical connections between adjacent coaches. Connections between coaches are essential since only one coach contains the batteries upon which the whole system depends. The problem is to find wires which are thick enough to conduct the fairly high currents involved but flexible enough not to cause derailments on tight curves with modern lightweight coaches. If you can obtain a supply of it, the wire used with personal earphones is ideal. You may be tempted to use Litz wire, intended for coil winding, but this is difficult to solder and may present heating problems when conducting currents in hundreds of milliAmps. If all else fails, use standard sleeved multi-strand connecting wire coiled up like the leads to telephone handsets. You can achieve this by winding it tightly around the shaft of a miniature screwdriver. These connecting wires can be fitted with a soldercon pin at each end which plug into further soldercon pins fixed beneath each end of each coach. This provides a means whereby coaches can be separated quite easily if the train formation is to be changed.

The last problem concerns the controller power supply. When you add 0.5 A of lighting load to the existing traction load you may find that your overload cut-out operates with rather less provocation than previously, eg whenever a lit train climbs a gradient. The only solution is to fit a higher-rated circuit breaker and, if your transformer starts to glow faintly, to use a higher rated power supply.

NiCad cells

The cells used are rated at 0.5 Ah. This means that in theory on a full charge each cell will deliver 0.5 A (500 mA) for one hour. The discharge rate should not exceed 0.5 A, hence the limit of ten 50 mA lamps. The charge rate should not exceed one tenth of the maximum discharge rate, ie, 50 mA for these cells. To charge the cells from a state of total discharge might be expected to take ten times the hourly maximum discharge rate, ie, 10 hours. In fact, owing to losses, it takes 14 hours at 50 mA. Lower charge rates may be used with a corresponding increase in charge time.

Part 8: Sound effects

Preamble

Sound effects on model railways are a controversial matter. To generate electronically a close simulation of the sound of a locomotive (complete with whistle or horn when required) is possible, but would demand complex circuitry beyond the scope of this present book. On the other hand, quite simple circuits will provide an approximation which can indeed add an extra dimension to model railway operations. Chapter 34 provides a whistle or horn sound and Chapter 35 a 'chuffer' that simulates exhaust steam sound.

A wide variety of sound effect ICs have been introduced — and subsequently withdrawn. Some were designed for use in computerized equipment, requiring connection to a microprocessor. In view of the problems regarding the availability of ICs, the circuits described here all use readily available discrete components. Maplin currently sells a 'Train sound generator' IC, the HT2830C (catalogue no. AZ46A) which can be used for on-board train sounds, including a bell or horn. See also Appendix 16.

One problem with sound effects is how to reproduce them. Ideally a miniature speaker should be installed on board the locomotive. The loco would need to carry its own amplifier and power supply in addition to the sound generator circuitry (all, of course, demanding precious space); monitoring track voltage could determine the chuff rate and train mounted reed switches activated by track mounted magnets could sound the whistle or horn at the right locations. Alternatively, the audio signal, already at a suitable level, could be piped to the loco from an off-board amplifier through the rails. This arrangement is quite feasible, but introduces its own complexities and compatibility problems. It is discussed in Chapter 36.

The alternative is to install one or more fixed speakers in or near the layout. A speaker in a tunnel mouth, for instance, could be used very effectively to reproduce a whistle or horn of a locomotive entering the tunnel. An array of hidden speakers at intervals along a line, driven by amplifiers fitted with faders could be used to 'carry' the sound effects along with the train. Such a system could be linked to track circuits or section bistables. Model railway audio could become a subject in its own right.

Any sound effect generator will need an amplifier. Its output could be amplified through a domestic hi-fi system or portable radio/recorder. Simple AF (audio-frequency) amplifiers can be made quite easily, are invaluable in railway modelling and provide an ideal introduction to the realm of audio. Such an amplifier is described in Chapter 33.

Chapter 33

Simple audio power amplifier

A loudspeaker can be thought of as a kind of electric motor in which the motion is not rotary but reciprocating, ie, back and forth. This motion applied to a paper cone sets up pressure waves in the air which our ears perceive as 'sound'. The quality of the sound is determined by its frequency (pitch), amplitude (strength) and rate of rise or fall of amplitude. The electrical input to the speaker needed to produce 'meaningful' sound, then, will consist of ac (alternating current) of varying frequency and amplitude. The range of audible frequencies extends from about 20 Hz to about 16,000 Hz.

In most of the projects in the earlier parts of this book transistors are employed as switches only. In these applications a transistor may be 'off', ie, not conducting so that its collector voltage approaches the supply voltage, or it may be 'on', ie, conducting flat out so that its collector voltage approaches zero. This kind of operation is not normally suitable for audio applications, because the transistor cannot respond to an ac input. For instance, an npn transistor that is 'off' can respond to a positive-going input by becoming conductive, but cannot respond to a negative-going input because it cannot be any further 'off'.

If however, we bias the transistor so that it is 'half-way on', a positive-going input will increase collector current (resulting in a fall in collector voltage) while a negative-going input will cause a diminution in collector current (resulting in a rise in collector voltage). In designing AF (audio frequency) amplifier stages care must be taken to bias the transistors so that the output voltage is free to rise or fall with varying input signal. It is wise to arrange for the quiescent (ie, no-input) output voltage to be approximately half the supply voltage, especially in the later stages of an amplifier. In the output stage any deviation of the quiescent output voltage from Vcc/2 (ie, half the supply voltage) would severely restrict the level of output available.

A practical 1 Watt amplifier

Figure 33.1 gives the circuit for an amplifier that is capable of running from a 9 V supply and delivering about 1 W into a 3 R to 8 R speaker. Voltage gain is 10 and input impedance about 50 K. One of the advantages of an AF signal being ac is that it will pass through capacitors, which isolate dc. So C1 at the input admits AF signals but prevents any dc from the signal source from upsetting the biasing of T1; this is set by R1/R2/R3. The potential divider R1/R2 sets the base voltage on T1 at about 1.1 V (upon which the AF input is superimposed). This 1.1 V puts about 0.4 V across R3 which sets the collector current at about 0.3 mA and the quiescent collector vol-

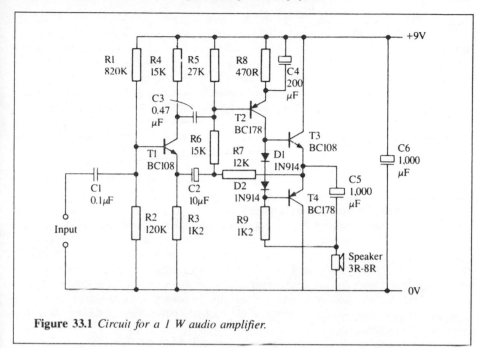

Figure 33.1 *Circuit for a 1 W audio amplifier.*

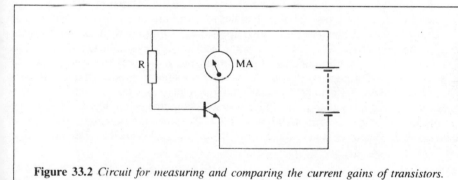

Figure 33.2 *Circuit for measuring and comparing the current gains of transistors.*

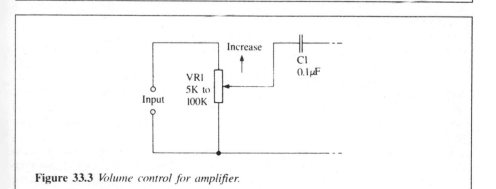

Figure 33.3 *Volume control for amplifier.*

tage at about 4.5 V. Ignore C2 for the moment.

The output from T1 is taken via C3 to driver T2, whose bias arrangements we will discuss later. Under quiescent conditions its base is at -2.25 V relative to the positive supply line and its emitter at -1.55 V, giving a collector current of 3.3 mA. Voltage at the top of R9 is 4.0 V, between D1 and D2 4.7 V and at the collector of T2 5.4 V. Bootstrapping R9 to the speaker rather than returning it to ground greatly increases the open-loop gain (ie, the gain without negative feedback) of the amplifier.

The output stage consists of the complementary pair T3/T4. T3 handles the positive-going excursions of input and T4 the negative-going ones. The two diodes compensate for the 0.7 V loss across the two base/emitter junctions and ensure that under quiescent conditions *both* transistors are *just* conducting.

To prevent the quiescent output voltage (at the emitters of T3/T4) from drifting too far from Vcc/2, it is used to derive the bias for T2. If the output voltage were, say, to fall, T2 would be biased (via R6/R7) further forward so that its collector voltage would rise (it being pnp type) restoring the required output voltage. Of course, this feedback loop would prevent the amplifier from amplifying at all if it were not *decoupled* to AF. The *decoupling* consists of capacitor C2, which could be taken straight to 'ground' from the junction of R6/R7. This filters most of the ac AF content out of the feedback loop so that nearly pure dc is fed back. Thus the output voltage is free to make the necessary *temporary* excursions associated with delivering power AF output, while any long-term tendency of the mean output voltage to deviate from that required is counteracted.

In fact C2 is taken not to ground but to the emitter of T1. The effect of this is to make R7 and R3 (via C2) an ac potential divider feeding a fraction (R7/R3) of the AF output back to the input. T1 now has the job not only of amplifying but also of comparing the scaled-down output signal applied to its emitter with the input signal being applied to its base. This kind of negative feedback is very important in AF amplifiers. Not only does it eliminate much distortion, but also it sets the voltage gain of the amplifier. Use of negative feedback makes it possible to produce large numbers of amplifiers having uniform performance, although there may be considerable differences between the individual performances of the components employed. The voltage gain of this amplifier is set at R7/R3 = 12/1.2 = 10. Since the maximum practicable excursion of the output voltage is about 4.0 V, the input signal needed to give full volume is 0.4 V.

Construction

Use Veroboard or similar. Construction is generally straightforward, but T3/T4 *must* be a matched complementary pair. Take a selection of suitable npn and pnp types and test them using the simple circuit shown in Figure 33.2. Use a 9 V battery and a selection of test resistors (R) between 10 K and 10 M. Write the collector current for each resistor against each individual transistor tested; remember to reverse the polarity of the battery and the meter for the pnp types. Hopefully you should find at least one pnp and npn transistor with similar gain characteristics. Use these as a matched complementary pair.

To test the amplifier, feed into its input some source of reasonable-quality audio material, eg the output of a record player, radio or cassette unit. Remember that even a signal as small as 0.5 V will overload the amplifier, causing distortion, so keep the input low. If necessary, fit a volume control as shown in Figure 33.3.

Power supply

All audio equipment must be operated from smoothed supplies. This amplifier was designed for 9 V operation and can be run from a battery. For satisfactory operation from other voltages the values of R1, R4, R8 and R9 must be amended in accordance with the table given below:

Vcc (supply)	R1	R4	R8	R9
6V	560K	10K	220R	680R
9V	820K	15K	470R	1K2
12V	1M2	18K	680R	1K5
16V	IM8	33K	1K0	2K2
22V	2M2	33K	1K5	3K3

Components

Maplin order codes as follows: BC108 QB32K, BC178 QB53H, 1N914 QL71N.

Chapter 34

Steam whistle or horn

A steam whistle generates sound by forcing high-pressure steam through a resonant pipe. Besides the musical note itself there is an accompanying hiss of escaping steam. The pitch of the note itself, however, is not constant. Its frequency is to some extent proportional to the pressure applied and, because it takes finite time to open and close the steam valve, there is a rise time (during which frequency rises) and a fall time at the end of the sounding (during which frequency falls).

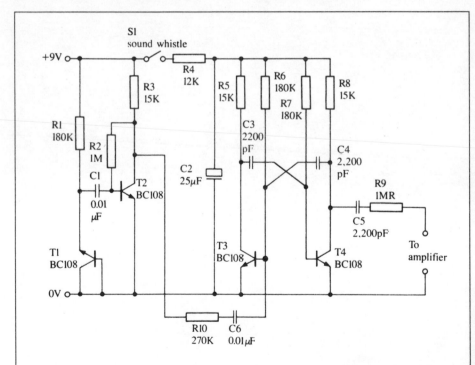

Figure 34.1 *Circuit for steam whistle simulator. A simple modification described in the text turns this into a diesel-type horn.*

The easiest way to generate a note electronically is to use a multivibrator similar to that used in Chapter 31 to generate the hf ac for coach lighting. The frequency, however, is rather lower: 1 kHz is suitable for a typical steam whistle — lower still for a horn. The multivibrator generates square waves which are not strictly the right *timbre* for a whistle (though not unlike a horn), but the unwanted harmonics tend to be drowned in the steam hiss, giving a final effect which is not unrealistic.

The frequency of a multivibrator is determined by a number of factors, including the supply voltage — frequency rises with voltage. Gradually (ie, over 0.3 second) building up the supply voltage on switch-on and letting it gradually decay on switch-off gives a realistic frequency shift — all that is required is to switch on the power via a suitable resistor (12 K) and shunt the supply lines via a suitable capacitor (25 µF).

The steam sound itself is generated by driving a pn junction into breakdown conditions; the most suitable junction is the base/emitter junction of a small signal npn transistor (T1 in Figure 34.1). This produces a random electronic signal, which, suitably amplified and applied to a speaker produces a loud 'steamy' hiss. T2 amplifies the hiss, a little of which is fed via R10/C6 into the multivibrator, where it partially modulates the whistle causing an attractive 'bubbly' sound. You may need to adjust the value of R10 — increase it to reduce modulation — if it causes distortion of the whistle sound. Some hiss will normally pass through C4 and into the output even when the whistle is not sounding.

Construction
Figure 34.1 gives the complete circuit. For the diesel horn omit the steam generator circuit around T1/T2 and also R4 and C2. Change the values of C3/C4 to 0.01 µF or to taste (higher for a lower note).

Veroboard construction is recommended. The circuit was developed in connection with the amplifier (Chapter 33) and the 'chuffer' (Chapter 35) and may share the same board and power supply. The recommended supply is 9 V.

Components
Maplin order code for the BC108 is QB32K.

Chapter 35

Exhaust steam sound ('Chuffer')

The rhythmic exhaust beat of a steam locomotive is part of the magic of steam-era railways and a part that most modellers reluctantly have to omit. The circuit described here used in conjunction with the steam generator from Chapter 34 (the circuit around T1/T2 in Figure 34.1) produces quite a realistic impression of the sound. The chuff rate is controlled by a voltage input which can be derived from the control voltage of an electronic controller (eg, Chapters 3 and 4) and, unlike some published chuffer circuits, at zero input voltage there will be no chuffs. As the train begins to move the chuffs start at about 1 per second and thereafter the rate rises with train speed. The 'cut-off', ie, chuff length (or width) can also be varied and indeed must be for realistic operation.

How it works
Refer to Figure 35.1. T2 and T3 form a rather unusual multivibrator circuit described by J.L. Linsley Hood (*Wireless World*, July 1976, p. 36), whose frequency is adjustable over a wide range by a single variable resistor. For this application, however, the variable resistor is replaced by FET T1, which can be regarded as a voltage-controlled variable resistor.

Field-effect transistors (FETs)
An FET is a semi-conductor amplifying device working on principles quite different to those of (bipolar) transistors and having very different characteristics. The term FET embraces a diverse range of devices; that used in this project is a *junction-gate* FET (JUGFET or JFET) and the following remarks apply to JUGFETs but not necessarily to other FET types such as the power MOSFETs in Chapter 31.

The two differences from bipolar transistors that make JUGFETs useful in this current are i) they are conductive when unbiased and ii) they will conduct current in either direction. Another useful difference is that input resistance is practically infinite under normal conditions, so no appreciable bias current flows.

The three terminals of a JFET corresponding to the collector, emitter and base of a bipolar transistor are called the drain, source and gate. Many JFETs, including the type used in this project, are electrically symmetrical and may be operated with their drain and source terminals interchanged. Like bipolar transistors JFETs are available in two polarities: n-channel corresponding to npn and p-channel corresponding to pnp. In an n-channel device the gate must be biased negative relative to the source to reduce drain current and in a p-channel device the gate must be biased positive to reduce drain current. When sufficient gate bias is applied, drain current becomes negligible and the device is said to be 'pinched off'.

When the circuit is first switched on, C1 is uncharged so the base of T2 is at about 0 V. Consequently T2 is non-conductive and T3 is fully on, so that its emitter voltage is at about 9 V. Now T1 is a symmetrical FET so both its designated source and drain terminals may be regarded as the source. One of these is connected to the emitter of T3 and so is at about 9 V. If the gate is low, at about 0 V, the FET will be pinched off so that C1 cannot begin to charge and the circuit will remain indefinitely in this state.

As the input voltage begins to rise (as the train begins to move), the FET will begin to conduct and C1 will begin to charge via the FET. The charge rate will, of course, be determined by the gate voltage on the FET. When a certain charge voltage has been reached, T2 begins to conduct. This causes T3 to cut off, whereupon its emitter voltage falls to a low value and C1 discharges via the FET, R4 and R5. When discharge is nearly complete, the cycle repeats. Thus the circuit 'multivibrates' at a rate determined by the input voltage and the value of C1.

To convert the output of the multivibrator to 'chuffs' involves using a diode as a switch. Output of the steam hiss generator is applied C3/R8 to the cathode of D1, while its anode is connected to a suitable amplifier via R9/C4. A diode is conductive when forward biased and non-conductive when reverse biased. The cathode of the diode is also connected via the network R6/C2/R7 to the output of the multivibrator. The anode is connected via R9 to the slider of VR2, the 'cut-off' or 'chuff width' control.

When the output of the multivibrator (ie, on the emitter of T3) is high, C2 charges up via R6 — this takes about 0.3 second. During this time the cathode of D1 is taken up to about 9 V, so is reverse biased at all except the very highest settings of VR2. When the output of the multivibrator goes low, C2 discharges gradually, so that the voltage on the cathode of D1 falls. When it falls below the voltage on its anode (set

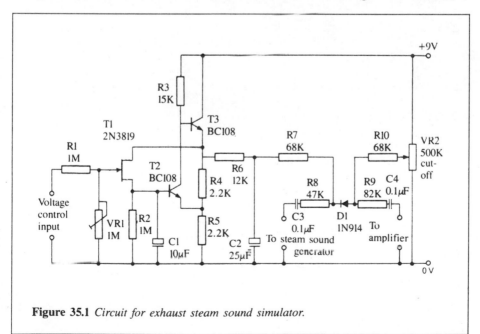

Figure 35.1 *Circuit for exhaust steam sound simulator.*

by VR2) it conducts and a 'chuff' begins. The 'chuff' continues until D1's cathode voltage rises again. By adjusting VR2 any chuff length from zero to continuous can be obtained. Different combinations of input voltage and VR2 setting will give effects varying from an express train at speed to a goods train struggling up a slippery gradient. For such a simple device the effect is remarkably lifelike.

Construction

Veroboard or similar is recommended. The project may share the same board and power supply as those described in Chapters 33 and 34 with which it was developed.

Operation

For testing, connect the input to the slider of a potentiometer (any value) across the supply. For normal use connect it to the control voltage of an electronic controller — adjust VR1 so that the chuffs start just as the train begins to move. Advance the cut-off control as the train accelerates or the chuffs will 'run into each other'. R9 sets the level of output (as does R9 of Chapter 34). You may need to adjust these values to give the correct relative loudness of whistle and exhaust steam sound.

Components

Maplin order codes are as follows: BC108 QB32K, 1N914 QL71N, 2N3819 QR36P.

Chapter 36

On-train sound reproduction

Sounds may be reproduced on board the train by installing in it a miniature loudspeaker or piezo-electric transducer. Ideally this should be situated in the locomotive itself, but it could alternatively be located in the tender or in an adjacent coach or wagon.

Remember that the loudspeaker will give a louder and richer output if it is mounted on some structure that acts as a baffle, ie, that prevents sound waves from the front of the speaker from 'short-circuiting' straight to the back of the cone. Also it is very desirable to have the cone exposed to the outside world, if at all possible. On a steam-outline locomotive it is sometimes possible to mount the speaker in the tender facing upwards through a loose sprinkling of coal over a gauze.

Through-the-rails sound

In this system the sound is applied to the track through the controller. In my experiments the controller was the same as that described in Chapter 31 in connection with high-frequency train lighting, except for the following differences: (i) the 'lower' power supply is stabilized at 9 V and (ii) the feedback loop bypass capacitor was increased to 100µF so that the feedback loop no longer functioned at audio frequencies. The audio input replaces the HF input from the 555 timer, giving the circuit shown in Figure 36.1, which delivers pure dc with superimposed audio. The audio may be electronically generated using circuitry like that described in Chapters 33 to 35 or may be via a cassette recorder or alternative source.

On board the train itself all we need, in theory, is the speaker with a blocking capacitor connected straight across the rails. The purpose of the blocking capacitor is to prevent dc from the controller from interfering with the speaker and indeed from burning it out. In practice, unfortunately, it is not as simple as that. The capacitor needs to be a high-value electrolytic type and non-polarized. These are expensive, so I used a pair of polarized types (400 µF, 40 V) 'back to back', which proved quite satisfactory. As a further precaution against damage to the speaker, I added a 6 V grain-of-wheat lamp in series with the speaker and capacitors, as shown in Figure 36.2. If the capacitors should become leaky so that controller's dc output reaches the lamp plus speaker, the lamp will light, absorbing most of the power and if the lamp should burn out, it will at least have served a useful purpose in protecting the rather more expensive speaker. In general use I have not had any failures with this circuit.

The lamp is also useful as an aid in setting the sound effect levels. A good level appears to correspond to the lamp glowing gently in time with the sound. In a steam-

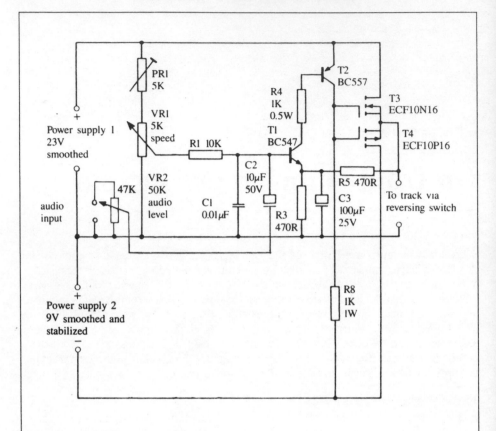

Figure 36.1 *Circuit for a controller for 'through-the-rails' sound effects. Compare this circuit with that shown in Figure 31.3.*

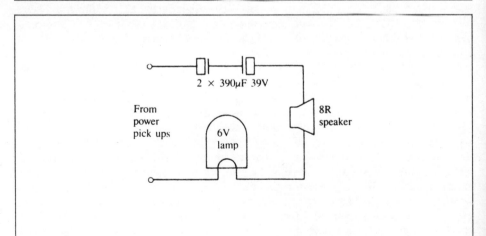

Figure 36.2 *On-train speaker arrangement for 'through-the-rails' sound.*

outline loco you might be able to use an orange-tinted lamp in the firebox which will glow prototypically in time with the chuffs.

If the sound is turned off, but the train is left running, the speaker does deliver some crackles and buzzes originating from the motor, but these are faint and are normally drowned by the mechanical sounds of the train as it runs.

Some locos will reproduce some through-the-rails sounds without even needing a speaker. Best for this purpose are those fitted with the Hornby X03/X04-type motor or the Airfix five-pole motors. Chuffs and hisses will be reproduced faintly but audibly at low settings of the speed control; this is caused by the armature 'rattling' as the ac component of the audio signal is applied to its coils. As the loco gathers speed, however, the armature gains momentum which counteracts the reciprocating tendency, so that the sound dies away.

An interesting spin-off from the through-the-rails sound is that the pure dc controller becomes compatible with live-rail track circuits. Even trains not fitted with speakers are detected normally by the live-rail track circuit provided that the sound is on. If the sound is turned off, train detection fails when the controller output is positive relative to the layout common return. Vehicles fitted with speakers and blocking capacitors are detected by track circuits in the absence of locos, provided that the sound is on. Through-the-rails sound, therefore, is compatible with all types of track circuitings, but not with speedo-meter circuits, nor, regrettably, with high frequency train lighting (Chapter 31). Although the controller circuit is almost identical to that described in Chapter 31, the HF generator causes intolerable interference with the audio system. Furthermore, the audio frequencies will in certain circumstances light lamps with blocking capacitors intended for HF light-ing. If you want through-the-rails sound *and* constant train lighting, you must opt for the battery-based lighting system described in Chapter 32.

Components
Maplin order codes as follows: ECF10N16 AY56L, ECF10P16 AY54J, BC557 QQ16S, BC547 QQ14Q.

Appendix 1

Tools needed for electronic projects

A number of tools are needed; as a railway modeller you may already have most of these, if not all.

A test meter
This is a meter having ac voltage, dc voltage, current and resistance ranges. The feature to look for in choosing a meter is a good selection of *current* ranges. You need ranges in multiples of 10 or less from 5 mA (or below) to 1 A (or above). Some cheaper instruments offer just two ranges: eg, 500 μA and 500 mA. This is not good enough because many of the currents used in electronics are in the range 1 to 10 mA, which would overload the lower range and barely register at all on the upper range. Do not spare the expense on your test meter; get a good one. It should give years of service and will be useful around the home and car as well.

A soldering iron
You need a conventional mains-operated iron with a miniature bit. The minimum useful element rating is 25 W; above that the higher the better. A warning lamp telling you that the iron is on is a practical safety feature.

A heavy, medium-grade file
You will need this to clean the bit of your soldering iron, which will rapidly become encrusted with oxide.

A pair of fine-nosed 'radio' pliers
These are useful for holding components while you solder them. You could use forceps, but the pliers are more comfortable and have the second valuable advantage over forceps in that, being comparatively massive, they act as a heat sink and conduct the heat away from sensitive components such as semi-conductors. If you want the heat-sinkage facility without the holding facility, put a thick rubber band around the handles of the pliers — they will 'cling' to anything.

Wire cutters
Use the proper tool for this job. I have never found the cutting edges built into pliers satisfactory. With a bit of practice you will also be able to use these for baring the ends of insulated wire, ie, stripping off the plastic or rubber sleeve at the end. Close

the cutters very gently on the sleeve until you feel the greater resistance of the wire itself. Then simply pull the main length of wire away. Practise this — once you have got the knack, you'll have it for life.

In addition you will also need a craft knife, a set of miniature screwdrivers and a set of miniature drills.

Appendix 2

How to make an effective soldered joint

The most common cause of failure in amateur electronic projects is badly soldered joints. A so-called 'dry joint' looks fine and yet there is an insulating barrier of flux or grease between the items supposedly connected. The author learned the hard way; spare yourself the trouble. *There is no short cut* — you ignore the following procedure at your (or your project's) peril.

1. Clean the items to be soldered by scraping with a blade or file. This removes dirt and grease and also breaks through the thin oxide layer that forms on many metal surfaces, exposing bare metal. It is only on bare metal that solder will 'take'.
2. Tin the items to be soldered. This means applying a thin layer of solder. Touch each item in turn together with a length of solder on the hot bit of the iron. The molten solder should wet the item and when cooled give a bright, silvery appearance.
3. If possible, make a physical connection between the items being soldered, eg, twist or hook one around the other.
4. Apply the iron with more solder to the items. The solder should run smoothly into the crevices and spaces.
5. Allow the joint a minute to cool down before applying any physical stress to it, eg, using wire cutters to trim off projecting ends.
6. For electronics work use only proper electronics solder with integral flux cores.
7. When soldering a semi-conductor device, apply a heat sink (which may be the pliers in which you are holding the device) between the body of the device and the part of the lead being soldered. Complete the joint as quickly as possible — the duration of the heating is more critical than the temperature of the iron; for this reason the hotter the iron, the better, since it will enable joints to be completed more quickly.

The acrobatics of soldering

If you are unused to soldering, you may wonder just how to hold everything. Ideally you need one hand for each item being soldered, one to hold the solder and another to hold the iron; even to join two items needs four hands, which most of us do not have. The answer lies in a mixture of dexterity and ingenuity. Two items can usually be manipulated in one hand, leaving the other free for the solder. I frequently wedge the soldering iron between my knees and bring everything else to it. I have even known those who advocate holding it in their mouth — caution! Never attempt this without first ensuring that the iron is adequately earthed, otherwise a short circuit in the iron could prove lethal. (Also do not hold the solder direct in your mouth — it contains lead. If your solder comes in a plastic dispensing tube, it is, of course, safe to hold that in your mouth.)

Undoing soldered joints

The most satisfactory method in the author's experience is the use of de-soldering braid. This is a wick of copper threads impregnated with flux. Apply the iron and the end of the braid to the joint to be undone. The molten solder runs up the braid by capillary action leaving the joint free of solder and ready for separation by hand. When the end of the braid is saturated with solder, cut it off and throw it away.

Warning

So far as is practicable do your soldering well away from your model railway. If this is not possible, keep polystyrene and white-metal models under cover. A drop of molten solder falling on one of these will leave a scar that you may never eliminate. Worse still, a dropped hot soldering iron falling on a model may melt its way clean through, a thought is almost too horrible to contemplate. So be very careful. Keep soldering irons away from young children, who find them fascinating. And be considerate of others; some people find the smell of solder flux irritating.

Appendix 3

Methods of construction

Nothing is more unsightly than a great tangle of components sprawling over the table top or floor. Such a construction is unsatisfactory also for more practical reasons. It is highly susceptible to breakage and to short circuits. A rigid construction method makes the circuit not only physically robust and therefore more reliable, but also more easily portable.

Many methods of construction are possible and this appendix does not claim to be comprehensive. The methods described are some that the author has tried and found satisfactory. Converting the circuit diagram into a practical reality should not prove too difficult. The physical layout need not be a copy of the layout of the circuit diagram. Provided the paths of continuity are the same, the physical layout itself is immaterial, although in practice it is generally more convenient for components electrically adjacent to be physically near.

Tagstrip

This is most appropriate for simpler circuits, eg, simpler controllers and bistables. The tagstrip is a strip of paxolin bearing at intervals metal tags to which components or wires can be soldered. The leads of power transistors may need to be *gently* splayed to equal the pitch of the tags.

Veroboard

Veroboard is paxolin sheet clad on the reverse with conductive copper strips at intervals (0.1 inch or 2.54 mm is the commonest pitch) with holes at the same intervals. Special boards are available for certain special applications, eg, for use with integrated circuits. The components are mounted on top of the board, their leads being inserted through the holes and soldered to the copper conductor beneath.

Breaks in the copper conductors can be made using a commercial 'spot face cutter' (stripboard cutter), which resembles a drill bit mounted in a handle. In fact you can use a ⅛ inch drill bit, but it is more awkward. Insert the point in a hole at a suitable point on the appropriate conductor and twist the device back and forth. The result is the removal of the copper and formation of a small dent in the undersurface of the board. *Always check carefully that the break is complete;* sometimes an almost invisible whisker of copper remains closing the gap and this can wreak havoc in a circuit. Small pieces of stray copper conductor can also come to rest, short-circuiting adjacent copper conductors. Oversize blobs of solder can also cause this.

Veroboard allows components to be packed at a very high density (especially if the resistors are mounted perpendicular to the board).

Blob board

This resembles Veroboard with a wider pitch (around 4 mm) and without holes. Intended for experimental rather than permanent projects, it can nevertheless be used for the latter. Components are mounted on the same side of the board as the conductors, which are pre-tinned. Conductors can be broken with a spot face cutter, but it is a time-consuming job. The system works tolerably well but guard against dry joints and blobs of solder short-circuiting adjacent conductors.

Printed circuits

Commercial electronic equipment uses printed circuit boards (pcbs), but there is no reason why amateurs and even beginners should not also make them up and use them for permanent projects. It is best — at least to begin with — to buy a printed circuit board kit from an electronics supplier or from Tandy, as this will contain more detailed instructions than can be given here.

To start with you need to plan — carefully! — the positions of the components on the board and the layout of the copper conductors. Double check your layout — mistakes after this stage cannot be easily rectified. Then take a piece of copper-clad board (as used for sleepers on home-made track) of the right size, clean the copper surface *thoroughly* using Vim or a similar abstergent cleaner and draw in the copper conductors using an etch-resist pen. This deposits on the board a substance rather like nail varnish. The pen will probably have a pump action to keep the etch resist flowing freely. Try to keep the thickness of the resist even.

When the etch resist has dried, float the board (copper-clad side down) in a solution of ferric chloride. Be careful with this — it is nasty stuff. The stronger and warmer the solution, the quicker the etching. The instructions in the kit will tell you how much of the crystals to dissolve in how much water, but take care as heat is generated as the solid goes into solution.

Ideally, after about five minutes, the ferric chloride will have etched the copper off the board except where it has been protected by the etch resist. Remove the board from the solution, wash it carefully in water and dry it. Remove the etch resist using nail varnish remover (acetone). Drill the holes for the component leads.

There are many variations on this process. Double-sided copper-clad board is available for especially complex circuits. Light-sensitive etch resist is available so that large numbers of identical boards can be made photographically from a master design drawn on acetate film. As on Veroboard, resistors may be mounted horizontally or vertically, depending on the space available. Printed circuit boards look good and are a robust way of assembling circuits.

Appendix 4

The resistance/capacitance colour code and preferred values

Most resistors and also some capacitors have their value marked not in figures but in an internationally accepted colour code giving the resistance in Ohms (R) or capacitance in picoFarads (pF); 1,000,000 pF = 1 μF. Colour coding makes it far easier to select the right component from a box of mixed values — it saves turning each device round until the markings are located, assuming they can be located at all!

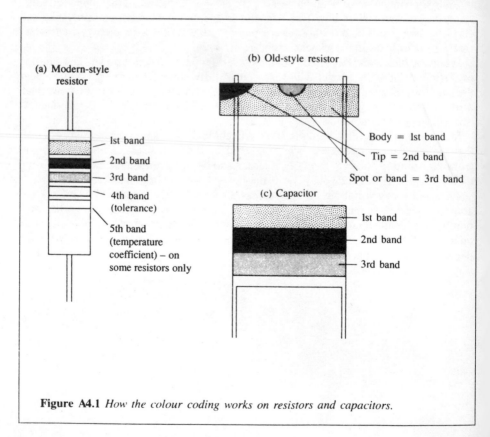

Figure A4.1 *How the colour coding works on resistors and capacitors.*

The colour code itself shows a logical sequence. Each colour represents a figure, thus

black	=	0	yellow	=	4	purple	=	7
brown	=	1	green	=	5	grey	=	8
red	=	2	blue	=	6	white	=	9
orange	=	3						

Figure A4.1 shows how these colours are applied in bands on the devices. The *first* band (or its equivalent) gives the first significant figure of the value. The *second* band gives the second significant figure. The *third* band gives the exponential, ie, the number of noughts that follow the two significant figures. The following examples show how these work for *resistors*.

	orange/orange/orange	= 3 3 000	= 33 000R = 33K
	brown/black/red	= 1 0 00	= 1000R = 1K = 1K0
	blue/grey/brown	= 6 8 0	= 680R
	orange/white/black	= 3 9 -	= 39R
BUT	yellow/purple	= 4 7	= 4.7R = 4R7
			(NOTE! No third band)

The *fourth* band on a resistor gives its tolerance, ie, a measure of how accurately the device's actual resistance conforms to that marked on it. Brown = ± 1%; red = ± 2%; gold = ± 5%; silver = ± 10%; no fourth band = ± 20%,

Some resistors carry a *fifth* band which specifies how its resistance varies with temperature. It is not significant in any of the circuits described in this book.

Capacitors

The colour code works in the same way giving the value in pF. Subtract 6 from the exponential to get the value in µF. Thus brown/black/yellow = 100000 = 100 000 pF = 0.1 µF. On Mullard polyester types there is no separation between bands, so a capacitor apparently coded red/yellow but with the red band double width is in fact red/red/yellow = 220000 pF = 0.22 µF.

Preferred values

Resistors and capacitors are made in standard ranges of values following a roughly logarithmic sequence. In the E12 series there are 12 values per decade; their significant figures are: 10, 12, 15, 18, 22, 27, 33, 39, 47, 56, 68, 82. In the E24 series there are 24 values per decade consisting of the E12 values given above and the following 12 intermediate values: 11, 13, 16, 20, 24, 30, 36, 43, 51, 62, 75, 91.

Resistors having all values in the E12 range from about 1 R0 to 10 M are quite easily obtainable; those in the other E24 values are less easy to find. Capacitors are available for all E12 values from a few pF up to about 1 µF; above this electrolytic and tantalum types are used in which working voltage also becomes important. Sometimes only alternate E12 values (ie, 10, 15, 22, 33, 47, 68) are available in any given series

In general in electronics the values of resistors and capacitors used are not very critical. Thus, where 1 K is specified 820 R or 1K2 or even 680 R or 1KS can often be used without adversely affecting the performance of the circuit.

Appendix 5

Characteristics of some popular semi-conductors

npn

Type	Case	Ptotal	Vceo	Ic	hfe	ft(MHz)	Remarks
BC 107*	TO 18	360 mW	45 V	100 mA	300	250	
BC 108*	TO 18	360 mW	20 V	100 mA	500	250	
BC 109	TO 18	360 mW	20 V	100 mA	500	250	low noise
2N 5136*	TO 105	n/a	20 V	500 mA	100	200	
BC 182*	TO 92 (A) or (B)	300 mW	50 V	200 mA	300	150	general purpose
BC 183*	TO 92 (A) or (B)	300 mA	30 V	200 mA	500	150	
BC 184*	TO 92 (A) or (B)	300 mW	30 V	200 mA	500	150	low noise
2N 3904*	TO 92 (C)	n/a	40 V	200 mA	200	300	general purpose
ZTX 300*	E line	300 mW	25 V	500 mA	200	150	general purpose
BC 337*	TO 92 (B) or (C)	625 mW	45 V	500 mA	400	200	
BFY 50	TO 39	800 mW	35 V	1 A	30	60	general purpose
BFY 51	TO 39	800 mW	30 V	1 A	40	50	
BFY 52	TO 39	800 mW	20 V	1 A	60	50	
2N 2222*	TO 18	500 mW	30 V	600 mA	150	300	
2N 3725	TO 5	800 mW	50 V	1 A	100	450	
BD 437	TO 126	36 W	45 V	4 A	40	3	
2N 5191	TO 126	40 W	60 V	4 A	100	2	
BD 201	TO 220	60 W	45 V	8 A	30	3	
MJE 3055	TO 127	90 W	60 V	10 A	50	2.5	
2N 3055	TO 3	115 W	60 V	15 A	50	2.5	

* Can be used as substitutes for BC 108 in circuits in this book.

pnp

Type	Case	Ptotal	Vceo	Ic	hfe	ft(MHz)	Remarks
BC 177*	TO 18	300 mW	-45 V	-300 mA	150	150	complement to BC 107/8/9
BC 178*	TO 18	300 mW	-25 V	-300 mA	200	150	
BC 179*	TO 18	300 mW	-25 V	-300 mA	500	150	
2N 5142*	TO 105	n/a	-20 V	-500 mA	100	200	complement to 2N 5136

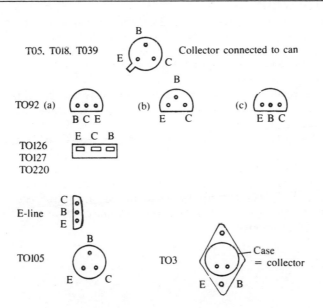

Figure A5.1 *Connections (pin outs) of some popular transistor types. Beware — many variations occur!*

BC 212*	TO 92 (A) or (B)	300 mW	-50 V	-200 mA	150	200	complement to BC 182/3/4
BC 213*	TO 92 (A) or (B)	300 mW	-30 V	-200 mA	200	350	
BC 214*	TO 92 (A) or (B)	300 mW	-30 V	-200 mA	300	200	
2N 3906*	TO 92 (C)	n/a	-40 V	-200 mA	200	300	complement to 2N 3904
ZTX 500*	E line	300 mW	-25 V	-500 mA	200	150	complement to ZTX 300
BC 327*	TO 92 (B) or (C)	625 mW	-45 V	-500 mA	400	260	complement to BC 337
BC 461*	TO 39	1 W	-60 V	-2 A	150	50	near complement to BFY 50/1/2
2N 2907*	TO 18	400 mW	-30 V	-600 mA	150	300	complement to 2N 2222
2N 5022	TO 5		-80 V	-1 A	100	450	complement to 2N 3725
2N 5194	TO 126	40 W	-60 V	-4 A	100	2	complement to 2N 5191
MJE 2955	TO 127	90 W	-60 V	-10 A	50	2.5	complement to MJE 3055
MJE 2955	TO 3	115 W	-60 V	-15 A	50	2.5	complement to 2N 3055

* Can be used as substitutes for BC 178 in circuits in this book.

Key to characteristics

P*total* = total power that may be continuously dissipated by the device. The power being dissipated by a transistor equals V*ceo* × I*c* (see below).

V*ceo* = maximum voltage that may be applied continuously to the collector relative to the emitter, the base being open-circuit (unbiased).

I*c* = maximum continuous collection current.

h*fe* = typical current gain. This figure varies enormously with conditions and between individuals even of the same nominal type. Many European general-purpose transistors (ie, those having type numbers beginning BC, eg, BC 108) are sometimes graded according to gain into A (low gain), B (medium gain) and C (high gain). Thus a BC 108 C should have higher gain than a BC 108 B. A device simply marked BC 108 is ungraded and its gain may fall anywhere in the possible range.

f*t* = transition frequency, not a figure liable to cause concern in model railway electronics, but useful in general electronics. The current gain of transistors falls with frequency of input signal (if ac); at f*t* gain becomes unity, above which amplification, of course, becomes impossible.

Appendix 6

Fault finding

So, you've built it and it doesn't work. What next? Tearing your hair or kicking the cat won't help.

How to get it right the first time

Prevention is better than cure, so let's see how to construct projects in such a way that they *do* work first time. The secret is to test everything at every stage as far as possible. Let's see how this works first for a simple project, *viz* the controller in Chapter 4.

Power Supply. You will need a power supply to run the finished controller, but it's a good idea to have it ready right at the beginning. Plug it in and switch it on. First, test its output voltage with a test meter and if that is satisfactory, put your test meter on the highest available current range (10 A is not too high) and connect it straight across the output. The meter should swing over to 1 or 2 A before the circuit breaker or current limiter comes into action. You now know that your power supply will deliver both the Volts and the Amps that your finished controller will need. This may sound trite, but it is amazing how many electronic projects have been built *correctly* but rejected as failures because they failed to work when connected to a faulty power supply.

Circuit Board. You must decide now on tag-strip, Veroboard or some other means of construction. We shall use the word 'board' loosely to indicate the assembly, whatever form it takes. Provide your positive and negative input connections, choose a suitable speed control potentiometer and wire its outer terminals to the positive and negative lines. Connect the board to the power supply. Select a suitable voltage range on the test meter; connect the black probe to the negative line and the red probe to the slider of the pot. Now run the slider from minimum to maximum and back a few times watching what happens on the meter. The indicated voltage should go up and down smoothly in unison with the movement of the slider. Again, I have seen controllers fail because the speed control pot was faulty. The carbon tracks in pots have been known to develop cracks, so the pot becomes in effect a two-position switch: with the slider below the crack the speed is zero; above the crack the speed is maximum. No wonder the circuit is rejected as a non-runner!

Select a resistor for R1 and check with the test meter that its resistance is what you think it is. Insert R1 and T1. *Temporarily* ground T1's emitter. Connect the test meter (voltage range) between T1's collector and supply positive. Now swing the speed control again. At minimum speed the meter should indicate no volts but at quite a low setting of the speed control the full supply voltage should appear as T1 goes into saturation. OK, you have a working T1. Disconnect T1's emitter from ground and insert D1. Repeat the last test. You should get no voltage reading at all — or perhaps a barely perceptible movement of the needle owing to a leakage current.

Insert IC1. Connect the test meter (voltage range) across the controller output, ie, across D1. Swing the speed control back and forth a few times. The results should be identical to those of the very first test when you were measuring the voltage on the slider of the pot. The circuit is, after all, a 'voltage follower'. The difference is, though the meter does not know it, that the controller will now deliver up to n Amps of current at any voltage you care to set when n is the threshold of the circuit breaker or current limiter in the power supply. If all is well, wire in the reversing switch and repeat the tests on both settings of the switch. You will need to transpose the probes when you operate the switch. If all is well, connect the controller to your railway and see how it handles a train.

If all is *not* well, by following this procedure you will at least know at what stage of construction things went wrong. Suppose, for instance, that you put in D1 the wrong way round. You would have quickly discovered that T1 was still behaving as though its emitter were grounded and, if in your haste to finish the controller and see it work, you forgot to carry out that test and proceeded to insert IC1, you would quickly discover things had run amok at the next test. Instead of following the input voltage obediently, it would follow it up to about 1 V and then the overload cutout would trip each time. The test suggests that we have a short circuit in the controller output, so we look at our output circuit and spot D1. D1 is supposed to be reverse biased, we tell ourselves, but when we look at our board we see that we have got it in the wrong way round. Exactly the kind of mistake that we all make when we're anxious to complete a project and see how it performs.

What applies to simple projects applies even more to complex ones. Probably the most complex project in this book is the progressive cab control unit (Chapter 29). The first prototype was built as follows.

First, IC4 was put in with the ties and connections needed for the *second* bistable only (IC4c/d). T2 with its LED was inserted. Power was applied and the bistable checked using the test meter on a current range to momentarily ground one bistable input, then the other. The bistable worked fine. This was repeated with the other bistable (IC4a/d) and its associated circuitry. This, too, worked fine. Next, IC3 was put in. There was no easy way of testing the bistable circuitry at this stage, but the 'unconnected train' LED should have lit when power was applied. It didn't, but I decided to press on and fit IC1 before further testing. With IC1 went the advise input switches which would help considerably in later testing. At this stage pressing either 'advise' input should illuminate the appropriate 'controller connected' LED. In practice, pressing 'advise A' brought on *both* LEDs, which correctly could be cleared using the 'isolate' switch. Pressing 'Advise B' did nothing. The 'unconnected train' LED still stubbornly refused to light under any circumstances.

An initial study of the board showed that a short circuit had joined the two transistors' collectors together. When separated, pressing the 'Advise A' button correctly brought on only the 'A connected' LED. Further examination showed a bad contact as responsible for the non-illumination of the 'unconnected train' LED, which now behaved. However, 'Advise B' still did nothing and this was worrying as both bistable circuits had worked perfectly.

At this stage I analysed the circuit using a logic probe. This is a very handy gadget which I unhesitatingly recommend to all who dabble with logic circuitry. It has two leads which are connected to the power supply of the circuit under investigation. The probe tip can be used to contact any part of the circuit. If it encounters a logical '0', one LED lights. If it encounters a logical '1' another LED lights. If it encounters an indeterminate voltage or is left open circuit, neither LED lights. It's much faster than a voltmeter because you do not have to look away from the circuit to the meter — the LEDs are at the base of the device's body — and it gives a nice 'digital' ('0' or '1') readout. The probe showed that one gate of IC4 and one gate of IC1 were not following their proper logic. IC1 was easy to check; it was in an IC socket, so out it came and in went a replacement. The performance was unchanged, suggesting that both ICs were fine; the fault was on the board. A very close scrutiny of the underside of the Veroboard, tracing the conductors away from the anomalously-behaving gates led me to the tiniest whisker of copper shorting two adjacent conductors together. With this removed, the circuit behaved perfectly, at last. IC2, IC5, IC6 and IC7 followed, fortunately without malfunction.

Faults in completed equipment

Never mind the how but you have a piece of equipment that does not work. Presumably you have a circuit diagram so reference to this should give you some idea of how much current the circuit should take from its power supply and also of what the voltages (or logic levels) should be at various points in the circuit.

First, check the current consumption. This may tell you everything or it may tell you nothing. If it is excessively high, this suggests some kind of short circuit. The affected components are likely to heat up quite quickly so that your sense of touch (and smell!) may enable you to locate them quite rapidly. If the current is too low, this suggests that the circuit, or part of it, is not making contact with the power supply. I built a radio receiver once which failed to work and which the meter told me at once was taking *no* current. The reason? I had correctly connected the earthy side of the battery to the frame of the tuning capacitor, but I had forgotten to insert a link from the said frame to the return line of the circuit! Once connected, the receiver worked perfectly. It's the real sillies like this that the current consumption test shows up. It's when the current consumption is more or less normal and the circuit still doesn't work, that the fault is more subtle and you must locate it by irregularities in the voltages or logic levels. There are a few 'tricks' that may help you locate a fault rapidly.

Remember that a transistor, when functioning normally, will have its base and emitter voltages 0.7 V apart. So, if you find a transistor where there is a great difference, say 3 V, between base and emitter, that transistor is suspect. The same is true for TTL gates. If you find a NAND gate with '1's on all inputs *and* on its output, something is very wrong. That is not to say that that gate has most definitely failed. It could be, for instance, that a solder blob or copper whisker is short circuiting its output terminal to supply positive.

These checks do not tell you *what* is wrong, but they help you to find *where* something is wrong. To spot what is actually causing the malfunction may still involve some tracing along the conductors. Never be afraid to search.

Kinds of faults

Let us now have a look at the kind of fault that we are likely to discover at the end of our quest.

Component failure is, in my experience, very rare. Most modern components are well tested before dispatch and remain serviceable even if subjected to considerable abuse.

Component wrongly inserted. The correct component has been used but with its leads interchanged, eg base and emitter interchanged. Watch out for this with transistors having unusual pin-outs, eg some variants of the BC182/212 family. Also watch out for the pin-out of the 7402 (74LS02) IC which is different from all other two-input gates (except the rarely used '01).

Wrong component. When the switching regulator for the battery-back-up train lighting system (Chapter 32) was first finished, it failed to work. The output transistor delivered the full input voltage and several components got very hot. I checked all connections and all were correct. Then I spotted that T2 was a BC557 (pnp) where the circuit demanded a BC547 (npn)! Substitution of the correct transistor made the circuit work. This kind of error is very easy to make especially where a one-digit difference in the component type number may make a world of difference to performance. Watch out for a similar problem with resistors. I have seen resistors apparently coded brown/black/brown (100 R) but with a barely perceptible difference in hue between the two brown bands. In fact the third band was supposed to be orange and the resistor was 10 K. Another common resistor error is to select brown/red/black (12 R) thinking you have brown/black/red (1 K). *Always* before using a resistor check it on the meter. You will be amazed at what you think is something else!

Bad contacts. These are normally the results of bad soldering. The joint may *look* fine and may even function properly for a while, but there is no fixed metal-to-metal contact and one day physical stress on one side of the joint causes the component to move and electrical contact is lost.

Circuit board faults. Nearly all of my circuits nowadays use Veroboard, an excellent medium and ideal for use with ICs but Veroboard lays the unwary constructor open to two faults, both very common. Firstly, when making a break in a conductor by means of a spot face cutter (stripboard cutter) make absolutely certain that you have fully separated the two parts of the conductor. It is easy to leave an almost microscopic trace of copper around the edge of the hole. Examine your break very carefully under a powerful light and don't feel a fool in checking the continuity (or rather, discontinuity) with the meter. Better to make certain now rather than waste hours later on looking for an elusive short circuit in the finished project. Secondly, it sometimes happens that the slivers of copper that result from the use of the spot face cutter come to rest so that they are shorting two conductors. They are very small, so easily go unnoticed. Molten flux from later soldering operations can even 'glue' such slivers into permanent short circuits (as on my prototype progressive cab control unit). The only evidence will be two adjacent conductors always at the same voltage. You must search diligently under a powerful lamp and a magnifying glass. The offending sliver, when located, can be hacked out using the blade of a miniature screwdriver. In fact, it is not a bad idea to score along between the conductors of a finished circuit board in the hope of breaking any such particles.

All that has been said above about copper particles applies equally to solder blobs which can also cause some hard-to-locate and harder-to-remove short circuits between conductors.

Conclusion

It has not been possible to give anything more than general hints, since every circuit and every method of construction has its own peculiar traps for the unwary. Yet I hope that I have encouraged you to look analytically at your failed project rather than throw it out of the window!

Appendix 7

Where to get electronic components

This is an age-old problem. There is no *one* answer. The following is a list of methods; no doubt you will use all of them from time to time.

Electronic components retailers

There was a time when a visit to London's Edgware Road would furnish all your needs, as there were then dozens of component shops there in close proximity. However, takeovers, mergers and moves up-market to more profitable hi-fi retailing have effectively stopped many outlets. Other shops have specialized in computer hardware and software. If you live outside London, look in *Yellow Pages* (also see below under 'Mail Order'). Many mail order suppliers also operate retail shops; there may be one near you.

Mail order

There is a multiplicity of mail order dealers throughout the UK. The best way to find their names, addresses and current prices is to consult the advertisements in popular electronics magazines that you will find in any newsagents. If you are a real miser, and unwilling to pay for a magazine, you may find some at your local public library.

In these advertisements you will see seemingly amazing bargains. I can only advise you to watch *carefully* what is being offered. The advertisers are scrupulously fair in their wording: a bag of '100 unmarked, untested transistors' will contain just that. Even if you establish which are working npn types, working pnp types and non-functional devices– which you can do with tedious testing — you will still not know the current ratings and voltage ratings of the working devices. My experience has been that devices from this kind of special offer are not reliable — many are manufacturers' rejects — and will give trouble if used in the kind of projects described in this book. Model railway circuits demand full-specification devices and readers are urged — for their own satisfaction and sanity! — to use only marked, tested devices. Even among these, there are still bargains to be had. By all means go for the bargains — but make sure that they *are* bargains — *know* what you are getting.

Compare mail order suppliers' prices with caution. Most charge extra for postage and packing. Some have a minimum order charge. Some include VAT in their advertised prices; with others you must add it. So when you see supplier A advertising an item at 10p and supplier B advertising the same at 12p, supplier B may nevertheless be cheaper.

Tandy (known as Radio Shack in the USA)
This is the closest that there is to an electronics chain store — the Tandy store is a familiar sight in High Streets throughout the UK and overseas. The range of electronic components stocked is limited and the regular prices tend to be high. Nevertheless if there is one item that you need, it may be cheaper and more convenient to buy it across the counter at your local Tandy than from a mail order supplier who adds a charge for postage and packing. In their sales there are genuine bargains to be had; also *some* items in the regular catalogue undoubtedly offer exceptional value for money. My experience with my local store (which I plague with requests for obscure items) has been that time and time again the staff have gone out of their way to be helpful.

MPS (Maplin Professional)
Maplin claims to have the UK's largest chain of electronic catalogue stores, with 42 outlets in the UK and distributors in some other countries. Maplin also operates a world-wide mail order service. The huge catalogue — a veritable treasury of information — is widely obtainable from newsagents and will, of course, list what is available, how much it costs and how to obtain it. Maplin welcomes enquiries and orders from hobbyists (unlike some other suppliers who prefer to serve business customers). In this book I have given the Maplin catalogue numbers for semi-conductors and other critical components, wher-ever possible. These were taken from the March 1997–August 1997 Maplin catalogue. Maplin also sells a range of electronic project kits, including several for railway modellers; these are described in Appendix 16.

Local radio shops
Radio shops which operate a repair service of necessity carry stocks of components, but they do not exist to serve the needs of electronics buffs! In dire emergency, when your project needs a certain component to finish it off, try your local radio shop, but his prices are likely to be high.

Ex-equipment components
Much old electronic equipment, especially old TV sets, is ditched — sometimes, regret-tably, literally in the local ditch! Nowadays a discarded TV set is quite likely to be tran-sistorized and to have up-to-date components. The local civic amenties tip is another source of these. Market stalls and junk shops sometimes sell ex-equipment circuit boards, often from computers. Remove the useful looking components following the procedure given near the end of Appendix 2. A warning — it gets a bit tedious after a while. On a purely economic basis you would probably be better off spending an equivalent time in paid employment and using your pay to buy new components. This is, of course, why these panels are often simply thrown away.

While there is no problem with the resistors and capacitors that you amass in this way, the semi-conductors may have unfamiliar type numbers. You will need access to a semi-conductor data book — there may be one in your local public library's reference section. Some radio and TV transistors will be unsuitable for most model railway applications, especially those having type numbers beginning with AF or BF, eg, AF117, BF194. Keep these — one day you might want to build a radio.

Friends

Unless you live on a lighthouse or in the middle of a desert, you probably have a large circle of friends and colleagues (at work, school, church, club, pub, next door, etc) which is nowadays *bound* to include at least one other electronics buff who has a stock of components. I suggest that you make yourself known to him and swop notes on what you are doing. While I *do not* recommend scrounging, there is nevertheless a fraternal bond that links electronics buffs, just as there is between railway modellers. One of the unwritten rules of this informal bond is that if you are desperate for a certain component and your friend has a spare one, he gives it to you. (That is unless it is a highly expensive item and so far as the projects in this book are concerned, none comes in that category.) This bond entails reciprocality when next week your friend is desperate for something that you have, you are obliged to give it to him, and so on. This kind of informal co-operation can help enormously, especially while you are wondering if that massive mail order consignment has gone astray in the post!

Warning

Electronics is a rapidly developing technology. Because of this some components (or even whole ranges) may have short production lives. Consequently, in a book such as this sometimes components specified in projects become obsolete and unobtainable, even before the book is in print.

74 and 74LS series TTL, for instance, are both technically obsolete, although still widely available at the time of writing (May 1997). It could be that these components may become hard to obtain during the next few years. When this happens, the projects which use their unique characteristics — such as the signal drivers — may simply become impractical.

Appendix 8

Current, voltage, resistance and power

Electric current

An electric current consists of a stream of electrons flowing along a suitable conductor. It is conventional to regard the current as flowing out of the positive terminal of the power supply, through the circuit (the *load*) and returning into the negative terminal of the power supply. In fact each electron bears a negative charge and the directon of flow of the electrons themselves is contrary to that of 'conventional current', ie, from the negative terminal of the power supply through the circuit to the positive terminal.

The unit of electric current is the *Ampère*, commonly abbreviated Amp or just A. Smaller units of current commonly used in electronics are the milliampere (mA) which equals 1/1,000 A and the microAmpere (μA) which equals 1/1,000,000 A or 1/1,000 mA. This *amperage* is an expression of the *rate of flow* of electricity — indeed 1 A corresponds to 6.24×10^{18} electrons per second passing the measuring point.

There are some simple rules relating to the behaviour of electric current. Current can neither be created nor destroyed at any point in the circuit. The current flowing into any component must equal that flowing out. More rules follow when we consider electromotive force and resistance.

Electromotive force (EMF)

Just as tractive force must be applied to railway vehicles to make them roll, so a force must be applied to the electrons in a conductor to set them moving. A force that sets electrons in motion is called simply an *electromotive force* (EMF) and its unit is the Volt (after Voltère), usually abbreviated V. Small units of voltage are the milliVolt (mV) equalling 1/1,000 V and the microvolt equalling 1/1,000,000 V or 1/1,000 mV.

Common sources of EMF in a circuit are a battery or a dynamo or the secondary winding of a transformer. Notice that *inside the source of EMF* the electrons arriving at the positive terminal (or the terminal that for the time being is positive in an ac circuit) are propelled to the negative terminal contrary to the normal direction of electron flow in the load circuit.

Resistance

When a source of EMF, eg, a battery, is connected to a circuit, the magnitude of the current that flows depends not only on the voltage of the EMF but also on the nature of the circuit. For many circuits, current is proportional to voltage, so that the ratio of voltage to current is constant for that circuit; such circuits are said to be *linear*. This voltage-divided-by-current figure is known as the *resistance* of the circuit and is measured in Ohms, abbreviated R or Ω. Larger units of resistance are the kilOhm (K) which equals 1,000 R and the megOhm (M) which equals 1,000,000 R or 1,000 K.

Notation

There is a convention that in writing values of resistance (and other electrical units) the unit sign replaces the decimal point. Thus 1500 R would normally be written 1K5 (for 1.5K).

Ohm's law

Ohm's law states that for linear circuits current is proportional to voltage and inversely proportional to resistance. This may be expressed algebraically:

$$I = \frac{E}{R} \text{ or } R = \frac{E}{I} \text{ or } E = IR$$

where *I* equals current, *E* equals EMF and *R* equals resistance.

Conveniently the equation holds good when *I* is in Amps, *E* in Volts and *R* in Ohms. So we would rewrite the equation as follows:

$$A = \frac{V}{R} \text{ or } R = \frac{V}{A} \text{ or } V = AR$$

Usefully in electronics it still holds good when *I* is in mA and *R* in K (and when *I* is in μA and R in M). So:

$$mA = \frac{V}{A} \text{ or } K = \frac{V}{mA} \text{ or } V = mAK$$

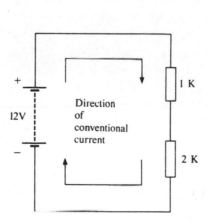

Figure A8.1 *Resistances in series add up — current flowing through 1 K and then 2 K has flowed through 3 K.*

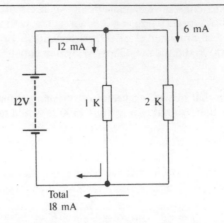

Figure A8.2 *Effect of connecting resistances in parallel — the* currents *add up.*

Ohm's law is of such fundamental importance in electronics that the above equations should be commited to memory. They appear over and over again.

Resistance in series

Figure A8.1 shows two resistors in series. The current flows through first 1 K then 2 K. It is not hard to see that this is equivalent to flowing through one 3 K resistor. (So, in this circuit, current by Ohm's law is 12 V/3 K = 4 mA.) For any number of resistances in series the general formula is:

$$R_{total} = R_1 + R_2 + R_3 + R_4 + R_5 + \ldots$$

Resistances in parallel

Figure A8.2 shows two resistors in parallel connected to the same power supply. We can therefore calculate the current flowing through each individually by Ohm's law.

$$\text{For } R_1 \ I_1 = 12 \text{ V/1 K} = 12 \text{ mA}$$
$$\text{For } R_2 \ I_2 = 12 \text{ V/2 K} = 6 \text{ mA}$$

The total current drained from the battery is 12 + 6 = 18 mA. So the two parallel resistors behave as one resistor having a resistance of 12 V/18 mA = 0.67 K = 670 R. Had the two resistors had the same value, the combined current would have been double the individual ones, making the combined resistance exactly half the individual values. Indeed for *n* parallel resistances each of value *R* the total resistances is *R/n*.

In fact when resistances are in parallel, their individual currents, each inversely proportional to resistance, add up to give a combined current inversely proportional to total resistance. This is summarized in the general formula for parallel resistances:

$$\frac{1}{R_{total}} = \frac{1}{R_1} + \frac{1}{R_2} + \frac{1}{R_3} + \frac{1}{R_4} + \frac{1}{R_5} + \ldots$$

There is a more convenient form for two resistances in parallel:

$$R_{total} = \frac{R_1 \times R_2}{R_1 + R_2}$$

By applying the appropriate equations the total resistance of any series/parallel resistance network can be calculated. This is of direct practical value to the experimenter, since it may enable him to make up a required resistance from series/parallel combinations when a suitable single component is unavailable.

Potential difference (PD)

When a current flows through a resistance, a voltage is set up across the resistance, which may be calculated by Ohm's law: $IR = E$. This voltage is known as a *potential difference* (PD). The distinction between PD and EMF is not always easy to understand, especially as both are measured in voltages. There are, however, several differences. An EMF is the force that drives a current and its voltage remains even if the current is switched off; a PD in contrast is the consequence of a current and disappears if the current is switched off. Inside the source of an EMF, electrons move from

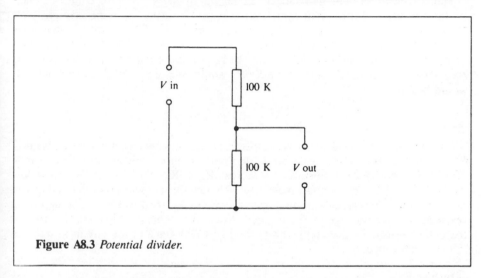

Figure A8.3 *Potential divider.*

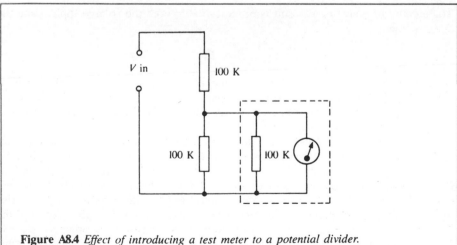

Figure A8.4 *Effect of introducing a test meter to a potential divider.*

the positive to the negative terminal; inside the reistance across which a PD is developed the electrons flow from negative to positive.

Potential dividers

Consider the circuit shown in Figure A8.3. Suppose V_{in} (the input voltage) is 12 V and both resistors are 100 K. The combined resistance of the two resistors is 100 + 100 = 200 K so the current flowing is 12 V/200 K = 60 μA. The PD raised across each resistor is 100 K $\times$ 60 μA = 6 V. In fact two series resistors form a *potential divider* in which any output voltage (V_{out}) between zero and V_{in} can be obtained by choice of values for R_1 and R_2.

$$V_{out} = \frac{R_2}{R_1 + R_2} \times V_{in}$$

There is, however, a hidden danger in potential dividers. Allowance must be made for the resistance of the circuit connected to V_{out}. For instance, in the example given above suppose that a voltmeter having input resistance of 100 K (a typical value) were connected to V_{out} to check the output of the potential divider. Its 100 K would now be parallel with R_2 and would upset the operation of the potential divider as Figure A8.4 shows. The parallel combination R_2/R_V would behave as a 50 K resistor and V_{out} would become:

$$\frac{50}{100 + 50} \times 12 = 4 \text{ V}$$

If the test were repeated taking the output from Rl, the same result would be obtained. So we should have the ludicrous but all-too-real situation: voltage across Rl = indicated 4 V, across R2 = indicated 4 V, across Rl + R2 = indicated 12 V; therefore 4 + 4 = 12! When using a test meter always allow for the possibility that the instrument itself may introduce inaccuracies into the circuit. With voltmeters a high input resistance is an advantage in this respect. When using potential dividers, ensure that the output resistor is low compared to the input resistance of the circuit to which it is to be connected.

Power

The amount of *power* in a circuit is proportional to both the voltage applied and the current flowing:

$$P = EI$$

where P is power. The unit of power is the *Watt* (after steam pioneer James Watt) abbreviated W; the milliwatt (mW) is also used — 1 mW = 1/1,000 W. Conveniently W = V A. So a model locomotive drawing 250 mA from a controller delivering 8 V (typical figures) is consuming 8 V $\times$ ¼A = 2 W.

Power calculations are important in determining choice of components. Many smaller resistors are rated for ¼ W (= 250 mW). Consider a 330 R resistor in a circuit where 6 V is applied across it. By Ohm's law the current is 6 V/0.33 K = 18 mA approximately. Power dissipation therefore is 6 V $\times$ 18 mA = 108 mW, well within the rating of a ¼ W device. But if the voltage were raised to 9 V, the current would also rise to 27 mA and the dissipation would now be 9 V $\times$ 27 mA = 243 mW, almost at the limits of the device's rating; any further increase would risk overloading the device. Many smaller transistors are rated for 200 mW or 300 mW dissipation and care must be taken to prevent overloading which could cause costly failures.

Appendix 9

Ac, capacitance and inductance

Alternating current (ac)

The EMFs considered in Appendix 8 were assumed to be sources of steady voltage, which drive steady currents through circuits having constant resistance; the direction of the current, of course, is determined by the polarity of the EMF. This kind of one-way current is called *direct current* (dc). It is the kind of current that a battery delivers.

The mains in the UK, most parts of Europe and the USA supplies *alternating current* (ac). This is current that keeps changing its direction. If we take a typical mains supply (240 V ac, 50 Hz), call one side of the supply zero and monitor the voltage on the other side relative to the first, we should obtain a pattern like that shown in Figure A9.1. The figure shows two complete *cycles*, each consisting of a positive-going peak and a negative-going trough. There are on average 50 such cycles per second; this figure is called the *frequency* and is measured in Hertz (Hz), the number of Hz being the number of cycles per second. Notice that the very tips of the peaks and the very bottoms of the troughs exceed the nominal mains voltage; they reach about 340 V for a 240 V nominal supply. This is because the nominal mains voltage is a calculated figure, known as the root mean square (rms). Since there are two instants in each mains cycle when the voltage delivered is zero, there must also be times when the voltage delivered exceeds 240 V if that rms value is to be maintained. The rms figure could be defined as the value of the dc supply which would deliver an equal amount of power into a circuit of given resistance over an appreciable period of time. It is also the figure indicated by a test meter switched to an ac range connected to an ac supply. This difference between the peak figure and the rms figure is important in the design of power supplies (see Appendix 11).

Capacitance

Capacitors and their ability to store electricity (their *capacitance*) were briefly introduced in Chapter 5. Some further information on their performance is given here. The unit of capacitance is the Farad (F), named after physicist Michael Faraday, but the Farad itself is a massive unit rarely encountered. Most capacitors used in general electronics have values in microFarads (μF) and in radio some have values in picoFarads (pF). 1,000,000 pF = 1 μF; 1,000,000 μF = 1 F.

When a capacitor is connected via a resistor to a dc EMF, it takes appreciable time to charge up. It would be most useful to know how long it takes to become fully charged. The question, however, is meaningless, because it *never* gets *fully* charged. As charge-

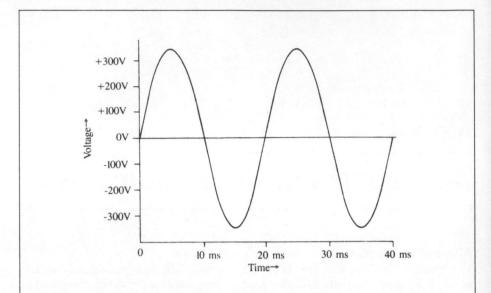

Figure A9.1 *Diagrammatic representation of the excursions of voltage in two full cycles of a 240 V ac 50 Hz mains supply.*

up proceeds, the charge current diminishes, slowing down the charging process. As full charge is approached, the rate of charge becomes negligible. So in theory *infinite* time would be needed to charge the capacitor fully. Exactly the same is true of its discharge.

Instead electronic engineers work on the basis of a 63% charge or discharge. The time taken for a capacitor to charge up to 63% of the charging EMF or to discharge (assuming that it was practically fully charged) by 63%, ie, to 37% of the original charging voltage gives a useful working parameter; moreoever, the mathematics is simple.

The time taken to charge a capacitor of *C* Farads to 63% (or to discharge it to 37%) of the charging EMF via a resistance of *R* Ohms is *RC* seconds. This figure is called the *time constant* for that resistor/capacitor combination and is independent of the EMF value. (Raising the EMF raises the charging current proportionately, but also raises the target voltage proportionately.) So in a voltage control system (Chapter 8), if the control voltage capacitor is 220 µF and the inertia control is set so that it introduces 50 K into its charge-up path, the time taken for the train to reach full speed from rest will be

$$220 \times 10^{-6} \times 50 \times 10^{3} = 11 \text{ seconds.}$$

As a capacitor charges, its opposition to the charge current rises. As it approaches full charge-up, its opposition becomes practically infinite. So any attempt to pass steady dc through a capacitor will be foredoomed to failure. However, capacitors *do* conduct ac. This is because each complete cycle of ac causes a charge-up, a discharge, a recharge with opposite polarity and a further discharge. In an ac circuit a capacitor behaves to some extent like a resistor. Its ac resistance is called its *reactance* and is measured in Ohms.

Increasing the capacitance means that a greater current will be consumed in charge-up, hence a *lower* reactance. So reactance is inversely proportional to capacitance, but reactance also depends on the frequency of the ac. There will inevitably be some resistance in the circuit so that it will have a time constant as described above. A low-frequency half cycle, occupying a period longer than the circuit's time constant will more completely charge the capacitor, raising its resistance, than a high-frequency half cycle which has ended with the capacitor only partially charged and still conductive. So reactance is inversely proportional to frequency. A constant, 2π, completes the formula for reactance (X).

$$X = \frac{1}{2\pi f C}$$

where X is the reactance in Ohms, f the frequency in Hz and C the capacitance in Farads.

So if we are using a high-frequency coach lighting system operating at 30 KHz and we wish to insert a 0.1 μF capacitor in series with a lamp, we can calculate its reactance as follows:

$$X = \frac{1}{2 \times 3.14 \times 30 \times 10^3 \times 0.1 \times 10^{-6}} = 53R$$

Capacitances in parallel and series

The values of capacitances in parallel add up, like resistors *in series*:

$$C_{total} = C_1 + C_2 + C_3 + C_4 + C_5 + \ldots$$

The values of capacitors in series follow the reciprocal law, like resistors in parallel:

$$\frac{1}{C_{total}} = \frac{1}{C_1} + \frac{1}{C_2} + \frac{1}{C_3} + \frac{1}{C_4} + \frac{1}{C_5} + \ldots$$

Inductance and inductors

When steady dc flows along a straight wire, it sets up a circular magnetic field in a plane at right angles to the wire. Normally this field is too weak to have any practical importance. However, if the wire is wound into a coil, the magnetic field is concentrated inside the core of the coil, greatly magnifying its effect. If a rod of soft iron or ferrite is inserted into the core, this further concentrates the magnetic field, turning the coil into an *electromagnet*.

A steady magnetic field has no effect on a stationary wire passing through it, but if the wire moves relative to the field or if the field varies in its strength, an EMF will be induced in it. Note that this *change* or *movement* of the field relative to the wire is essential to the induction of an EMF. If the wire is formed into a coil and the magnet moves along the axis of the coil or parallel to it, the induced EMF will be greatly magnified, since each turn of the coil acts as a separate 'generator' and all act in series. The ability of a magnetic field to set up an EMF in a conductor is called *inductance*.

Even in the absence of an external magnet a coil exhibits electrical properties different from those of the same length of wire if it were not coiled. This is because the magnetic field set up by a varying electric current within each turn of the coil varies in proportion with the current and, being a varying magnetic field, it acts upon adjacent turns of the coil and induces in them an EMF *of opposite polarity to the EMF driving the original current*. Of course, this is of no consequence when steady dc is flowing through the coil, since the magnetic field will be steady and therefore without effect.

But when an EMF is first applied to the coil and when it is disconnected, there is an effect.

Let us assume that the dc resistance of the coil is low, as is likely. When an EMF is first applied, the current flowing in the coil will attempt to rise very rapidly from zero to that which one would expect from the strict application of Ohm's law. This rapidly rising current sets up around each turn of the coil a magnetic field of rapidly rising intensity. This magnetic field of rapidly rising intensity acts on adjacent turns of the coil to induce in them a rapidly rising EMF which opposes the external EMF and reduces the current. However it does not succeed in completely stopping the current; if it did, the current could not begin to flow in the first place. Once the current has begun to flow the *rate of change* of flow declines and the induced contrary EMF fades away. So the effect of the inductance of the coil is to make the current build-up gradual.

When the external EMF is disconnected, the current passing through the coil is reduced to zero instantaneously, causing an instantaneous collapse of the magnetic field. This induces in the coil a considerable EMF *of the same polarity* (relative to the coil) as the original external source of EMF; this is known as the *inductive overshoot or inductive kickback*. This phenomenon can cause problems with certain designs of pulsed controller; this is considered in Part 2.

Inductance is measured in Henrys (H) but inductors (coils) as discrete components are rarely met in model railway electronics. As coils form part of transformers, relays and electric motors, however, some knowledge of their properties is useful. When an ac EMF is applied to an inductor, the same 'delay' is experienced as with dc, but now that 'delay' assumes far greater importance, since the current may hardly have begun to flow before the half cycle finishes and an opposite-polarity half cycle begins, whereupon the 'delay' begins all over again. Consequently an inductor which appears to have a low resistance to dc may nevertheless present a very high opposition to ac. This opposition to ac like that of capacitors is known as *reactance*; it is proportional both to inductance and to frequency.

$$X = 2\pi f L$$

where X is reactance in Ohms, f is frequency in Hz and L is inductance in Henrys.

Transformers

If two separate coils are wound on the same core so that there is efficient magnetic

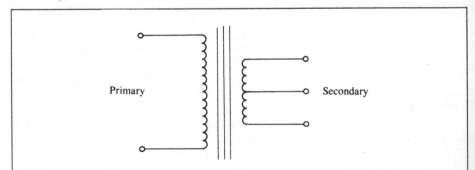

Figure A9.2 *Symbol for a transformer. This symbol suggests a step-down transformer with a centre-tapped secondary.*

coupling between them, the application of an ac EMF to one winding (called the *primary*) will result in an ac EMF being induced in the other winding (called the *secondary*). Moreoever, the voltages in the two windings will be in proportion to the numbers of turns. Thus, if a primary having 240 turns is connected to a mains supply of 240 V ac, a secondary having 16 turns, will deliver 16 V ac. Such a combination of two coils is called a *transformer*.

If the secondary of a transformer is left *open circuit*, ie, not forming part of a complete circuit so that no current can flow, very little current will flow in the primary; the primary will in fact exhibit the high reactance that one would expect in a massive inductor. If the secondary is connected to a suitable load so that the magnetic field set up by the primary can be used to induce current in the secondary, the reactance of the primary will be lower and more current will flow in it. Most commercial transformers are efficient exchangers of power; little power is wasted in them, so the current flowing in the primary and secondary will be inversely proportional to the voltages across them. To return to the example quoted earlier; if the primary voltage is 240 V and the secondary 16 V and if the secondary is delivering 240 mA, then the current in the primary should be 16 mA.

Transformers are used extensively for stepping high mains voltages down to lower voltages for such applications as power supplies for model railways and electronic equipment. Figure A9.2 shows the circuit diagram symbol for a typical transformer; it is quite usual for transformers to have tappings on both primary and secondary windings (or to have more than one secondary winding) so that they can be used with a variety of primary voltages (generally mains supplies) to obtain a variety of output voltages. In the diagrammatic symbol it is usual to draw one winding with a greater number of turns than the other (assuming it is a step-down or step-up transformer) but in the diagram the ratio need not be the same as that of the device represented.

Electromagnets, solenoids and relays

As we have seen, an electric current flowing in a coil produces a powerful magnetic field in the core. One useful application for this is as an *electromagnet* ie, a magnet whose magnetism can be switched on and off. Polarity of the magnetic field will depend on the polarity of the supply, but if it is simply the device's ability to attract ferrous metal objects that is wanted, polarity is immaterial and the electromagnet will work satisfactorily on ac or dc power supplies. Electromagnets suspended from cranes are used on scrap metal dealers for separating ferrous and non-ferrous metals. In a model railway a working electromagnet can be used to great effect to add interest to a lineside scrapyard.

It is as a *solenoid* that an electromagnet is most likely to be encountered by the railway modeller (setting aside for the moment its crucial role in the heart of every dc motor). A solenoid consists of an electromagnet with a captive iron bolt in its core. The bolt is free to slide in and out of the core. When current is applied to an electromagnet, the bolt is drawn further into the core. When the current is stopped, the bolt may return to its former position by spring action or gravity or it may remain in its new position until a second electromagnet is energized which draws it back. Solenoids are widely used in model railways as turnout (point) motors and for operating semaphore signals and other accessories. Electronic circuitry for their operation is described in Chapter 16.

One particular application of a solenoid is a *relay*. In a relay the moving bolt (the *armature*) is used to operate a bank of switches (usually electrically insulated from the coil). Relays were at one time widely used in telephone exchanges and for other

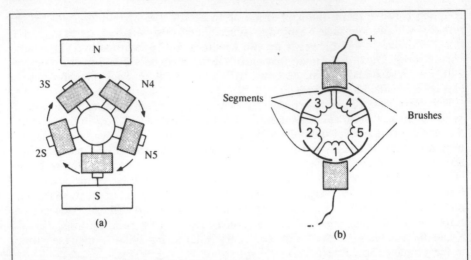

Figure A9.3 *Five-pole, single-magnet dc motor: (a) cross-section through poles and (b) cross-section through commutator at the same moment. Pole 1 is not energized; arrows indicate magnetic forces, hence direction of rotation. Poles 2 and 3 are connected in series at the moment, as are poles 4 and 5.*

applications that involved complex multiple switching. They are still common in model railway electrical systems, but for many of these applications they may be replaced by electronic switching which offers lower cost, lower power consumption and greater reliability.

Electric motors

Electric motors are, of course, of fundamental importance to model railways and therefore, although not strictly a part of electronics, their operation needs some consideration. There are many types of electric motor, but only dc types as used in model locomotives will concern us here.

A dc motor has essentially two parts: a fixed *stator* consisting of one or two permanent magnets and a rotating *armature* positioned within the magnetic field. Mounted on the armature are three or five (or occasionally seven) coils called, confusingly, the *poles*. Also mounted on the armature are the segments (as many as the poles) of the *commutator* to which the ends of the pole windings are connected. The segments contact the *brushes*, two in number, mounted on the stator and connected to the terminals of the motor.

When an EMF is applied to the terminals of the motor all but one of the pole windings is energized. The energized poles act as electromagnets, being attracted to one (side of the) permanent magnet and repelled from the other. Consequently, they begin to move, causing the armature to rotate. As an energized winding approaches a magnet to which it is attracted, the switching action of the commutator removes its power supply so that the attraction disappears. (If this did not happen, the energized pole would stop adjacent to the magnet, preventing further the rotation.) As its supply disappears, another pole winding is energized and the process is repeated. So rotation continues as long as sufficient power is supplied, all the poles becoming energized in turn by the commutator. Reversing the polarity of the power supply reverses the polarity of the pole windings, but not that of the permanent magnet(s), so that all the former attractions become repulsions and *vice versa* and the direction of rotation is reversed. Reference to Figure A9.3 may clarify the sequence of operation.

An electric motor will, of course, demonstrate all the electrical properties to be expected of a predominantly inductive device. For instance it will exhibit inductive overshoot and in certain circuits precautions must be taken to prevent this from interfering with the operation of the controller. Since a motor includes coils rotating in a magnetic field, it also behaves as a generator, even when it is being used as a motor. Its rotation causes it to generate an EMF which opposes that of the power supply and tends to reduce the current consumed; this is called the *back EMF* and, other factors being equal, the back EMF is proportional to motor speed. This is useful, since it is possible to design an electronic controller which monitors the back EMF and compares it with a control voltage in order to achieve highly accurate speed control.

Appendix 10

Electrical properties of dc motors

In a dc motor the external supply voltage V_{cc} is balanced by two internal voltages which behave as though they are in series: E_b the motor EMF (often called the 'back EMF') and IR. IR is simply the potential difference raised across the motor's 'ordinary' resistance R by the power current I and so is proportional to that current. Since these three voltages form a closed loop we may say:

$$V_{cc} = E_b + IR$$

A firm grasp of this relationship is essential to understanding the operation of dc motors and their control systems.

Motor EMF

Every dc motor can and does also act as a generator. Even when being used as a motor, as its poles move within the magnetic field provided by the permanent magnet(s), a voltage proportional to speed is induced in them and this opposes the supply voltage. This voltage is called the *motor EMF* or *back EMF* and it plays a crucial role in the operation of the motor.

At high speeds E_b is high; this makes IR low and, since R is constant, limits the motor current I. To put it another way, the only force that can drive current through the motor resistance R is V_{cc} from which must be subtracted the opposing motor EMF, E_b. We see this if we rearrange the earlier equation:

$$I = (V_{cc} - E_b)/R$$

You can easily test this for yourself. Set up a motor on a test bed and monitor its current. Unloaded and spinning fast it draws comparatively little current (typically about 70mA for the motors used in OO/HO-scale trains). Gently squeeze the spindle between your fingers to load the motor and you will see the current rise (to 500mA or more) before the motor stalls.

This is a useful phenomenon, albeit with limitations. It means that, as the motor's load rises reducing the speed — so its current rises, increasing the torque. Of course, stalling the motor is risky since, with the motor EMF reduced to nil, the entire supply voltage appears across the motor resistance and is dissipated in it as heat — or even as incineration!

Since slowing the motor results in a *rise* in current and motor speeding results in a *fall* in current, it follows that dc motors possess a degree of inherent speed stability.

Indeed they are sometimes called 'constant-speed motors'. The speed that is 'constant' however, varies with the supply voltage and load; it will attempt to approach the speed at which IR equals E_b; under these conditions the motor has the greatest efficiency (highest value of $I \times E_b$).

This inherent speed regulation mechanism, however, has a somewhat limited range. On our model railways we all know how a train running under any but the most sophisticated speed control systems will slow down on tight curves or gradients. This is because these conditions increase the load, raising IR and reducing E_b so slowing the motor. To keep the speed constant under these conditions it is necessary to substantially raise the controller output voltage to compensate for the higher IR; there are electronic methods of doing this and these will be considered shortly.

IR

Every dc motor presents 'ordinary' electrical resistance in its pole windings and in the commutator. This resistance, R, fluctuates somewhat even in the same specimen, since there are many different paths through the poles, depending on the position for the time being of the commutator segments relative to the brushes.

As the motor runs, the current I which is powering it raises a potential difference across R, whose voltage by Ohm's law is IR. This voltage opposes the supply voltage and reduces the proportion of it available for traction power.

Some control circuits, especially those used in industrial equipment, incorporate IR compensation by monitoring the current flowing through the motor and raising the controller output proportionately. This may sound as though it is likely to result in some kind of positive feedback or runaway phenomenon, but in practice other factors limit the output current. The advantage of IR compensation is that it effectively 'locks' the control voltage to the motor EMF giving precise control of speed.

Motor heating

Another unpleasant consequence of IR is motor heating. IR, as we have seen, is a *voltage; $I \times IR$ (= $I^2 R$)* is power dissipated as heat in the motor resistance. Clearly this heating is proportional to the *square* of the motor current. The value of this current depends on both the supply voltage and the motor EMF *($I = (V_{cc}-E_b)/R$)*, but at very low speed when motor EMF is negligible, heating may be regarded as proportional to the square of the supply voltage.

This has unfortunate repercussions for users of square-wave pulse width-modulation (PWM) control systems. Let us assume for the sake of argument that we have a motor which presents a constant resistance of 10 R. Suppose that we have the choice of connecting it to a steady 6 V supply or a 12 V supply pulsed with a 50 per cent duty cycle, ie pulse width equals space width. On a volt meter these two supplies would appear identical, the meter reading 6 V. Ignoring for the moment all inductive and motor EMF effects, we can say that with the 6 V supply $I = 6/10 = 0.6$ A and $I^2 R = 3.6$ W. *During* the 12 V pulses $I = 1.2$ A and $I^2 R = 14.4$ W. Allowing for the 50 per cent duty cycle, the motor under pulsed control will be dissipating on average 7.2 W, double the heat for the same nominal controller output. So PWM causes more motor heating than other systems.

In the example just described we ignored motor EMF. This is indeed negligible when the motor is stationary or turning very slowly, ie under stalled or starting conditions. So it is under these conditions that a motor is most vulnerable, ie most likely to burn out. As soon as it gathers speed the motor EMF rises, reducing IR and limiting the potentially dangerous current consumption.

Some PWM control systems reduce the *voltage* of the pulses as well as the pulse width at lower speed settings and this reduces the risk of overheating. Two controllers of this type are described in Chapters 5 and 6.

Self-inductance

Besides resistance, the poles of a dc motor like all coils, exhibit *self-inductance*. That is to say, they react against any change of input current. This is because such changes in the coil set up a changing magnetic field which induces an opposing EMF within the coil.

Although this reactance is measured in Ohms, it is not actually *resistive*. It does not result, as ordinary resistance does, in electrical energy being dissipated as heat. Instead it acts as though it were a 'temporary battery' of dwindling voltage inserted into the circuit in such a way that it opposes the motor's power supply.

Because the self-inductance of the poles is comparatively low and the frequency of the commutator's switching action is also comparatively low, self-inductance is not normally a major factor in determining the electrical properties of model train motors. The only exception is when the supply is switched off suddenly, eg at the end of a power pulse from a PWM controller. The almost instantaneous collapse of the current in the poles causes an equally sudden demise of the magnetic field whose effect is to induce in the poles a temporary voltage almost equal to that which collapsed (but of the opposite polarity as measured by a voltmeter or oscilloscope connected to the motor terminals).

This inductive kickback or overshoot is responsible for many seemingly anomalous effects which occur when model railways and electronics get together, For instance, it can cause LED status indicators connected across the controller output to remain illuminated when they would be expected to be off. With PWM controllers it is impossible to use direction-sensing headlamps and tail lamps on the train — invariably *all* will be on. A popular remedy is to connect a normally reverse-biased diode across the controller output (before the reversing switch of course); this harmlessly short-circuits away the inductive kickbacks.

Types of electronic control

Electronic controllers (throttles) for dc motors fall into two broad categories representing the digital and the analogue approach. These are respectively pulse-width modulation (PWM) and closed-loop (voltage source) systems. A diversity of designs is possible in both categories; it is even possible to combine both categories in one controller; examples of all types are given in chapters 3-6.

PWM controllers deliver pulses of high power. Generally pulse frequency is constant in the range 50 to 120 Hz. Speed is controlled by adjusting the duty cycle, ie the pulse width/space ratio. At low settings of the speed control pulses are brief and spaces are long. Turning up the speed control lengthens the pulses, shortening the spaces. At top speed the pulses may merge, the spaces disappearing, so that continuous full power is delivered.

Closed-loop controllers deliver an output that may be steady (pure dc controllers) or pulsed. In the pulsed variety the pulses are often introduced by virtue of an un-smoothed rectified ac power supply. The speed control simply sets the output voltage which is either the steady voltage from a pure dc controller or the peak voltage in a pulsed closed-loop system. Closed-loop controllers always include a measure of feedback to hold the output voltage constant under all load conditions (hence the term *closed-loop*).

Speed compensation systems

Even using simple PWM and closed-loop electronic controllers, train speeds are not constant, although their constancy is far better than under old-fashioned variable-resistance controllers. The reason for this will be seen in the following example.

Suppose our train is cruising on level track with the controller delivering 6 V and the motor consuming 300 mA. Let us assume the mean motor resistance R is 10 R. Consequently $IR = 3$ V and E_b is $6 - 3 = 3$ V. Our train now comes to a gradient. The load increases to 500 mA, so IR is now 5 V and E_b is 1 V. This means that the speed has fallen to one-third of its original level.

The only way to hold this speed steady is by means of a servo which causes the controller to actually *raise* its output voltage as the load increases and to lower it when the load falls so that the speed, and therefore E_b, remain constant.

There are two ways of doing this. The first which is applicable primarily to PWM controllers reads E_2 directly using a sample-and-hold technique between the controller's output pulses. While the controller output is 'off' any voltage present on the output terminals must be motor EMF. This is then compared with the control voltage and, if the motor EMF is found to have dropped, the mark/space ratio is increased to counteract the fall in speed.

The second method, more appropriate to closed-loop controllers, is IR compensation. The controller's output current is monitored and a voltage proportional to this current is added to the control voltage. So, in the example cited above, when our controller senses that the current has risen by 200 mA (and therefore IR by 2 V) it adds 2 V to the control voltage to bring E_b back to the required 3 V, restoring the original speed.

Appendix 11

Semi-conductor diodes

Strictly speaking the term *semi-conductor* refers to a group of substances including silicon, germanium and alloys of gallium with phosphorus or arsenic or both, which are intermediate in conductivity between those substances normally considered conductors and those regarded as insulators. From the substance, however, the term has come to be applied to a diversity of electronic components which utilize the peculiar properties of semi-conducting materials; those that we shall be considering are junction diodes, bipolar transistors and field-effect transistors (FETs).

Semi-conductor action

The mode of action of semi-conductor devices is exceedingly complex and the reader wishing to have a detailed explanation should consult more comprehensive works on the subject. An exact understanding, however, is not needed in order to apply the devices correctly in electronic circuitry, so only a brief explanation will be given here. Silicon is the semi-conducting material in most general use, but references here to silicon can generally be take to apply to other semi-conductor materials and devices, unless differences are specified.

Chemically pure silicon is a poor conductor of electricity because its atoms interlock in its crystal structure in such a way that there are no free electrons available to act as 'carriers' of electric current; in this respect it resembles those materials generally termed insulators. It is possible, however, to introduce trace impurities into silicon which affect its electrical properties. The atoms of these impurities replace silicon atoms in the crystal structure, but they have different numbers of electrons. Certain impurities, such as arsenic, have surplus electrons thereby introducing 'free' electrons into the silicon, giving it a negative charge; such silicon is called *n-type*. Other impurities, such as boron, have a deficit of electrons and introduce what are called *holes* into the silicon. These holes are the positively charged gaps into which electrons fit and which attract electrons; such silicon has an overall positive charge and is called *p-type*. When an electron enters a hole, their opposite charges cancel each other. When an atom with a hole succeeds in attracting an electron from a neighbouring atom, a new hole is created in the atom which it left. Thus holes appear to wander through a p-type silicon, just as electrons do through n-type silicon. Since the flow of holes is a consequence of the movement of electrons, this too constitutes an electric current, but since holes bear effective positive charges, the flow of holes is in the same direction as conventional current flow.

Both n-type and p-type silicon are, of course, conductive, because of the presence in them of carrier electrons or holes. Individually their electrical properties are unremarkable, but if, say, an n-type impurity is introduced into one end of a piece of p-type silicon, an interface between n-type and p-type regions is formed. Such an interface is called a *pn junction* and its electrical properties are remarkable.

Some electrons, naturally enough, migrate from the negatively charged n-region across the junction of the p-region and some holes similarly from the p-region to the n-region. Thus the n-region, having lost electrons and gained holes, becomes positively charged relative to the p-region — it acts as if a battery were connected across it with its positive terminal to the n-type region. This charge cannot be measured directly on a voltmeter, but its effect is felt when the junction is being used in a circuit. This charge is responsible for the *offset voltage*, for which allowance must be made when designing circuits and choosing component values. For a silicon junction the offset voltage is around 0.7 V, for a germanium junction around 0.2 V and for a gallium-arsenic-phosphide junction around 1.8 V.

This PD across the junction establishes an effective barrier across it — the negative charge on the p-type material deters further electrons from crossing from the n-region, while the positive charge on the n-region deters further holes from making the crossing. Indeed such is the charge that electrons in the n-region tend to stay away from the junction, as do holes in the p-region. So a zone is established around the junction which is largely free of carriers (electrons and holes). Such a zone is called a *depletion area* and, since it lacks carriers, it is, like pure silicon, a very poor conductor of electricity.

This, then, is the state existing in a silicon junction *in vacuo*. Let us now see what happens when an external EMF is connected to it. If a pn junction is connected to a battery with its positive terminal to the n-region and its negative terminal to the p-region, the external battery's EMF will reinforce the internal charge which established the depletion zone around the junction, making it even wider and the junction will

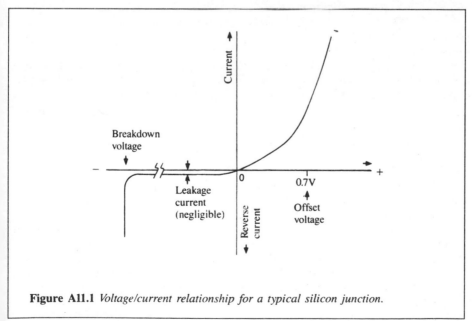

Figure A11.1 *Voltage/current relationship for a typical silicon junction.*

be even less conductive. The junction is now said to be *reverse-biased*; the only current that flows is a leakage current which for practical purposes is negligible.

If the reverse bias across the junction is increased, at a certain critical reverse voltage depending on the design of the junction the potential barrier will break down and current will flow. This is called the *breakdown* point and the reader may be excused for supposing that operating a junction beyond its breakdown point causes irreparable damage to it. Provided that precautions are taken to limit the breakdown current (and hence the power dissipated as heat in the junction), there is no damage. When the reverse bias is removed, the potential barrier is restored and the junction will function normally again. Junctions can be designed to have any breakdown voltage from zero to minus several hundreds of volts. Use is made of this property in voltage-reference ('Zener') diodes.

If we now reverse the connections to the external battery, so that its positive terminal is connected to the p-region and its negative terminal to the n-region, the junction is said to be *forward-biased*. The external EMF now reduces that of the internal fictitious battery and therefore the depletion zone becomes smaller. If the external EMF exceeds the offset voltage, the depletion zone with its potential barrier disappears altogether, so that electrons can cross freely from the n-region to the p-region and holes can cross in the opposite direction. Electrons leaving the n-region and crossing to the p-region are replaced by electrons flowing from the negative terminal of the battery, while those arriving in the n-region flow on towards the positive terminal of the battery. So a substantial electric current flows.

To summarize, then, a pn junction when reverse biased is hardly conductive (provided its breakdown voltage is not exceeded) — it presents a very high resistance. When forward biased it becomes conductive and, when its offset voltage is exceeded, it presents a very low resistance. Figure A11.1 shows in graphic form the current-voltage relationship of a typical pn junction. Since the current flowing is not proportional to the voltage applied, a pn junction does not obey Ohm's law; its resistance varies according to the EMF applied so is non-linear.

The junction diode

The simplest semi-conductor device is called a *junction diode*; it consists simply of a pn junction in a glass or epoxy resin or metal capsule. Diodes are used for a diversity of applications including power rectifiers, voltage regulators, indicator lamps and even as variable capacitors. Their most common application, however, is in switching.

Most small-signal diodes are encapsulated in glass envelopes, the cathode end (the n-type region) being marked by a coloured band or spot on the body of the device. Bags of unmarked, untested diodes can often be purchased more cheaply than branded, tested diodes; in general most of the devices in the bag will prove to be serviceable. They should be tested using a resistance meter. In the reverse direction the reading should be infinite, ie, no deflection whatsoever. Do not handle both leads of the device simultaneously while testing or you may get a spurious reading. Discard any devices that show a leakage current — you will probably find suitable non-electrical uses for them on your model railway. In the forward direction, if your resistance meter uses a 1.5 V battery, you should get a resistance reading of about half-full-scale deflection for a silicon diode and nearly full-scale deflection for a germanium diode. As diodes are non-linear the actual resistance reading obtained will vary widely according to the characteristics of the test meter. When the diode is forward biased, the red or positive lead of the test meter is connected to the *cathode* lead of the device; this should now be marked with a blob or band of paint. Doing this now will save a lot of frustrat-

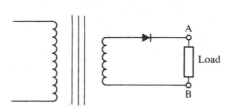

Figure A11.2 *The simplest possible transformer/rectifier circuit.*

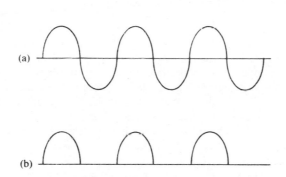

Figure A11.3 *Waveforms of (a) ac mains supply and (b) half-wave rectified ac obtained at the output of the circuit in Figure A11.2.*

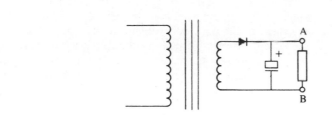

Figure A11.4 *The circuit of Figure A11.2 with a smoothing capacitor added.*

ing polarity checking later when you suddenly need a number of diodes in a complex project.

Rectifiers and power supplies

One of the most frequent switching applications for diodes is rectifying, ie converting an ac supply either to steady dc (with the aid of one or more capacitors) or to pulses of uniform polarity. The power supply used to enable an item of electronic equipment (such as an electronic controller) to be operated from an ac mains supply usually consists of a transformer which steps the high mains voltage down to a suitable voltage, say 16 V ac, one or more rectifier diodes and probably one or more electrolytic capacitors to help keep the resultant dc free from ripples and hums. For certain delicate electronic equipment a power supply may incorporate a voltage stabilizing circuit employing voltage-reference diodes and a number of transistors possibly in an integrated circuit (a 'chip'), but such sophistication is unnecessary for normal model railway purposes.

The simplest circuit for converting the ac output from a mains transformer secondary to pulsed dc is shown in Figure A11.2; a single rectifier diode is connected in series with the transformer secondary. During that part of each positive-going half cycle when the voltage at A relative to that at B exceeds the offset voltage (0.7 V for a silicon diode), the diode will conduct. The output from this simple transformer/rectifier combination, as was stated, is not steady dc, but a series of pulses, known — for obvious reasons — as *rectified ac*. The reason for this is demonstrated in Figure A11.3. The output consists, to all intents and purposes, of alternate half cycles of ac. Such rectification in which only half of the available ac waveform is utilized is called *half-wave rectification*.

The voltage output from such a half-wave rectifier circuit will be lower than one might expect. If the transformer in Figure A11.2 delivers 16 V ac (the actual peak excursions being around ± 23 V), the output from the rectifier as measured on a dc volt meter is likely to be around 7.3 V, this representing the rms figure divided by two (since only half the 'waves' are used) less the offset voltage of 0.7 V (a silicon rectifier is assumed). Nevertheless, within this indicated 7.3 V there are peaks of over 22 V and if used as a power supply for an electronic controller almost certainly a better performance will be obtained than from a power supply which delivered a steady 7.3 V dc.

Some electronic circuits, including some types of electronic controller, operate well from a pulsed power supply such as that described above. Others, however, must have a smooth, continuous dc supply. One way of obtaining a smooth dc output from the circuit shown in Figure A11.2 is to add a *smoothing* capacitor across its output terminals, giving the circuit shown in Figure A11.4. If the same transformer is used that was described in the last paragraph, we should be perhaps surprised to find that adding the capacitor raises the indicated voltage on a dc voltmeter across the output from 7.3 V to around 22 V! It should not surprise us really — the new reading represents the *peaks* of excursion of the ac in the transformer secondary. Each peak of input causes the capacitor to charge up to that voltage. The capacitor discharges comparatively slowly through the output load and so most of that peak voltage is retained between cycles; any diminution in voltage is replenished at the next peak; this is shown in Figure A11.5, which demonstrates how much 'smoother' the output has become. The rate of dis-

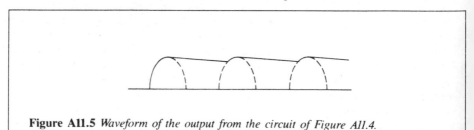

Figure A11.5 *Waveform of the output from the circuit of Figure A11.4.*

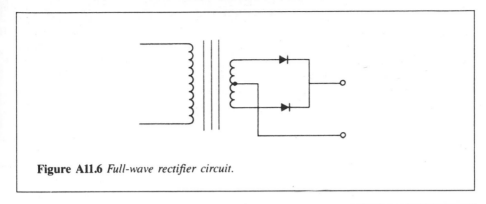

Figure A11.6 *Full-wave rectifier circuit.*

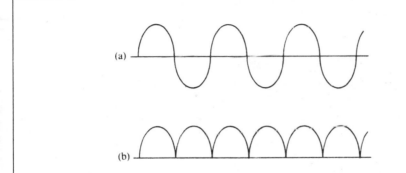

Figure A11.7 *Waveforms of (a) ac mains supply and (b) full-wave rectified ac obtained at the output of the circuit in Figure A11.6.*

charge of the capacitor (indicated by the gently falling slope between cycles in Figure A11.5) is determined by the load, ie the resistance of the circuit being driven, and by the value of the smoothing capacitor. Obviously the lower the resistance or the smaller the capacitor, the more rapidly it will discharge, resulting in a lower mean output voltage. In practice the minimum value of capacitor that will maintain an adequate average supply voltage is chosen. For many electronics applications this will be a high-value electrolytic type, eg, 1,000 μF.

Full-wave rectification

Another way of obtaining a smoother power supply is to arrange for both positive- and negative-going half cycles of ac to be combined to give pulses of uniform polarity. One way of achieving this is shown in Figure A11.6, in which the transformer secondary has a centre tap. The two diodes conduct alternately so that the ac output of the transformer becomes full-wave rectified ac; see Figure A11.7 for its waveform. Some types of electronic controller (Chapters 5 and 6) depend for correct operation on a rectified ac power supply having this waveform. A dc voltmeter across the output of the circuit shown in Figure A11.6 would indicate around 16 V dc if the transformer secondary were rated 16 V ac. For some electronics applications a smoothing capacitor would still be needed (as otherwise there are still two instants in each ac cycle when the output of this circuit is zero; this will upset some circuits, such as bistables).

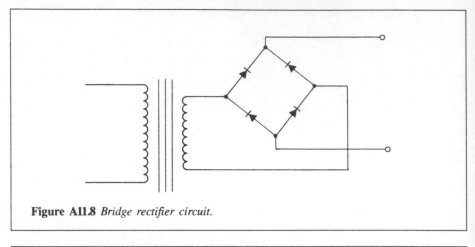

Figure A11.8 *Bridge rectifier circuit.*

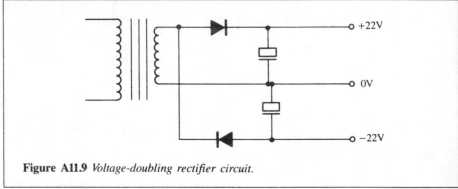

Figure A11.9 *Voltage-doubling rectifier circuit.*

A capacitor across the output of the 16 V circuit described will raise its output voltage to around 22 V, as in the half-wave rectifier circuit.

An alternative method of obtaining full-wave rectification, in which a centre-tapped secondary is not needed, is to use what is known as a *bridge rectifier circuit*; a typical example is shown in Figure A11.8. Opposite pairs of diodes conduct alternately, the output waveform being identical to that of the circuit shown in Figure A11.6. Output voltage, however, will be very slightly less, because the current must always pass through two diodes and therefore two doses of offset voltage must be subtracted. Nevertheless, the bridge rectifier is one of the commonest rectifier configurations. It may be made up from four separate diodes or from one four-terminal device containing the four silicon junctions.

Voltage doubler

Consider again the smoothed half-wave rectifier circuit shown in Figure A11.4; remember that the diode conducts, charging the capacitor, during positive-going half cycles of input only. Now imagine a second diode being added to the circuit with its cathode to the anode of the first diode and a second capacitor from its anode to 'ground' providing a second output. The circuit is shown in Figure A11.9. This second diode will clearly conduct only on negative-going half cycles of input and its output voltage relative to 'ground' will clearly by analogy with the first diode be around -22 V. So now we have a three-terminal output: the terminals offer + 22 V, 0 V and -22 V. For certain types of electronic controller such a symmetrical power supply is very useful. If we measure the PD from the +22-V terminal to the -22-V terminal, we find of course that it is 22(-22) V = 44 V. The 22 V nominal supply has been effectively doubled, hence the name of this type of circuit. Note that if the capacitors were removed no voltage doubling would occur; the diodes would conduct alternately providing half-wave rectified ac on either 'live' output terminal, but never on both simultaneously.

Diodes as voltage stabilizers

The voltage/current relationship for a silicon junction was given in Figure A11.1. Examination of this reveals that over a wide range of forward currents the PD across a silicon junction approximates to 0.7 V, its offset voltage. This means that a forward-biased diode can be used as a *voltage reference*, ie, as a stable source of a known voltage. The current passing through may be subject to fluctuations, but the voltage should remain fairly constant. Arrays of diodes in series could be used to provide any reference voltage that is a multiple of 0.7 V; Figure A11.10 shows how eight such diodes could be used to provide a reference source of 5.6 V. Such an array, however, is clumsy and in practice would be replaced by one 'Zener' diode for the required voltage — Figure A11.11. Such a voltage-reference diode is reverse-biased and operates under controlled breakdown conditions.

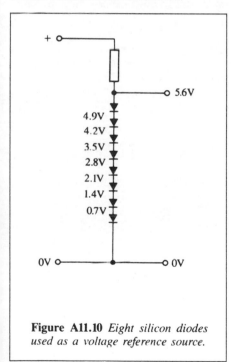

Figure A11.10 *Eight silicon diodes used as a voltage reference source.*

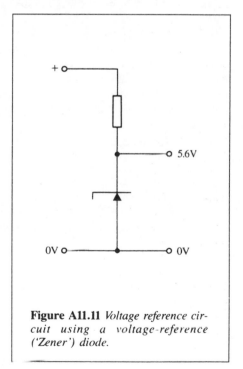

Figure A11.11 *Voltage reference circuit using a voltage-reference ('Zener') diode.*

Appendix 12

Transistors

Transistors are divided into several classes of which just two will be considered in this book: *bipolar transistors* (usually called simply 'transistors') and *field-effect transistors* (usually called FETs or even 'fets' rhyming with 'nets'). Of the two, bipolar transistors are more useful to the railway modeller; only occasionally will the peculiar properties of FETs come to the aid of the railway modeller with an electronics problem.

The operation of bipolar transistors

A junction diode consists of one pn junction; a bipolar transistor consists of two. It has either two regions of n-type conductivity separated by a very thin layer of a p-type material or two regions of p-type material separated by a thin layer of n-type. For obvious reasons such transistors are referred to as npn and pnp respectively. The mode of operation is identical for both, but all the polarities concerned are, of course, reversed.

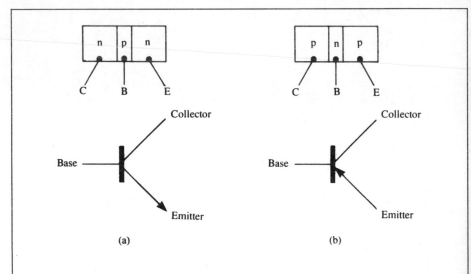

Figure A12.1 *Structures (above) and symbols (below) for (a) an npn and (b) a pnp transistor.*

The chemistry of silicon is such that it favours the production of npn devices, although silicon pnp types are by no means uncommon and many circuits demand the use of both.

The thin layer at the centre of the transistor is called the *base*; the other two zones are called the *collector* and the *emitter*. Connections are made to each. The symbols for npn and pnp transistors are shown in Figure A12.1. Note that the polarity of the device represented is indicated by the direction of the arrow on the emitter; this points in the direction of conventional current flow.

Consider an npn transistor connected to a 9 V battery *via* a milliameter as shown in Figure A12.2. The base is connected via an 82 K current-limiting resistor to a change-over switch by which it can be connected to either the positive or the negative terminal of the battery; we begin with it connected to the negative side of the battery. The milliameter will indicate no current (except for a leakage current so tiny that for practical purposes it may generally be ignored). It is not hard to see why this should be so. The collector-base junction is reverse biased and behaves like a reverse-biased diode. The base-emitter junction is effectively unbiased. Both junctions are virtually non-conductive.

If we throw the switch so that the base is connected to the *positive* side of the battery via the 82 K resistor, the transistor will behave very differently. The base-emitter junction is now forward-biased; consequently the pd across it will be around 0.7 V and the current flowing in the base circuit can be calculated by Ohm's law as (9.0-0.7) V/82 K = 0.1 mA (approximately). Our milliameter will now indicate that a very much larger current is also flowing in the collector circuit, even though the collector-base junction is supposedly reverse-biased; for a high-grade transistor a typical collector current under these condtions would be 20 mA (showing a current gain of 20/0.1 = 200), although this varies widely, even among devices of nominally the same type. This collector current is stimulated by the base current and will stop as soon as the base current is stopped, eg, by throwing back the switch in the circuit of Figure A12.2. So a small base current (0.1 mA in our example) is seen to

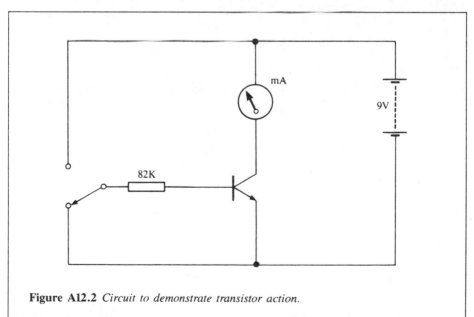

Figure A12.2 *Circuit to demonstrate transistor action.*

control a much larger collector current (20 mA in our example).

When the base-emitter junction is forward-biased, electrons flow from the n-region (the emitter) across the junction and into the p-region (the base). But the base is a very thin region so that these electrons are bound to pass very close to the collector-base junction. Although there is around the collector-base junction — as around any reverse-biased junction — a depletion area, its extent is limited by the thinness of the base and this, together with the powerful attraction of the positive potential on the collector, ensures that *most of the electrons crossing the base-emitter junction reach the collector.* Only a minority actually emerge on the base terminal. Consequently the small base current is capable of controlling the much larger collector current. In some transistors under favourable conditions the current amplification factor may be as high as 500, ie:

$$I_c = 500 \ I_b$$

where I_c is the collector current and I_b the base current. The current gain $(I_c)/I_b)$ of any transistor, however, is not constant, but varies with collector current. It is obvious that:

$$I_e = I_b + I_c$$

where I_e is emitter current.

Biasing of transistors

To employ a transistor in a circuit correctly it is, of course, necessary to ensure that the base-emitter junction is suitably forward-biased and the collector-base is suitably reverse-biased. As a very general guide a transistor is connected as shown in Figure A12.3. Resistor R_e in the emitter circuit is clearly common to both base and collector current and acts as a feedback loop to stablize the collector current. Since the base current is negligible compared to the collector current, we may say that by Ohm's law:

$$V_e = I_c R_e$$

But V_e is determined by V_b; since the base-emitter junction is forward-biased:

$$V_e = V_b\text{-}0.7$$

(a silicon transistor is assumed) and, since I_b is small compared with the current flowing in the potential divider R_{b1} and R_{b2}, V_b is fixed by the potential divider (or any other source of potential on the base).

We can see now how the current regulation mechanism works. If the collector current should fall, V_e must fall (by Ohm's law), but V_b stays constant. So the pd across the base-emitter junction will become greater than 0.7 V, significantly increasing the base current. This in turn will bring about a significant increase in collector current. Should the collector current rise too high V_e will also rise (by Ohm's law) and the pd across the base-emitter junction will become less than 0.7 V, significantly reducing the base current. This in turn will reduce the collector current. So, substituting for V_e in the two equations above:

$$I_c = \frac{V_b\text{-}0.7}{R_e}$$

The collector current may be said, therefore, to be determined by the base voltage and the emitter resistance. A change in either will alter the collector current. For this

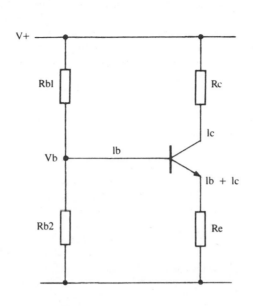

Figure A12.3 *Circuit to illustrate the biasing of a transistor.*

reason both base and emitter are said to present a low input resistance.

However the collector resistance, R_C, is different. Its value has no effect on the collector current provided, of course, that it is not made so great that the supply voltage cannot (by Ohm's law) drive the collector current through it. The voltage on the collector will be the supply voltage less the pd across the collector load resistor. Even changing the supply voltage will not affect the collector current, provided the base voltage is constant. Consequently the collector is said to have a high output resistance.

It was said earlier that a transistor's input consists of a base *current*. Then reference was made to a base *voltage*. In Figure A12.3 the base of the transistor is connected to a potential divider, essentially a voltage source. The base current is often so small that the base input resistance can be regarded as high. This can be seen if we take the circuit Figure A12.3 and assign values to the components, as shown in Figure A12.4.

We shall assume that the base input resistance is so high compared with the 33 K lower arm of the potential divider that it does not significantly affect the operation of the potential divider; shortly we shall demonstrate that this is indeed so. So the voltage on the base of the transistor is determined purely by the potential divider as:

$$\frac{33 \times 12}{33 + 68} = 4.0 \text{ V appx}$$

Therefore the voltage on the emitter is 4.0-0.7 = 3.3 V. Since this voltage is applied across the 3K3 emitter resistor, the collector current is stabilized at 3.3 V/3K3 = 1 mA. The pd across the 6K8 collector load resistor is therefore:

$$1 \text{ mA} \times 6\text{K8} = 6.8 \text{ V}$$

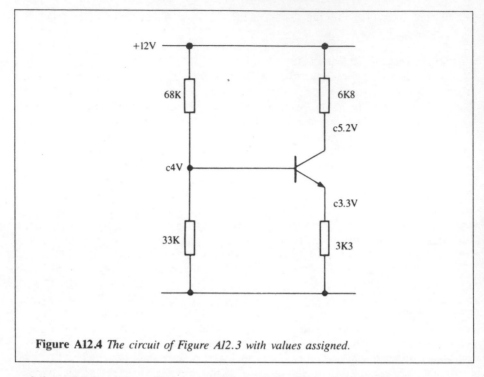

Figure A12.4 *The circuit of Figure A12.3 with values assigned.*

and the voltage on the collector (relative to the negative line) is 12.0-6.8 = 5.2 V.

We can see now that a transistor is capable of giving voltage gain besides current gain. If the base voltage were to fall from 4.0 V to 2.4 V, the emitter voltage would now be 2.4-0.7 = 1.7 V, the collector current 1.7/3.3 = 0.5 mA (approximately), the pd across the collector load 0.5 × 6.8 = 3.4 V and the collector voltage would *rise* from 5.2 V to 12.0-3.4 = 8.6 V. Thus a change of 1.6 V on the base causes a change of 3.4 V on the collector. This is only a doubling of 'signal voltage'; far greater voltage amplification can be achieved if required.

However, transistors primarily give *current amplification*; the base *current* controls the collector *current*. Indeed, the voltage amplification just described is simply a side effect of the current amplification. If the current gain of the transistor in the circuit of Figure A12.4 were 200 at a collector current of 1 mA, the base current under those conditions would be 1/200 mA = 5 μA. We can now calculate the base input resistance. Since a base voltage of 4.0 V drives a base current of 5 μA, the input resistance is:

$$\frac{4.0 \text{ V}}{5 \text{ } \mu\text{A}} = 0.8 \text{ MR (or 800 K)}$$

This is indeed high compared with the lower arm of the potential divider (33 K) and therefore does not significantly affect its voltage output. It is, however, important always to ensure that any resistors in the base circuit of a transistor are *low* compared to the input resistance.

If in the circuit of Figure A12.4 the collector of the transistor were disconnected, transistor action would cease and the base-emitter junction would function as an ordinary silicon diode. The 33 K resistor would now have in parallel the equivalent of a forward-biased diode in series with a 3K3 resistor. This is equivalent to about an

8 K resistor in parallel with the 33 K and the output of the potential divider would fall to about 1 V.

Transistor amplifying circuits

A transistor, as we have seen, has three terminals. The input circuit uses two and the output circuit uses two. It follows that one terminal is always common to input and output circuits. There are, in fact, three kinds of amplifying circuit: common-collector (more generally known as emitter follower), common-emitter and common-base amplifiers, depending upon the terminal that is common to input and output circuits.

The *emitter follower* is the simplest kind of transistor amplifying stage and is frequently used in model railway electronics; a simplified diagram of a typical emitter follower stage is shown in Figure A12.5. Input is applied to the base of the transistor and output taken from the emitter. The collector is effectively 'grounded' and therefore is common to input and output. There is no voltage gain, since the output voltage must always be equal to the input voltage less 0.7 V (for a silicon transistor), but there is current gain. The transistor might perhaps be the output stage of an electronic controller delivering 250 mA controlled by a base current of, say, 10 mA.

The emitter follower offers high input resistance (current gain × emitter load resistance) and low output resistance, since any changes in the resistance of the emitter load will affect the biasing of the transistor and thus the emitter current. An emitter-follower output stage in a controller will show 'sensitivity' to motor back EMF which will help to improve speed regulation. A disadvantage of the emitter follower as an output stage is that, while the output voltage can be reduced to zero by bringing the base voltage down to zero (or near it), the output voltage can never equal the full supply voltage, since, even if the base voltage is raised to the supply voltage, the output from the emitter will still be 0.7 V lower.

The *common-emitter* stage closely resembles the emitter follower, as a comparison of Figure A12.6 with Figure A12.5 will show. The principal difference is in the placing of the load. In the emitter follower this was common to input and output circuits, reducing voltage gain to unity. In the common-emitter stage there is no such limit to voltage

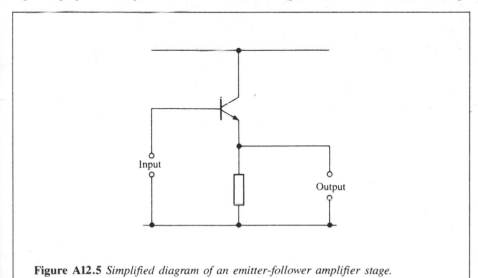

Figure A12.5 *Simplified diagram of an emitter-follower amplifier stage.*

gain. Indeed the way in which such a circuit gives voltage gain was described earlier when we were considering bias. We noticed that collector voltage *rises* as base voltage *falls*; conversely, of course, collector voltage will fall as base voltage rises. The output voltage is therefore said to be *antiphase* with input voltage.

Like the emitter follower, a common-emitter stage gives current gain, the current output rising as the base voltage (and current) rise. As an output stage a common-emitter amplifier has an advantage over an emitter follower in that the full power-supply voltage is available: collector voltage will equal power supply voltage when the base bias is zero (and the transistor is not conducting) but can also fall to equal the emitter voltage when sufficient current flows through the collector load; interestingly, when this happens both junctions in the transistor are simultaneously forward biased and the transistor is then said to be operating under *saturation conditions*. Since the collector presents a high output resistance, this kind of amplifier circuit does not exhibit the same kind of 'sensitivity' to changes in the output conditions as does an emitter follower. In a practical multi-stage circuit, however, such 'sensitivity' can be provided, if required, by a separate feedback loop to an earlier stage.

The *common-base* amplifier is rarely used in model railway electronics; T2 in Figure 14.2 is an interesting example. As Figure A12.7 shows, input is applied to the emitter and taken from the collector, the base being common. We have already noticed that the emitter, like the base, is sensitive to changes in operating conditions. Since the collector current is nearly equal to the emitter current (the difference being the almost negligible base current), there can be no current gain. However, there is voltage gain; since effectively the same current flows in R_e and R_c, it follows that the voltage gain equals R_c/R_e. Since a positive-going bias on the emitter is equivalent to a negative-going bias on the base, this will decrease collector current and *raise* collector voltage. Thus, unlike that given by a common-emitter stage, this voltage gain is in phase with the input. Since the output is taken from the collector, it shows the same high output resistance as does a common-emitter stage.

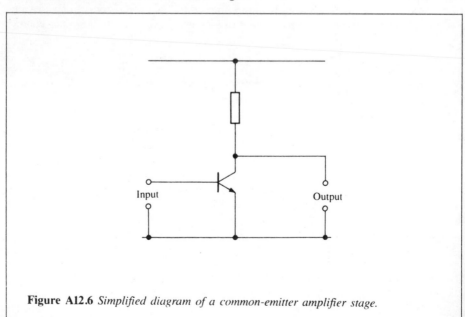

Figure A12.6 *Simplified diagram of a common-emitter amplifier stage.*

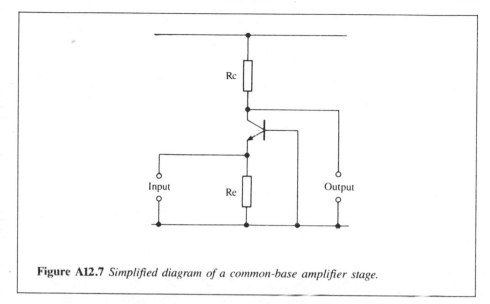

Figure A12.7 *Simplified diagram of a common-base amplifier stage.*

Summary table of characteristics of transistor amplifier stages

Type	Emitter follower	Common emitter	Common base
Input between	base and collector	base and emitter	emitter and base
Output between	emitter and collector	collector and emitter	collector and base
Input resistance	high	medium	low
Output resistance	low	high	high
Voltage gain	unity (less offset)	high	high
Current gain	high	high	unity (less base current)
Output voltage relative to input voltage	in phase	antiphase	in phase

Direct coupling of transistors

In many applications — and especially in electronic controllers — it is essential to cascade two or more transistors, ie, they must be connected so that all (or most) of the output of the first transistor is used as the input for the second transistor and similarly all (or most) of the output of the second transistor is used as the input for the third transistor if used. Since current output is available from both the collector and emitter of a transistor and devices of either polarity must be used, there are a number of ways in which two transistors may be coupled.

Figure A12.8 shows what is known as a *Darlington pair*. The two collectors are bonded and the emitter current of the first transistor is the base bias of the second. It has the advantages of very high input resistance and of high efficiency: even the collector current of the first transistor forms part of the output current. Output may be taken from the collectors or the emitter of the second transistor; if the latter, there will, of course, be no voltage gain. The Darlington pair may be regarded as one compound transistor having very high current gain.

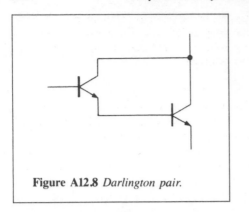

Figure A12.8 *Darlington pair.*

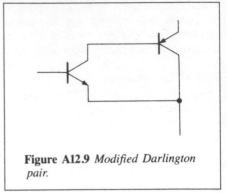

Figure A12.9 *Modified Darlington pair.*

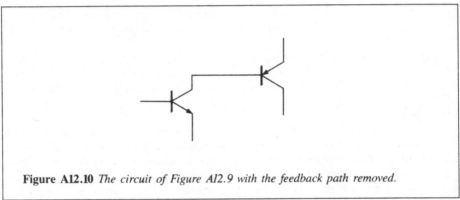

Figure A12.10 *The circuit of Figure A12.9 with the feedback path removed.*

Figure A12.9 shows a modified Darlington circuit in which the second transistor is of opposite polarity to the first. Output would normally be taken from the collector of the second transistor, which is also the emitter of the first. Because the output load is also part of the emitter circuit of the first transistor, this circuit exhibits a remarkable ability to compensate for changes in load. It is incapable of providing voltage gain therefore; it behaves like an emitter follower having very high current gain.

The configuration shown in Figure A12.10 resembles the previous one except that the feedback path between the output and the emitter of the first transistor has been removed. Output may be taken from the collector of the second transistor, where there will be both high voltage gain and high current gain; output voltage will be in phase with input, since phase is inverted twice, the circuit being essentially two common-emitter stages in cascade. Alternatively output may be taken from the emitter of the second transistor, where there will be moderate voltage gain and high current gain; output will be antiphase with input, having been inverted in the first transistor.

The circuit shown in Figure A12.11 is known rather quaintly as a *long-tailed* pair. It resembles two stages of common-emitter amplification having a common emitter resistor. Indeed, if either transistor is left without an input on its base, the other will function as a normal common-emitter stage. The emitter coupling ensures that signals applied to the base of T1 also appear at the emitter of T2, which now functions as a *common-base* amplifier. Thus any signal applied to input 1 will give an antiphase amplified voltage output from the collector of T1 and a similar but in-phase output at the collector of T2. Since the circuit is symmetrical a similar result will be obtained by applying a signal to input 2. If identical signals are applied to both inputs, in theory they cancel each other giving zero output. A long-tailed pair is sometimes used for comparing two voltages; in an electronic controller, for instance, it could be used to compare the controller output with a control voltage.

Field-effect transistors

A field-effect transistor (FET) is a semi-conductor amplifying device working on principles quite different from those of bipolar transistors and consequently having somewhat different characteristics. The properties of FETs, however, render them rather less useful to the railway modeller than are bipolar transistors, so that they are likely to be encountered only in certain specialist applications (see Chapters 31 and 35). Perhaps the greatest importance of FETs is their application in many integrated circuits ('chips'), such as COS/MOS types, which are beyond the scope of this book. Consequently, although FETs are a very much more diverse group of devices than bipolar transistors (and represented by a corresponding diversity of diagrammatic symbols), there is no need for the railway modeller to master them all; the junction-gate types will suffice.

The free electrons and holes in n-type and p-type silicon respectively make these materials fair conductors of electricity in contrast with pure silicon. If electrical connections are made to each end of a strip of, say, n-type silicon, it will behave as a linear resistor, ie, current may flow in either direction and will be proportional to the EMF applied.

Now imagine that a zone of p-type material encircles our strip of n-type material like a belt and forms a circular junction with it. If a connection is made to the p-type zone, we have a three-terminal device. If no bias is applied to the p-type zone, the strip will continue to show normal, linear conductivity. If *reverse* bias is applied to the junction, ie, the p-region is made negative relative to the n-type strip, a depletion zone will be established in the strip making it effectively narrower and therefore increasing its resistance. If the reverse bias is made greater, the depletion zone will constrict the conductive region of the strip even more, making it even more resistant. If the

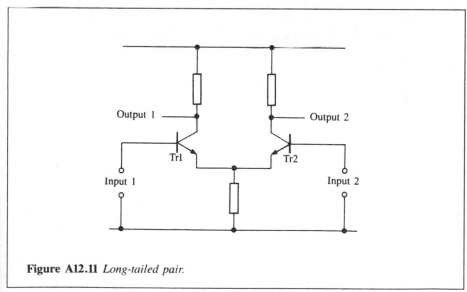

Figure A12.11 *Long-tailed pair.*

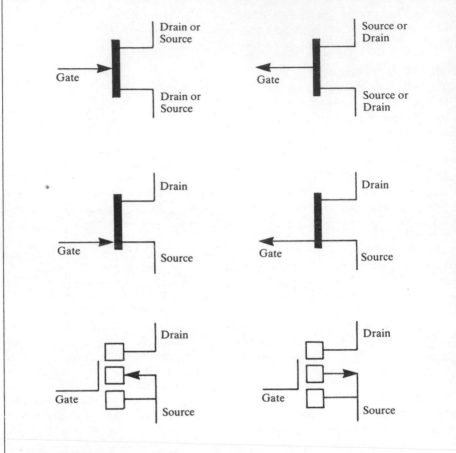

Figure A12.12 *Symbols for FETs: (left) n-channel and (right) p-channel; (top) symmetrical JUGFET, (middle) asymmetric JUGFET, (bottom) enhancement-mode MOSFET.*

reverse bias is great enough, the depletion zone will spread right across the strip cutting off current altogether; the device is now said to be 'pinched off'. Thus a current is being controlled by a voltage applied across a reverse-biased junction. This type of device is called a *junction-gate FET* (JUGFET or JFET).

The junction itself is not, however, an essential part of an FET. There are also insulated-gate FETs (IGFETs), in which the control electrode is insulated from the conductive channel by a thin layer of metal oxide; such devices are often called Metal Oxide/Silicon FETs (MOSFETs) or, simply, MOSTs. These are very widely used in integrated circuits, but are also used as power output devices, eg the VMOS devices encountered in Chapter 31. The 'V' stands for *vertical* and is a reference to the internal architecture of the device.

The normally-conductive strip is called the *channel*; if it is of n-type material, the device is said to be *n-channel* (cf npn); if it is of p-type material, the device is said to be *p-channel* (cf pnp). The terminals at the ends of the channel are called the *source* (corresponding to the emitter) and the *drain* (corresponding to the collector). The control terminal is called the *gate* (and corresponds to the base). Many JUGFETs, including the types most likely to be encountered in model railway applications, are electrically symmetrical, the drain and source terminals being interchangeable. Because of this there are four symbols for JUGFETs as shown in Figure A12.12.

At once several practical differences between the operation of FETs and bipolar transistors are apparent:

i) An unbiased JUGFET is conductive, reverse bias being applied to control the drain current by reducing it; this is known as *depletion-mode* operation. In contrast, an unbiased bipolar transistor is non-conductive, forward bias being needed to establish collector current; this is known as *enhancement-mode* operation. Most MOSFETs, in contrast, are enhancement-mode devices.

ii) An FET will conduct current in either direction (hence the reversibility of symmetrical types), whereas a bipolar transistor will not function normally with collector and emitter leads interchanged.

iii) The gate input resistance of an FET under normal conditions is very high and for practical purposes may be regarded as infinite. Input current is infinitesimal; the input signal may be regarded as an electrostatic charge.

As with bipolar transistors current is stabilized by a resistor in series with the source and by returning the gate to a fixed potential. There can be no set formula for determining the drain current; this is best found by experiment. Amplifier circuits having common-drain (source follower), common-source and common-gate configurations are all possible; the following table summarizes their characteristics.

Summary table of characteristics of FET amplifier stages

Type	Source follower	Common source	Common gate
Input between	gate and drain	gate and source	source and gate
Output between	source and drain	drain and source	drain and gate
Input resistance	infinite	infinite	low
Output resistance	low	high	high
Voltage gain	unity	medium	medium
Current gain	infinite*	infinite*	unity
Output voltage relation to input voltage	in phase	antiphase	in phase

*Current gain must be regarded as infinite since input current is zero (input resistance being infinite) but output current is finite.

Appendix 13

Transistor/transistor logic (TTL)

Many domestic and industrial appliances now demand for their operation the ability to 'reason', albeit on a minor scale. Examples range from automatic washing machines offering a range of 'programmes' through automobile electrical systems to video games. These items and many more make use of the 'families' of electronic logic ICs now available. These ICs contain transistors (MOSFETs in CMOS logic) configured to perform various logic functions that will be described later.

These ICs are ideal for use in automatic signalling systems and certain other model railway equipment which is fundamentally 'logical' in its operation. This is why Parts 5 and 6 of this book bristle with them.

A consequence of the very widespread use of this technology is that the ICs are universally available and very cheap. One supplier's catalogue drawn at random quotes the BC108B, the archetypal silicon npn small-signal transistor, at 10p but the 74LS00 quad two-input NAND gate (the archetypal TTL IC) at 9p and this contains the equivalent of 20 transistors!

Logic families

There are several 'families' of transistor/transistor logic (TTL) devices. Best known is the 74 series having four- or five-digit numbers beginning with 74, eg 7400, 7408, 74157. These are now officially obsolete, but are still widely available. This was superseded by the 74LS series, whose numbering and pin-out is in general the same as the 74 series, but the letters LS are inserted after the 74, eg 74LS00, 74LS08, 74LS157. The LS stands for low power Schottky and this series is characterized by being more miserly on current than the older 74 series.

The 74 LS is in turn being replaced by the 74ALS series (advanced low-power Schottky) and 74HC series which will one day be the industry standard. 74LS is still available and is most useful for our purposes. With certain limitations (explained later under the heading 'Fan out') 74 and 74LS can be used interchangeably, although I recommend that, as far as possible, you should stick to one family or the other, 74LS being preferable. Wherever in this book a 74 series is specified, use the 74LS equivalent if possible.

Another widely used family is CMOS logic. The devices have four- or five-digit numbers beginning with 4, eg 4007, 4029. Although CMOS is flexible in its power supply requirements (3 V to 18 V), its use is not recommended because certain precautions must be taken to avoid accidental damage to the MOSFETs of which the logic circuits are composed. Furthermore, the output current available from most CMOS devices is very limited, often less than 1 mA. So you cannot normally drive LEDs direct from CMOS outputs as you can from 74 or 74LS outputs.

Other logic families you are less likely to encounter are ECL (emitter coupled logic), 74C (CMOS with pin-outs as 74 series), 74S (Schottky) and 74L (low power).

Power requirements

The 74 and 74LS devices require what to railway modellers is the slightly awkward 5 V DC smoothed and *stabilized* supply. The easiest way to provide this is to take an unstabilized but smoothed supply delivering 7 V to 12 V and feed this through a 7805 (or similar) 5 V regulator (see Figure 13.1). The 7805 will deliver up to 1 A with very accurate regulation. *On no account should you attempt to operate TTL from any kind of unstabilized power supply.*

All your TTL devices may share the power supply. You are recommended to include 0.1 µF smoothing capacitors from supply positive to ground at intervals through your circuitry, about one capacitor for every five ICs.

Logic levels

The active devices in the 74 and 74LS ICs are bipolar transistors. In logic circuitry these transistors are used as switches only. Consequently each transistor is either fully

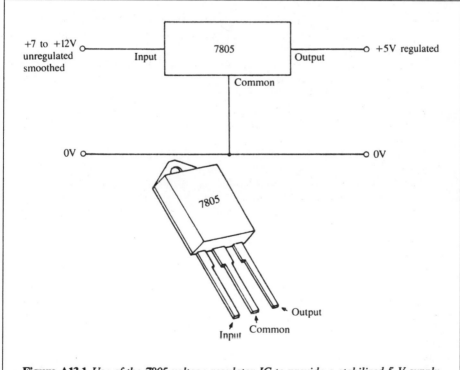

Figure A13.1 *Use of the 7805 voltage regulator IC to provide a stabilized 5 V supply for TTL. The 7805 should be bolted to a heat sink if the total dissipation $\frac{V_{in} - V_{out}}{I}$ exceeds 1 W.*

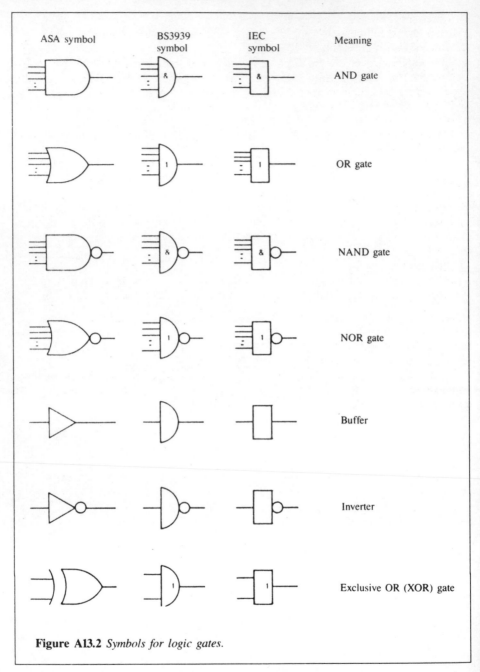

ASA symbol	BS3939 symbol	IEC symbol	Meaning
	&	&	AND gate
	1	1	OR gate
	&	&	NAND gate
	1	1	NOR gate
			Buffer
			Inverter
	1	1	Exclusive OR (XOR) gate

Figure A13.2 *Symbols for logic gates.*

'on', ie saturated or near saturated in the 74LS series, or it is 'off', ie not conducting. So inputs to and outputs from the ICs are either *high* or *low*. A high output is typically 2.4 V or higher while low output is typically 0.4 V or below. The maximum input that a device will read as low is 0.8 V and the minimum output that a device will read as high is 2.0 V.

A high input or output is often called a logical '1' and a low input or output is often called a logical '0'. These '1's and '0's are often collectively called *data*, a plural word of which the singular is *datum*. They are called *data* because they convey useful information which the whole logic circuit processes. For example, a '0' from a track circuit output may indicate 'train in section' which we feed into a signalling system; this processes the data and acts upon it by illuminating the appropriate signal aspects. The smallest unit of data, ie a single 'slot' which may be (indeed *must* be) occupied by a '0' or a '1', is called a *bit*, short for *binary digit*.

The simplest TTL devices, and those of most immediate use in model railway electronics, are known as *gates*.

Gates

A *gate* in logic circuitry is a device having a number (often 1, 2, 3, or 4) of identical inputs and one output. The logic level on the output is determined by the combination of levels on the inputs.

There are three basic types of gates and others that are combinations of the basic three. The basic three are called AND, OR and NOT gates. Each is recognized by its own symbol. (Actually a profusion of different symbols are used — see Figures A13.2 and A13.4 — of which the American Standard symbols are in most general use and these are used throughout this book. The AND and OR symbols are used apart from electronics, eg in critical path analysis.) These symbols are used in circuit diagrams as though each gate were a single component. This is just a 'shorthand' to save drawing out the complete internal circuit for the gate; we shall look at the internal circuitry of some gates later on (Figure A13.5 and A13.6).

An AND gate is a gate having two or more inputs which gives a '1' output only when there is a '1' on *every* input, ie on input 1 AND input 2 AND input 3 AND *ad infinitum*. A corollary of this is that, if there is a '0' on *any* input, the output is '0'.

An OR gate is a gate having two or more inputs which gives a '1' output if there is a '1' on any input or inputs, ie on input 1 OR input 2 OR input 3 OR *ad infinitum*. So, it follows that the output is '0' only if there is a '0' on *every* input.

A NOT gate is more commonly known as an *inverter*. It has only one input and the output is the complement of the input. That is to say, if the input is '0', the output is '1'. And if the input is '1', the output is '0'. The output is whichever the input is NOT.

Three very commonly used gates are combinations of these three basic functions: the NAND gate, the NOR gate and the exclusive OR (XOR) gate. A NAND (NOT

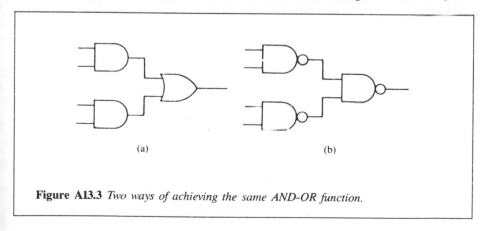

(a)   (b)

Figure A13.3 *Two ways of achieving the same AND-OR function.*

AND) gate is an AND gate incorporating an inverter before its output terminal. So, if there is a '1' on every input, the output will be '0'. And if there is a '0' on any input, the output will be '1'. Similarly a NOR (NOT OR) gate is an OR gate having an inverter before its output terminal. So a '1' on any input will give a '0' on the output. And when there is a '0' on every input there will be a '1' on the output. An exclusive OR (XOR) gate is a variant of the OR gate. It is a two-input gate in which a '1' on one input *but not both* gives a '1' output. It gives a '0' output if both inputs are '0's or both '1's. You could say that it gives a '0' output if the inputs are similar and a '1' if they are dissimilar. There is also a version which has an inverter before its output and is known as an exclusive NOR (XNOR) gate.

Generally the inverting gates (NAND and NOR) are more useful than the non-inverting gates (AND or OR). NAND, NOR and AND gates are all available with 2, 3 or 4 inputs, some with more. OR gates are only available with 2 inputs.

It may seem that the OR gates get a raw deal, but there are other ways of achieving the OR function, as we shall see.

De Morgan's Theorem

If you look again at the description of the gate types given above, you will see that there are two ways in which each gate can be used. The AND gate, for instance, only behaves as an AND gate when we are considering inputs that are '1's, that is to say, when we are using *positive-true* logic. Alternatively, we could decide that the inputs in which we are interested are '0's (as indeed we do in the signal driver circuits in Chapter 15). This is called *negative-true* logic. Inputs or outputs which are negative true are designated either by a bar over the name, eg section occupied, or a prime (') after the name, eg advise A'.

Now, if the data that we are processing consist of '0's, we find that the gates behave differently. For instance, to quote what I said about AND gates earlier, 'if there is a '0' on any input, the output is '0'. Thus our AND gate behaves as though it were an OR gate when dealing with '0's, which is how AND gates are used in Chapters 17, 18 and 19. Indeed, in general, if you use negative-true logic, an AND gate behaves as an OR gate, an OR gate behaves as an AND gate, a NAND gate behaves as a NOR gate and a NOR gate behaves as a NAND gate. This is the basis of what is called *De Morgan's Theorem*.

You do not have to stick to one convention (positive-true or negative-true) through-out one circuit; you can mix them. Indeed, there is a lot to be said for mixing them.

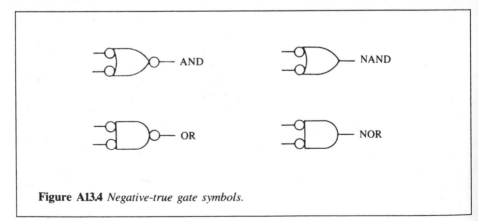

Figure A13.4 *Negative-true gate symbols.*

If you use inverting gates, you change convention at every stage. This permits much greater flexibility and therefore economy in the selection of your gates. For example, in the progressive cab control unit (Chapter 29) there is a function as follows: we want a '1' output (to activate the interlock) if the train is moving forwards *and* and the next section is unavailable *or* if the train is moving backwards *and* the previous section is unavailable. The inputs are all '1's, so at first thought the obvious arrangement is two ANDs feeding an OR as in Figure A13.3(a). However, we do not use AND or OR gates anywhere else in this unit and it would be wasteful to specify a 7408 (quad AND) and a 7432 (quad OR) and then to leave five of the eight gates unused, even if the two ICs together do cost only a few pence. If you examine the circuit of the three-controller version, you will see a most elegant alternative arrangement reproduced in Figure A13.3(b). Two NAND gates provide the AND function, but their outputs are inverted of course. However, since the OR function is being applied to '0's, by De Morgan we now need an AND gate and because we want to invert its output back to a '1', it is in fact a further NAND gate that we choose. The three NAND gates are identical and indeed are on the same 7400 IC.

So important is De Morgan's Theorem that many authors use a second set of graphic symbols for the various gate types when their inputs are negative-true. These are shown in Figure A13.4 and they reflect the *function* that the gate is fulfilling rather than the name by which you would ask for it in a shop. However, throughout this book, for simplicity, only the positive-true symbols are used, whether the logic is positive-true or negative-true. I take the view that where the circuit diagram shows a NAND gate, that is what you must order from your supplier, whether it is being used as a NAND or a NOR or even, as often happens, as an inverter.

Using the gates

Figure A13.5 shows the internal circuit diagram of one of the four two-input NAND gates in a 7400 IC. The gates in the 74LS00 are rather different, as we shall see shortly. All the devices in the 74 family have similar input arrangements and most have similar output facilities. Exceptions to the latter are units having open-collector output and three-state output, which we shall consider later (under the heading 'Fan in').

Transistor T1 is a transistor with two emitters. In discrete components transistors having more than one emitter are rare, although they do exist. In fact there is no limit to the number of emitters a transistor could have. Our two-emitter transistor is perhaps best considered as two separate conventional transistors having their bases and collectors connected in parallel.

Here's how the NAND gate works. If both inputs are held high or left unconnected, no emitter current can flow. So T1's base/collector junction is *forward biased*, providing base bias for T2, whose emitter current in turn provides bias for T3, which conducts, holding the output low; because T2 is saturated, T4's base voltage is held low, barely above T3's base voltage. Now D1 pushes T4's emitter voltage higher than its base voltage, so T4 is cut off. The output of the gate is therefore low, a logical '0'. Yet, if a low voltage is applied to either input, or both, T1 functions as an ordinary transistor under saturation conditions. Its collector voltage falls almost to the low input voltage, so T2 and, in turn, T3 are cut off. Resistor R3 now provides base bias for T4 which conducts, delivering (via D1) a high voltage at the output, a logical '1'.

Figure A13.6 shows the circuit of a NAND gate in a 74LS00 IC. The principal differences between this and a 7400 NAND gate are: (i) that the input is provided by a matrix of Schottky diodes: (ii) that the transistors are all Schottky transistors and (iii) that the resistor values are generally higher than in the 7400, reducing all the current flows.

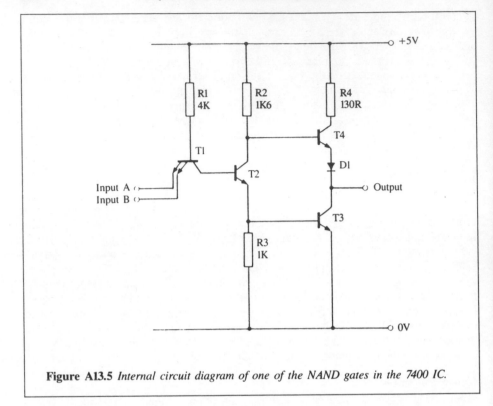

Figure A13.5 *Internal circuit diagram of one of the NAND gates in the 7400 IC.*

Note the different symbols used to distinguish Schottky diodes and transistors. Schottky diodes use a mixture of metal (often aluminium) and semiconductor in their junctions, which gives them a lower forward voltage, typically less than 0.2 V, compared with 0.6 to 0.7 V for a normal silicon diode. Consequently Schottky diodes are ideally suited for use in logic circuits.

Schottky *transistors* are ordinary silicon transistors, which incorporate a Schottky diode parallel to their base/collector junctions (cathode to the collector of an npn transistor). The function of this diode is to prevent the transistor from becoming fully saturated. As the saturation point is approached, the diode comes into conduction, short-circuiting away the excess base bias. The reason for the undesirability of saturation is that it affects the speed at which a transistor can respond to a change of bias. A saturated transistor takes longer to turn off than a transistor that is held just short of saturation by a Schottky diode. The difference is a fraction of a microsecond, irrelevant in the average model railway application, but it makes an appreciable difference to the speed at which gates can be switched in high-speed computing applications. So Schottky logic can work faster than 'plain' 74-series TTL.

A consequence of this kind of circuitry is that the input to a TTL device, 74 series or 74LS, *sources* current; it never sinks it. When an input is high, *no current flows* and when an input is low, *current flows out of it*. Experienced designers unfamiliar with the peculiarities of TTL have been baffled by its input characteristics and projects have failed when the designers have mistakenly expected current to flow *into* inputs at logical '1', as it would if the input were to the base of an npn transistor. This arrangement was chosen because it gives TTL considerable immunity to noise and other electrical interference. It is also easier to analyse circuitry when the difference between '0' and '1' is 2.4 V or so, rather than only 0.7 V as it would be if the input were to the base of an npn transistor.

You may wonder why, having this kind of input arrangement, it was considered necessary for TTL to be given a push-pull-type ('totem-pole') output which can source or sink current. In fact it is not necessary. Open-collector versions are available (see later under 'Fan in') in which the output transistor equivalent to T4 in Figure A13.5 (or T5 in Figure A13.6) is omitted. This type of output can sink current when in the low state, but cannot source current in the high state. For some applications these units can be used interchangeably with the normal push-pull output types. TTL is sometimes used at high frequencies up to 45 MHz, although not normally so in model railway applications. At such high frequencies the internal capacitance of the devices has a signifcant effect upon their efficiency of operation and a push-pull-type output allows more rapid charge and discharge of the internal capacitance, so that it can work faster.

From the railway modeller's viewpoint, speed of operation is generally irrelevant, as a response time in milliseconds would be adequate but the push-pull type output is useful in allowing the driving of common-anode or common-cathode LEDs.

Typical total input current for 74 series is 1 mA and for 74LS series is 200 μA; typical maximum output current to ground with output high is 20 mA for 74 series

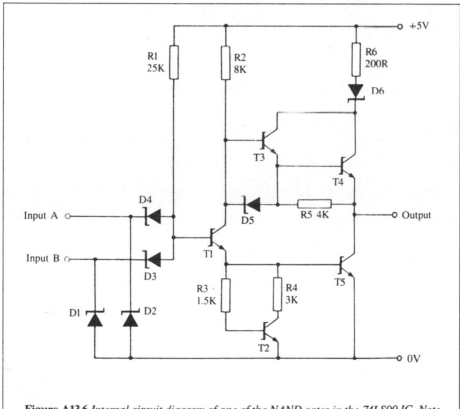

Figure A13.6 *Internal circuit diagram of one of the NAND gates in the 74LS00 IC. Note the special symbols used for Schottky diodes and transistors (explained in the text).*

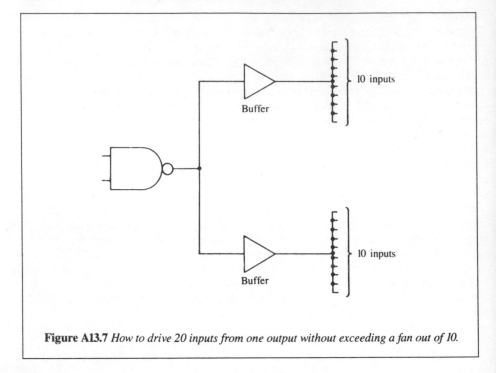

Figure A13.7 *How to drive 20 inputs from one output without exceeding a fan out of 10.*

(10 mA for 74LS) and to supply positive when at logical '0' is about 55 mA (28 mA for 74LS).

Fan out

TTL devices are so designed that the output of one device can be connected directly to the input(s) of other device(s) without need for any intermediary components. This greatly simplifies circuit design and construction. There is, however, a limit to the number of inputs that can be serviced from one output. This figure is called the *fan out*. For a circuit consistently using 74 series, fan out is quoted as 10. That is to say, one output can feed up to 10 inputs. For 74LS, fan out is quoted as 20 and if you mix 74 and 74SL, you must allow for the differences between them. So if a 74 output is feeding 74LS inputs, fan out rises to 40 to 50 and for a 74LS output feeding 74 inputs, fan out falls to 5.

There may be occasions (although none occurs in any of the circuits described in this book) when you need to feed more inputs than the fan out permits, eg 20 inputs from one output (assuming consistent use of the 74 series). The solution is to use intermediary *buffers* (not the railway type!). These are TTL gates having one input and one output in which the output simply 'follows' the input, '0' for '0' and '1' for '1'. We can now connect two buffer inputs to our 'feeder' output and 10 inputs to each buffer output (Figure A13.7).

If you do exceed the fan out, you may find that the driving device cannot handle the output current and gives indeterminate outputs, eg, its '1's are too low and some receiving devices read them as '0's or its '0's are too high and some receiving devices read them as '1's. So beware! Those who break the rules of the game are liable to incur penalties.

Fan in

The *fan in* of a TTL device is the number of other devices which may feed data directly into it. Normally this is the same as its number of inputs, eg a four-input NAND gate (on the 7420 IC) may receive inputs from each of four other gates, one output to each input. Therefore it has a fan in of four.

Although one output may feed several inputs (fan out), great care must be taken if more than one output is connected to the same input terminal. An electrical problem is liable to arise if you connect two normal (totem-pole) TTL outputs in parallel. All is fine as long as both outputs agree and deliver the same logic level, but if they disagree, one will short-circuit the other, leading to an indeterminate reading. There are three ways of overcoming this problem: (i) avoid the problem altogether by using an additional AND or OR gate to perform this combining function; (ii) the use of open-collector devices and (iii) the use of three-state devices.

Open-collector devices have already been mentioned. These do not have the normal output; the output is the open collector of T3 in Figure A13.5 or of T4 in Figure A13.6, the upper output transistor having been removed. Many TTL gates, buffers and inverters arc available with open-collector outputs. In this book and in some other publications an open-collector output is distinguished in circuit diagrams by an asterisk adjacent to the output terminal.

Open collector outputs may be connected in parallel, whereupon a '0' on *any* output will be read as a '0' by any input(s) connected to this point. Only if all the outputs are at '1', ie non-conductive, will the input(s) read a '1'. Therefore, this arrangement behaves as though it were an AND gate; sometimes it is called a 'wired AND' or a 'wired OR' because most often it is handling negative-true logic in which, by De Morgan's Theorem, AND behaves as OR.

Several examples of open-collector NAND gates are used in the progressive cab control modules described in Chapter 29. For example, all the 'advise' outputs are from this type of device because they are likely to be paralleled or short-circuited in normal use.

It is recommended that open-collector outputs be equipped with a pull-up resistor (1 K to 10 K) to supply positive. Its function is to pull the output up to the logic '1' level when the output transistors are off. Although in theory the circuit should work without the pull-up resistor, in the electrically noisy environment of a working model railway, its inclusion will help to eliminate interference.

Three-state devices sound as though they employ a third logic level in addition to '0' and '1', but the truth is simpler. They have a push-pull-type output, but both output transistors are normally open-circuit, so that neither a '0' or a '1' is delivered. These devices incorporate a separate 'enable' input, to which a '1' in some devices or a '0' in other devices must be applied to activate the output stage and enable the output data to be read. Consequently any number of three-state outputs may be connected in parallel, provided that no more than one at a time is enabled. Only the selected and enabled (the proper term is 'addressed') device's output will be read by any inputs connected to the common data line (the proper term is 'bus'). The system functions somewhat like a data selector (see below). The number of three-state devices is limited and there are probably not many occasions on which their characteristics are likely to render them useful to railway modellers.

Data selectors (Multiplexers)

Some of the most useful 'gate variants' in model railway electronics are the data selectors, sometimes called multiplexers. One example, the 74LS157 is put to good model

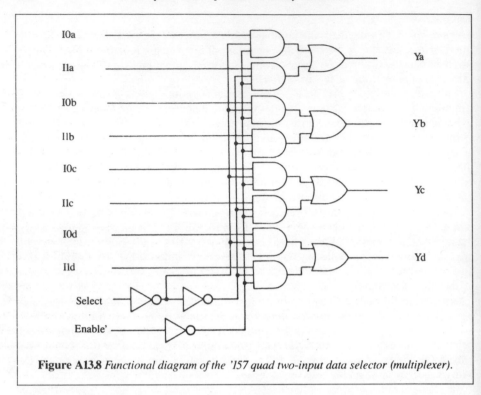

Figure A13.8 *Functional diagram of the '157 quad two-input data selector (multiplexer).*

railway use in Chapter 20. As the name suggests, these devices select logical data from a choice of sources. The 74LS157 is a quad two-input selector; that is to say, it functions rather like a four-pole two-way switch, except that it is only *inputs* that are selected. It cannot be used (as a two-way switch can) to *distribute* data to selected receivers, which is the function of a *demultiplexer*. The 74LS157 is ideally suited for switching the inputs to a multiple-aspect signal driver at a running junction; which is how it is used in Chapter 20. A functional diagram of the 74LS157 is given in Figure A13.8.

Other multiplexers in common use are the 74LS151 (single 8-input, 74LS153 (dual 4-input) and the 74LS158 (as the '157 but with the inverted outputs). A useful feature on all these devices is their enable input. If a logical '1' is applied to this input, all the outputs go to '0', irrespective of the other inputs. So normally this input is kept 'low'. In Figure 20.5 you will see it used to provide a manual override for the signal.

Demultiplexers and decoders

The 'opposite' of a data selector or multiplexer is called a *demultiplexer* or sometimes, incorrectly, a *decoder*. It has an input terminal, an array of output terminals and one or more address terminals. The input data are transmitted exclusively to the output terminal selected by the code applied to the address terminals.

A *decoder*, using the term in its strict sense, is similar to a demultiplexer, but lacks the input terminal. It simply has address inputs and outputs. Two of the best known TTL decoders, a pair of extraordinarily useful ICs, are the 7442 and 74145 (74LS42 and 74LS145) binary-code-decimal (BCD) to decimal decoders. These are 16-pin ICs with four address inputs called D, C, B and A and ten outputs numbered 0 to 9. Each of the ten outputs is addressed by a unique combination of address inputs designed to perform the arithmetical function of BCD to decimal conversion. The one addressed output is a logical '0' while all others are '1'. If the input code has a decimal value exceeding 9, *all* outputs are '1's. The following table shows the behaviour of these decoders.

Input DCBA	Output	Input DCBA	Output
0000	0 low; others high	1000	8 low; others high
0001	1 low; others high	1001	9 low; others high
0010	2 low; others high	1010	all high
0011	3 low; others high	1011	all high
0100	4 low; others high	1100	all high
0101	5 low; others high	1101	all high
0110	6 low; others high	1110	all high
0111	7 low; others high	1111	all high

Although these ICs may have been intended originally for arithmetical functions, their applications are far broader. They may be regarded as 'universal three or four input gates'. Suppose we want to identity those situations in which the logic levels at three points are 1, 1 and 1 respectively and we want a logical '0' output. This is easy: we use a three-input NAND gate with inputs from those points. However, suppose the three levels are 1, 1 and 0. We could apply an inverter to the third point and still use the three-input NAND. We might just happen to have a spare inverter somewhere, or a spare NAND that could be used as one, or we might not, but we *could* use a '42 instead. We apply the 1, 1 and 0 points to inputs C, B and A respectively and tie input D to ground. Now 110 is BCD for 6, so we take our output from output 6. Then suppose we also need to identify those situations when the same points are at 1, 0 and 1 respectively. 101 is 5, so we take the new output from output 5. Any of the eight possible combinations of three inputs A, B and C can be detected in this way, provided input D is tied to ground. Many combinations of *four* inputs can be handled, provided that input D is wanted as a '0', unless it happens to form part of the two valid input codes in which it is high, ie, 1000 (= 8) and 1001 (= 9).

The '145 is an interesting IC. It has the same pin-out and functions as the '42 but the outputs are open-collector type and rated to carry up to 80 mA and tolerate up to 15 V. Thus it is ideal for driving relays or grain-of-wheat bulbs. Equally valid outputs can be paralleled and this enables such fascinating circuits to be made up as the signal drivers shown in Figures 15.5 and 15.6.

Combinational and sequential logic

All the logic circuitry considered so far in this Appendix — and indeed most of the logic circuitry in this book — involves what is called combinational logic. That is logic in which the output is dependent only on the inputs being applied at that time, so that, if the status of all the inputs is known, the output can be deduced. Gates and multiplexers are examples of combinational-logic devices and the signal driver circuits in Chapter 15 (which, after all, are only combinations of gates) are examples of whole circuits displaying combinational logic.

A further dimension is added to logic circuitry by the use of *sequential logic*. This is logic circuitry in which the output is determined not only by the status of the inputs currently being applied, but also by past inputs which have subsequently disappeared.

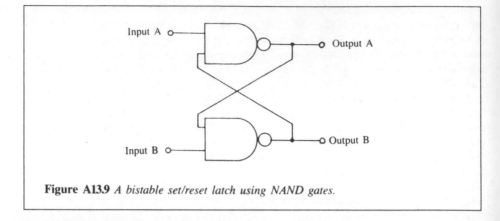

Figure A13.9 *A bistable set/reset latch using NAND gates.*

In other words, it is circuitry which has *memory*.

Consider the simple circuit shown in Figure A13.9. The two NAND gates may well be on the same 7400 IC. If we apply '0's to both inputs, we can predict the outputs; both will be '1's, since a '0' applied to any input of a NAND gate will always ensure a '1' output. But what if both inputs are '1's? We can no longer predict the output, for there are two possibilities. *Either* output B will be 'high' and (since both inputs of IC1a are 'high') output A will be 'low' (holding output B 'high'), *or* output A will be 'high' and (since both inputs of IC1b are 'high') output B will be 'low' (holding output A 'high'). So both states are inherently *stable*. That is to say, the circuit if left alone will stay in the same state. This kind of circuit is called a *bistable* (or 'flip-flop'). (In Chapter 12 bistables composed of pairs of discrete transistors are described.)

The useful feature of this kind of bistable is that we can force it into whichever state we choose — and it will, of course, stay in that state until we decide to force it into the other state. In Figure A13.9, if we apply a '0' to input A, that gate's output will go high, so that IC1b will now have '1's on *both* inputs. Its output now goes low, holding the other input of IC1a low and this state will be maintained if we let input A return to '1'. If we now apply a '0' to input B, the bistable will go into its other state — and that similarly will be maintained until input A is activated again.

The two inputs of this bistable are often called the $\overline{\text{set}}$ and $\overline{\text{reset}}$ ($\overline{\text{S}}$ and $\overline{\text{R}}$) inputs. Since the circuit, at least in the form in which it is shown in Figure A13.9, is symmetrical it might appear to be an arbitrary decision which input is $\overline{\text{S}}$ and which is $\overline{\text{R}}$. When the bistable is used as a part of a functional system, however, it is usually obvious which is which: the $\overline{\text{S}}$ input initiates the *active* state, eg section occupied, flashing yellow aspects on, controller A engaged.

Notice that the two outputs of this bistable are antiphase. That is to say, *in normal use* one is always at '0' and the other is at '1': This must be so since each output is also an input to the other gate; the output that is at '0' will cause a '1' to be delivered at the other output. Often, however, only one output is used — the one that gives a '1' output when the $\overline{\text{S}}$ input has been activated. There are TTL ICs containing arrays of such bistables, generally having a single output and often sharing a common reset input.

There is a drawback to this kind of bistable. As mentioned earlier, if a '0' is applied to both inputs simultaneously, a '1' will appear on both outputs. This is the one exception to the rule given in the last paragraph that in normal use the outputs are antiphase. So, in a device having a single output, even if the $\overline{\text{R}}$ input is being held at a steady

'0', a '0' on the $\overline{S}$ input will give a '1' on the output. Because the output can 'see' the input in this way, this kind of bistable is sometimes called a 'transparent latch'.

This 'transparency' can be eliminated by gating the $\overline{S}$ input, ie, feeding the input through a gate which is disabled by a '0' on the $\overline{R}$ input. Figure A13.10 shows one way of doing this; a similar arrangement is used in the progressive cab control units described in Chapter 29. Note that the $\overline{S}$ input is now positive-true.

There are however, various more sophisticated bistable types which eliminate the 'transparency' problems by various means. Generally these units have an additional input called the 'clock' input to which a train of pulses is applied; these lock pulses enable changes of state. Examples are the D-type and JK bistables, both of which are widely used in electronics. Further details of their construction and use will be found in textbooks of digital electronics.

Interfacing TTL with other systems

Care must be taken when interfacing TTL to switches or other electronic circuits because of its input characteristics. Switch contacts should always be connected between ground (supply negative line) and the TTL device input, so that the closing of the contacts is read as a logical '0'. A pull-up resistor (1 K to 10 K) should always be provided from the gate input to supply positive; its omission would render the TTL system susceptible to noise and spurious activation. See Figure A13.11. In the same way an npn transistor in place of the switch contacts is particularly useful in interfacing TTL to other electronic circuits, especially if these operate from a different supply voltage. This is shown in Figure 13.12.

Another method of using a transistor as an interface is shown in Figure A13.13. Although this configuration is possible, that of Figure A13.11 is preferable for a number of reasons. For example Rc must be a low value to sink the TTL input current: recommended maximum values are 470 R with 74 series and 2K2 with 74LS. These low values, especially with 'plain' 74 series, lead to heavy current consumption when the transistor is conductive.

TTL outputs are more flexible. The standard push-pull outputs can source or sink current up to 10 mA or more. LEDs can be driven direct in either mode. Auxiliary transistors or Darlingtons should be used where higher output currents or voltages or both are needed, eg for relay driving.

Some TTL ICs are available with outputs rated for heavier duties. Examples are the 74LS37 and 74LS38. Both are quad two-input NAND gates which can handle up

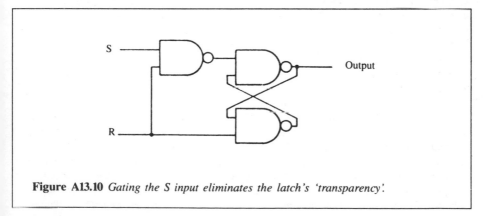

Figure A13.10 *Gating the S input eliminates the latch's 'transparency'.*

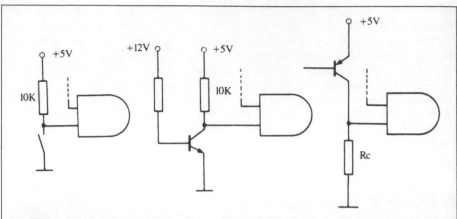

Figure A13.11 *(Left) Switched inputs to TTL should be between input and ground and should include a pull-up resistor.*

Figure A13.12 *(Middle) An npn transistor used as an input to a TTL system.*

Figure A13.13 *(Right) An alternative system of using a transistor to interface to TTL. This system is less satisfactory than that of Figure A13.12 for reasons given in the text.*

to 50 mA of output current; the '38 has open-collector output. They are intended for applications where they are called upon to drive large numbers of other TTL inputs exceeding the normal fan out, but can also be used for other applications, eg grain-of-wheat lamp driving, provided that the output voltage limit (about 7 V) is not exceeded.

Handling TTL devices

Most common TTL ICs come in 14-pin DIL (dual-in-line) plastic packages. Pin 14 is generally supply positive and pin 7 supply negative. This leaves 12 pins for inputs and outputs. Consequently the number of gates per chip is generally as follows:

1-input gates (buffers and inverters):	6 per chip
2-input gates	4 per chip
3-input gates	3 per chip
4-input gates	2 per chip
8-input gates	1 per chip

Due to the positions of the positive and negative supply pins, the gate connections are generally staggered, so that the output of one gate is invariably opposite the input of another. This is often very useful when constructing circuits on Veroboard or similar stripboard, since one gate can be made to feed another of the same type by simply leaving the strip intact between the pins.

Devising the simplest Veroboard arrangements for complex TTL circuits is a gruelling task. Perhaps one day someone will invent a computer program to do this!

TTL ICs are, in general, robust, trouble free and they will withstand considerable misuse. On one occasion a circuit of mine that had begun malfunctioning proved to have been hooked up to the *input* of its supply voltage regulator, so was being operated from 7.5 V unregulated. When restored to its correct supply voltage, the circuit functioned normally again, so no damage had been done. On another occasion, an IC was grossly overheated when it took 30 minutes to remove a particularly stubbon solder blob that was shorting adjacent Veroboard conductors. For several minutes the IC package itself was too hot to handle but it still performed perfectly afterwards. Nevertheless, as with all ICs, I recommend the use of IC sockets. These should be soldered in place at the same time as the passive components; afterwards the ICs themselves can be inserted (a fiddly job). This not only protects the ICs against overheating when soldering (however unlikely this may be to actually cause damage) but also offers the facility for swopping ICs. In the unlikely event of the project not working (most TTL projects work perfectly well first time) and of your suspecting the IC of being less than perfect, you can easily take it out and try another.

Pin-outs

On the following pages are pin-out diagrams of some of the most popular TTL ICs, including all those mentioned in this book. Note that the diagrams are all *top views*. The drawings are reproduced from the Maplin catalogue by kind permission of Maplin Electronic Supplies Ltd.

Table 13.1 Gate selector guide *NB Numbers must be prefixed 74 or 74LS etc.*

	Normal output	Open-collector output	Special
AND gates			
Quad 2-input	08	09	—
Triple 3-input	11	15	—
Dual 4-input	21	—	—
OR gates			
Quad 2-input	32	—	—
NAND gates			
Quad 2-input	00	01	26*h**
		03	37*b*
			38*b**
			132*s*
Triple 3-input	10	12	—
Dual 4-input	20	22	13*s*
Single 8-input	30	—	—
NOR gates			
Quad 2-input	02	33*b*	38*b*
Triple 3-input	27	—	—
Dual 4-input	25*a*	—	—
XOR gates			
Quad	86	136	—
XNOR gates			
Quad	—	266	—
Buffers			
Hex	—	07	17*h**
Inverts (NOT)			
Hex	04	05	06*b**
			14*s*
			16*h**

Notes

* = open-collector output; *a* also has strobe inputs; *b* buffer output (has higher than normal current handling capacity); *h* high-voltage tolerance; *s* Schmitt trigger.

Semiconductors

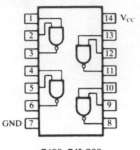

7400, 74LS00
Quad 2-input
NAND gate

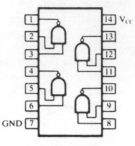

7401, 74LS01
Quad 2-input
NAND gate
Open collector
outputs

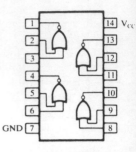

7402, 74LS02
Quad 2-input
NOR gate

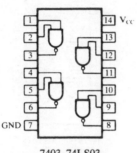

7403, 74LS03
Quad 2-input
NAND gate
Open collector
outputs

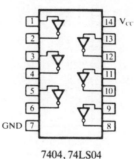

7404, 74LS04
Hex inverter

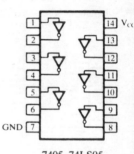

7405, 74LS05
Hex inverter
Open collector
outputs

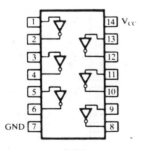

7406
Hex inverter buffer/
drive
Open collector outputs

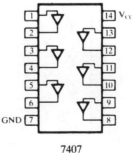

7407
Hex buffer/driver
Open collector outputs

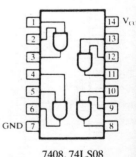

7408, 74LS08
Quad 2-input AND gate

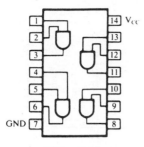

7409, 74LS09
Quad 2-input AND gate
Open collector outputs

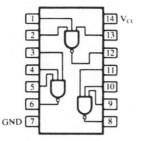

7410
Triple 3-input NAND gate

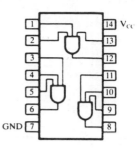

7411, 74LS11
Triple 3-input AND
gate

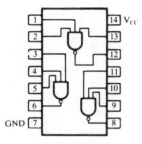

74LS12
Triple 3-input NAND gate
Open collector outputs

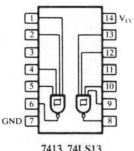

7413, 74LS13
Dual Schmitt Trigger

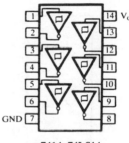

7414, 74LS14
Hex Schmitt Trigger

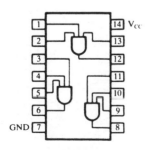

74LS15
Triple 3-input AND gate
Open collector outputs

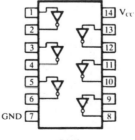

7416
Hex inverter buffer/
driver
Open collector outputs

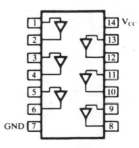

7417
Hex buffer/driver
Open collector outputs

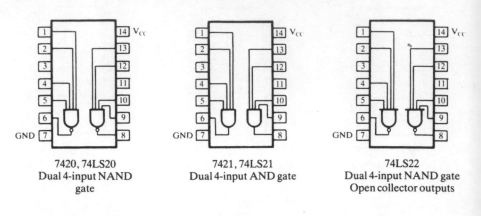

7420, 74LS20
Dual 4-input NAND
gate

7421, 74LS21
Dual 4-input AND gate

74LS22
Dual 4-input NAND gate
Open collector outputs

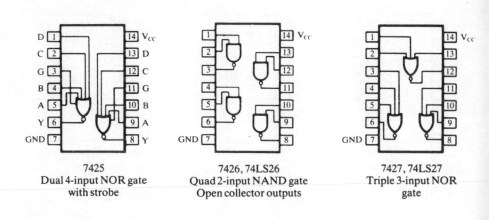

7425
Dual 4-input NOR gate
with strobe

7426, 74LS26
Quad 2-input NAND gate
Open collector outputs

7427, 74LS27
Triple 3-input NOR
gate

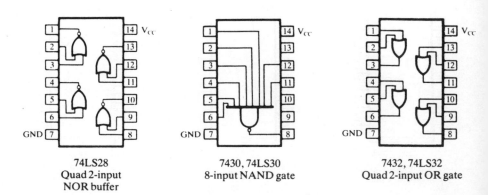

74LS28
Quad 2-input
NOR buffer

7430, 74LS30
8-input NAND gate

7432, 74LS32
Quad 2-input OR gate

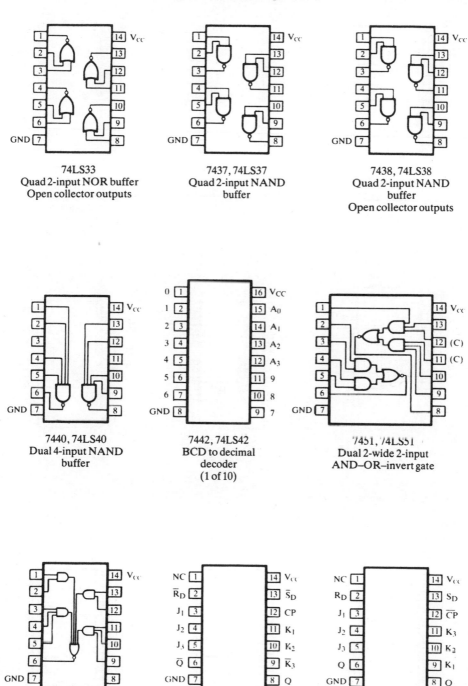

74LS33
Quad 2-input NOR buffer
Open collector outputs

7437, 74LS37
Quad 2-input NAND
buffer

7438, 74LS38
Quad 2-input NAND
buffer
Open collector outputs

7440, 74LS40
Dual 4-input NAND
buffer

7442, 74LS42
BCD to decimal
decoder
(1 of 10)

7451, 74LS51
Dual 2-wide 2-input
AND–OR–invert gate

74LS54
4-wide 2 and 3 input
AND–OR–invert gate

7470
JK edge-triggered
flip-flop

7472
JK pulse-triggered
flip-flop

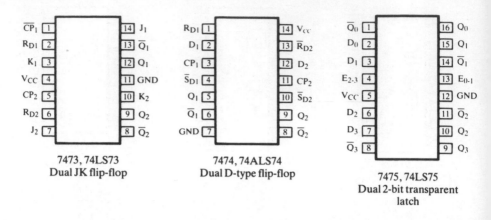

7473, 74LS73
Dual JK flip-flop

7474, 74ALS74
Dual D-type flip-flop

7475, 74LS75
Dual 2-bit transparent
latch

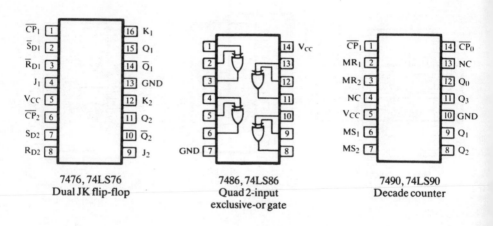

7476, 74LS76
Dual JK flip-flop

7486, 74LS86
Quad 2-input
exclusive-or gate

7490, 74LS90
Decade counter

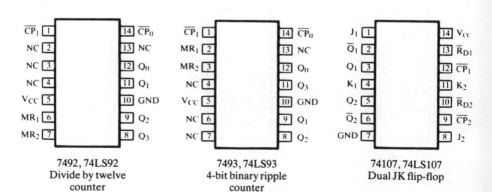

7492, 74LS92
Divide by twelve
counter

7493, 74LS93
4-bit binary ripple
counter

74107, 74LS107
Dual JK flip-flop

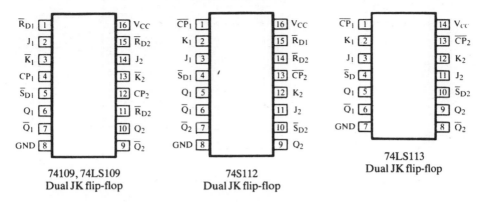

74109, 74LS109
Dual JK flip-flop

74S112
Dual JK flip-flop

74LS113
Dual JK flip-flop

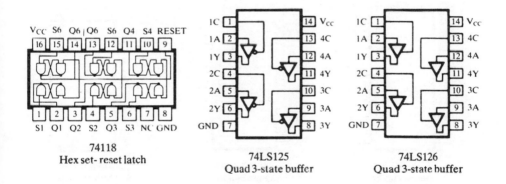

74118
Hex set- reset latch

74LS125
Quad 3-state buffer

74LS126
Quad 3-state buffer

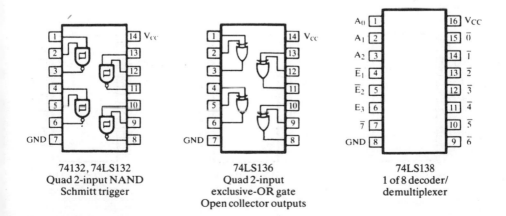

74132, 74LS132
Quad 2-input NAND
Schmitt trigger

74LS136
Quad 2-input
exclusive-OR gate
Open collector outputs

74LS138
1 of 8 decoder/
demultiplexer

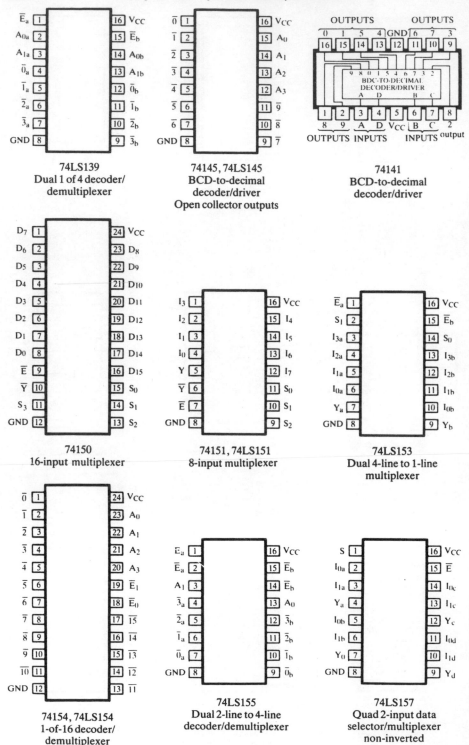

74LS139
Dual 1 of 4 decoder/
demultiplexer

74145, 74LS145
BCD-to-decimal
decoder/driver
Open collector outputs

74141
BCD-to-decimal
decoder/driver

74150
16-input multiplexer

74151, 74LS151
8-input multiplexer

74LS153
Dual 4-line to 1-line
multiplexer

74154, 74LS154
1-of-16 decoder/
demultiplexer

74LS155
Dual 2-line to 4-line
decoder/demultiplexer

74LS157
Quad 2-input data
selector/multiplexer
non-inverted

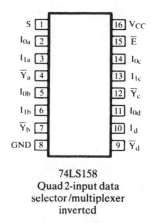

74LS158
Quad 2-input data
selector/multiplexer
inverted

Reprinted by permission of Maplin Electronic Supplies Ltd.

Appendix 14

Timers

CA555, CA555C Types

Timers: For Timing Delays and Oscillator Applications in Commercial, Industrial, and Military Equipment.

The RCA-CA555 and CA555C are highly stable timers for use in precision timing and oscillator applications. As timers, these monolithic integrated circuits are capable of producing accurate time delays for periods ranging from microseconds through hours. These devices are also useful for astable oscillator operation and can maintain an accurately controlled free-running frequency and duty cycle with only two external resistors and one capacitor.

The circuits of the CA555 and CA555C may be triggered by the falling edge of the wave-form signal, and the output of these circuits can source or sink up to a 200-milliampere current or drive TTL circuits.

The CA555 and CA555C are supplied in hermetic IC Gold-CHIP 8-lead dual-in-line plastic packages (G Suffix), standard 8-lead TO-5 style packages (T Suffix), 8-lead TO-5 style packages with dual-in-line formed leads (DIL-CAN, S suffix), 8-lead dual-in-line plastic packages (MINI-DIP, E suffix), and in chip form (H suffix). These

Maximum Ratings, Absolute-Maximum Values:

DC SUPPLY VOLTAGE	. . .	18	V
DEVICE DISSIPATION:			
Up to $T_A = 55°C$	. . . . .	600	mW
Above $T_A = 55°C$ Derate linearly		5	mW/°C
AMBIENT TEMPERATURE RANGE (All Types):			
Operating			
CA555	. . . .	-55 to +125	°C
CA555C	. . . .	0 to 70	°C*
Storage	. . . .	-65 to +150	°C
LEAD TEMPERATURE (During Soldering)			
At distance 1/16" + 1/32"			
(1.59 + 0.79 mm) from case			
for 10 seconds max.	. . . . . .	+265	°C

*The CA555E, S, J, and T can be operated over the temperature range of −55°C to +125°C although the published limits for certain electrical specifications apply only over the temperature range of 0 to +70°C.

types are direct replacements for industry types in packages with similar terminal arrangements eg SE555 and NE555, MC1555 and MC1455, respectively. The CA555 type circuits are intended for applications requiring premium electrical performance. The CA555C type circuits are intended for applications requiring less stringent electrical characteristics.

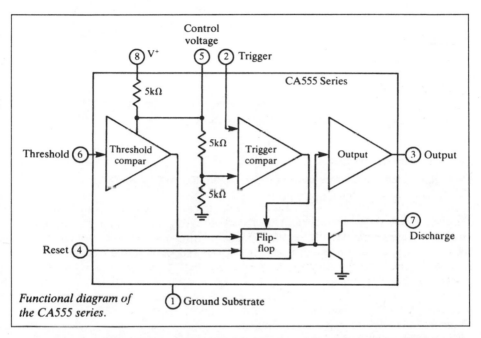

Functional diagram of the CA555 series.

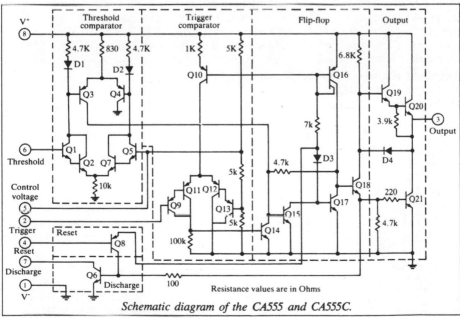

Schematic diagram of the CA555 and CA555C.

CA555G, CA565CG:
Hermetic Gold-CHIP 8-lead Dual-In-Line Plastic Package (MINI-DIP)

CA555T, CA555CT:
Standard 8-Lead TO-5 Style Package.

CA555S, CA555CS:
Standard 8-Lead TO-5 Style Package With Formed Leads (DIL-CAN).

CA555E, CA555CE:
8-Lead Dual-In-Line Plastic Package (MINI-DIP).

Features
- Accurate timing from microseconds through hours.
- Astable and monostable operation
- Adjustable duty cycle
- Output capable of sourcing or sinking up to 200 mA
- Output capable of driving TTL devices
- Normally ON and OFF outputs
- High-temperature stability — 0.005%/°C
- Directly interchangeable with SE555, NE555, MC1555 and MC1455

Applications
- Precision timing
- Sequential timing
- Time-delay generation
- Pulse generation
- Pulse-width and position modulation
- Pulse detector

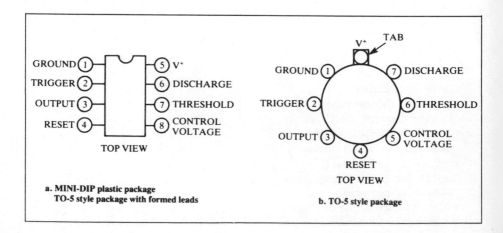

a. MINI-DIP plastic package
   TO-5 style package with formed leads

b. TO-5 style package

Electrical Characteristics *At $T_A = 25°C$, $V^+ = 5$ to 15 V unless otherwise specified.*

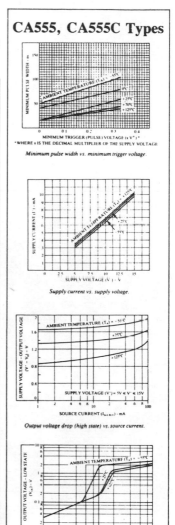

CA555, CA555C Types

Characteristic	Test conditions	CA555 Min.	CA555 Typ.	CA555 Max.	CA555C Min.	CA555C Typ.	CA555C Max.	Units
DC Supply Voltage V^+		4.5	—	18	4.5	—	16	V
DC Supply Current (Low State)*. I^+	$V^+ = 5$ V, $R_L = \infty$	—	3	5	—	3	6	mA
	$V^+ = 15V$, $R_L = \infty$	—	10	12	—	10	15	mA
Threshold Voltage V_{TH}		—	(2/3) V^+	—	—	(2/3) V^+	—	V
Trigger Voltage	$V^+ = 5$ V	1.45	1.67	1.9	—	1.67	—	V
	$V^+ = 15$ V	4.8	5	5.2	—	5	—	
Trigger Current		—	0.5	—	—	0.5	—	µA
Threshold Current I_{TH}		—	0.1	0.25	—	0.1	0.25	µA
Reset Voltage		0.4	0.7	1.0	0.4	0.7	1.0	V
Reset Current		—	0.1	—	—	0.1	—	mA
Current Voltage Level	$V^+ = 5$ V	2.9	3.33	3.8	2.6	3.33	4	V
	$V^+ = 15$ V	9.6	10	10.4	9	10	11	V
Output Voltage Drop: Low Stage, V_{OL}	$V^+ = 5$ V, $I_{SINK} = 5$ mA	—	—	—	—	0.25	0.35	V
	$I_{SINK} = 8$ mA	—	0.1	0.25	—	—	—	
	$V^+ = 15$ V, $I_{SINK} = 10$ mA	—	0.1	0.15	—	0.1	0.25	V
	$I_{SINK} = 50$ mA	—	0.4	0.5	—	0.4	0.75	
	$I_{SINK} = 100$ mA	—	2.0	2.2	—	2.0	2.5	V
	$I_{SINK} = 200$ mA	—	2.5	—	—	2.5	—	
High State, V_{OH}	$V^+ = 5$ V, $I_{SOURCE} = 100$ mA	3.0	3.3	—	2.75	3.3	—	V
	$V^+ = 5$ V, $I_{SOURCE} = 100$ mA	13.0	13.3	—	12.75	13.3	—	
	$I_{SOURCE} = 200$ mA	—	12.5	—	—	12.5	—	
Timing Error (Monostable): Initial Accuracy	$R_1, R_2 = 1$ to 100 kR $C = 0.1$ µF Tested at $V^+ = 5$ V $V^+ = 15$ V	—	0.5	2	—	1	—	%
Frequency Drift with Temperature		—	30	100	—	50	—	p/m/°C
Drift with Supply Voltage		—	0.05	0.2	—	0.1	—	%/V
Output Rise Time, t_r		—	100	—	—	100	—	ns
Output Fall Time, t_f		—	100	—	—	100	—	ns

*When the output is in a high state, the dc supply current is typically 1 mA less than the low-state value.

The threshold current will determine the sum of the values of R_1 and R_2 to be used in Fig 16 (astable operation): the maximum total $R_1 + R_2 = 20$ MR.

Minimum pulse width vs. minimum trigger voltage.

Supply current vs. supply voltage.

Output voltage drop (high state) vs. source current.

Output voltage-low state vs. sink current at $V^+ = 5$ V.

Typical application

Reset Timer (Monostable Operation)

One of the diagrams overleaf shows the CA555 connected as a reset timer. In this mode of operation capacitor C_T is initially held discharged by a transistor on the integrated circuit. Upon closing the 'start' switch, or applying a negative trigger pulse to terminal 2, the integral timer flip-flop is 'set' and releases the short circuit across C_T which drives the output voltage 'high' (relay engerized). The action allows the voltage across the capacitor to increase exponentially with the time constant $t = R_1 C_T$. When the voltage across the capacitor equals 2/3 V^+, the comparator resets the flip-flop which in turn discharges the capacitor rapidly and drives the output to its low state.

CA555, CA555C Types

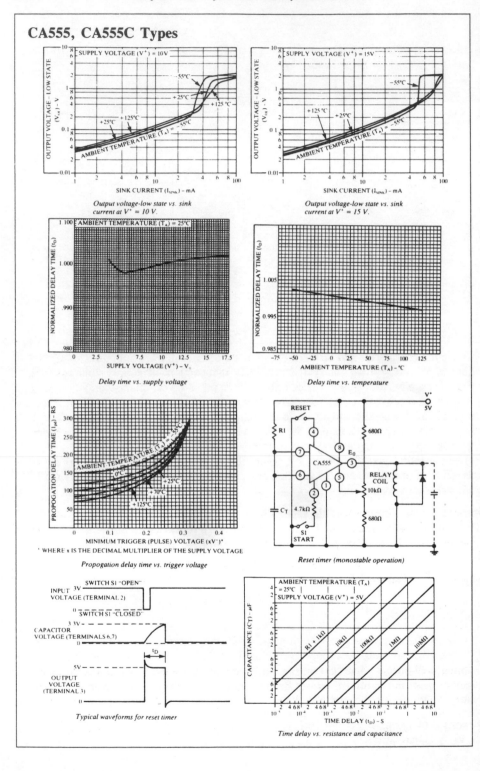

Output voltage-low state vs. sink current at $V^+ = 10$ V.

Output voltage-low state vs. sink current at $V^+ = 15$ V.

Delay time vs. supply voltage

Delay time vs. temperature

Propogation delay time vs. trigger voltage

' WHERE x IS THE DECIMAL MULTIPLIER OF THE SUPPLY VOLTAGE

Reset timer (monostable operation)

Typical waveforms for reset timer

Time delay vs. resistance and capacitance

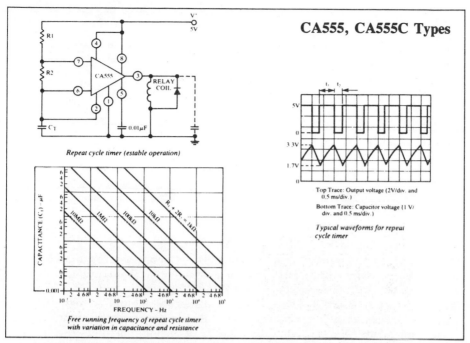

Repeat cycle timer (estable operation)

Top Trace: Output voltage (2V/div. and 0.5 ms/div.)

Bottom Trace: Capacitor voltage (1 V/div. and 0.5 ms/div.)

Typical waveforms for repeat cycle timer

CA555, CA555C Types

Free running frequency of repeat cycle timer with variation in capacitance and resistance

Since the charge rate and threshold level of the comparator are both directly proportional to V^+, the timing interval is relatively independent of supply voltage variations. Typically, the timing varies only 0.05% for a 1 volt change in V^+.

Applying a negative pulse simultaneously to the reset terminal (4) and the trigger terminal (2) during the timing cycle discharges C_T and causes the timing cycle to restart. Momentarily closing only the reset switch during the timing interval discharges C_T, but the timing cycle does not restart.

The diagram opposite bottom left shows the typical waveforms generated during this mode of operation, and the adjacent diagram gives the family of time delay curves with variations in R_1 and C_T.

Repeat Cycle Timer (Astable Operation)

The diagram above shows the CA555 connected as a repeat cycle timer. In this mode of operation, the total period is a function of both R_1 and R_2.

$$T = 0.692(R_1 + 2R_2) \, C_T = t_1 + t_2$$

where $t_1 = 0.693(R_1 + R_2) \, C_T$

$$\text{and } t_2 = 0.693 \, (R_1 + R_2) \, C_T$$

The duty cycle is:

$$\frac{t_2}{t_1 + t_2} = \frac{R_2}{R_1 + 2R_2}$$

Typical waveforms generated during this mode of operation are also shown above, together with the family of curves of free running frequency with variations in the value of $(R_1 + 2R_2)$ and C_T.

Appendix 15

Operational amplifiers

CA741, CA747, CA748, CA1458, CA1558 Types

Operational amplifiers: High-Gain Single and Dual Operational Amplifiers For Military, Industrial and Commercial Applications

The RCA-CA1458, CA1558 (dual types); CA741C, CA741 (single-types); CA747C, CA747 (dual types); and CA748C, CA748 (single types) are general-purpose, high-gain operational amplifiers for use in military, industrial and commerical applications.

These monolithic silicon integrated circuit devices provide output short-circuit protection and latch-free operation. These types also feature wide common-mode and differential-mode signal ranges and have low-offset voltage nulling capability when used with an appropriately valued potentiometer. A 5-megohm potentiometer is used for offset nulling types CA748C, CA748 (See Fig. 10); a 10-kilohm potentiometer is used for offset nulling types CA741C, CA741, CA747CE, CA747CG, CA747E, CA747G (See Fig. 9); and types CA1458, CA1558, CA747CT, have no specific terminals for offset nulling. Each type consists of a differential-input amplifier that effectively drives a gain and level-shifting stage having a complementary emitter-follower output.

This operational amplifier line also offers the circuit designer the option of operation with internal or external phase compensation.

Types CA748C and CA748, which are externally phase compensated (terminals 1 and 8) permit a choice of operation for improved bandwidth and slew-rate capabilities. Unity gain with external phase compensation can be obtained with a single 30-pF capacitor. All the other types are internally phase-compensated.

RCA's manufacturing process makes it possible to produce IC operational amplifiers with low-burst ("popcorn") noise characteristics. Type CA6741, a low-noise version of the CA741, gives limit specifications for burst noise in the data bulletin, File No. 530. Contact your RCA Sales Representative for information pertinent to other operational amplifier types that meet low-burst noise specifications.

"G" Suffix Types — Hermetic Gold-CHIP in Dual-In-Line Plastic Package
"E" Suffix Types — Standard Dual-In-Line Plastic Package
"T" and "S" Suffix Types — TO-5 Style Package

Features:

● Input bias current (all types): 500 nA max.

- Input offset current (all types): 200 nA max.

Applications:

- Comparator
- DC amplifier
- Integrator or differentiator
- Multivibrator
- Narrow-band or band-pass filter
- Summing amplifier

MAXIMUM RATINGS, *Absolute-Maximum Values at T_A = 25°C:*

DC Supply Voltage (between V^+ and V^- terminals):

CA741C, CA747C ▲, CA748C, CA1458 ▲	36 V
CA741, CA747 ▲, CA748, CA1558 ▲	44 V
Differential Input Voltage	±30 V
DC Input Voltage*	±15 V
Output Short-Circuit Duration	Indefinite

Device Dissipation:

Up to 70°C (CA741C, CA748C)	500 mW
Up to 75°C (CA741, CA748)	500 mW
Up to 30°C (CA747)	800 mW
Up to 25°C (CA747C)	800 mW
Up to 30°C (CA1558)	680 mW
Up to 25°C (CA1458)	680 mW
For Temperatures Indicated Above	Derate linearly 6.67 mW/°C

Voltage between Offset Null and V^- (CA741C, CA741, CA747CE,

CA747CG)	±0.5 V

Ambient Temperature Range:

Operating — CA741, CA747E, CA748, CA1558	−55 to +125°C
CA741C, CA747C, CA748C, CA1458 . . .	0 to +70°C†
Storage	−65 to +150°C

Lead Temperature (During Soldering):

At distance 1/16 ± 1/32 inch (1.59 ± 0.79 mm) from case

for 10 seconds max	265°C

▲ Voltage values apply for each of the dual operational amplifiers.
* If Supply voltage is less than ± 15 volts, the Absolute Maximum Input Voltage is equal to the Supply Voltage.
† All types in any package style can be operated over the temperature range of −55 to +125°C, although the published limits for certain electrical specifications apply only over the temperature range of 0 to +70°C

RCA Type No.	No. of Ampl.	Phase Comp.	Offset Voltage Null	Min. A$_{OL}$	Max. V$_{IO}$ (mV)	Operating-Temperature Range (°C)
CA1458	dual	int.	no	20k	6	0 to +70 ▲
CA1558	dual	int.	no	50k	5	−55 to +125
CA741C	single	int.	yes	20k	6	0 to +70 ▲
CA741	single	int.	yes	50k	5	−55 to +125
CA747C	dual	int.	yes*	20k	6	0 to +70 ▲
CA747	dual	int.	yes*	50k	5	−55 to +125
CA748C	single	ext.	yes	20k	6	0 to +70 ▲
CA748	single	ext.	yes	50k	5	−55 to +125

* In the 14 lead dual-in-line plastic package only.
▲ All types in any package style can be operated over the temperature range of −55 to +125°C, although the published limits for certain electrical specifications apply only over the temperature range of 0 to +70°C.

Ordering information

When ordering any of these types, it is important that the appropriate suffix letter for the package required be affixed to the type number. For example: If a CA1458 in a straight-lead TO-5 style package is desired, order CA1458T.

Type No.	PACKAGE TYPE AND SUFFIX LETTER									FIG. No.
	TO-5 STYLE		PLASTIC	Gold-CHIP PLASTIC		CHIP	Gold-CHIP	BEAM-LEAD		
	8L	10L	DIL-CAN	8L	14L	8L	14L			
CA1458	T		S	E	G		H	GH		1d, 1h
CA1558	T		S	E	G					1d, 1h
CA741C	T		S	E	G		H	GH		1a, 1e
CA741	T		S	E	G				L	1a, 1e
CA747C		T		E		G	H	GH		1b, 1f
CA747		T		E		G				1b, 1f
CA748C	T		S	E		G	H	GH		1c, 1g
CA748	T		S	E		G				1c, 1g

CA741, CA747, CA748, CA1558 Types

Electrical characteristics: *For Equipment Design*

CHARACTERISTIC	TEST CONDITIONS Supply Voltage V⁺ = 15 V V⁻ = −15 V	Ambient Temperature, T_A	LIMITS CA741 CA747* CA748 CA1558*			UNITS
			Min.	Typ.	Max.	
Input Offset Voltage, V_{IO}	$R_S = \leqslant 10kR$	25°C	—	1	5	mV
		−55 to +125°C	—	1	6	
Input Offset Current, I_{IO}		25°C	—	20	200	nA
		−55°C	—	85	500	
		+125°C	—	7	200	
Input Bias Current, I_{IB}		25°C	—	80	500	nA
		−55°C	—	300	1500	
		+125°C	—	30	500	
Input Resistance, R_I			0.3	2		MR
Open-Loop Differential Voltage Gain, A_{OL}	$R_L \geqslant 2kR$ $V_O = \pm 10$ V	25°C	50,000	200,000	—	
		−55 to +125°C	25,000	—	—	
Common-Mode Input Voltage Range, V_{ICR}		−55 to +125°C	±12	±13	—	V
Common-Mode Rejection Ratio, CMRR	$R_S \leqslant 10kR$	−55 to +125°C	70	90	—	dB
Supply Voltage Rejection Ratio, PSRR	$R_S \leqslant 10kR$	−55 to +125°C	—	30	150	µV/V
Output Voltage Swing, V_{OPP}	$R_L \geqslant 10kR$	−55 to +125°C	±12	±14	—	V
	$R_L \geqslant 2kR$	−55 to +125°C	±10	±13	—	
Supply Current, $I^\pm$		25°C	—	1.7	2.8	mA
		−55°C	—	2	3.3	
		+125°C	—	1.5	2.5	
Device Dissipation, P_D		25°C	—	50	85	mW
		−55°C	—	60	100	
		+125°C	—	45	75	

*Values apply for each section of the dual amplifiers.

TOP VIEW

NOTE PIN 4 IS CONNECTED TO CASE

a. *CA741CS, CA741CT, CA741S, and CA741T with internal phase compensation.*

TOP VIEW

b. *CA747CT and CA747T with internal phase compensation.*

TOP VIEW

NOTE PIN 4 IS CONNECTED TO CASE

c. *CA748CS, CA748CT, CA748S, and CA748T with external phase compensation.*

Functional diagrams.

CA741C, CA747C, CA748C, CA1458 Types
Electrical characteristics: *For Equipment Design*

CHARACTERISTIC	TEST CONDITIONS Supply Voltage V⁺ = 15 V V⁻ = −15 V	Ambient Temperature, T_A	LIMITS CA741C CA747C* CA748C CA1458* Min.	Typ.	Max.	UNITS
Input Offset Voltage, V_{IO}	$R_S = \leqslant 10kR$	25°C	—	2	6	mV
		0 to 70°C	—	—	7.5	
Input Offset Current, I_{IO}		25°C	—	20	200	nA
		0 to 70°C	—	—	300	
Input Bias Current, I_{IB}		25°C	—	80	500	nA
		0 to 70°C	—	—	800	
Input Resistance, R_I			0.3	2	—	MR
Open-Loop Differential Voltage Gain. A_{OL}	$R_L \geqslant 2kR$ $V_O = \pm 10$ V	25°C	20,000	200,000	—	
		0 to +70°C	15,000	—	—	
Common-Mode Input Voltage Range, V_{ICR}		25°C	±12	±13	—	V
Common-Mode Rejection Ratio, CMRR	$R_S \leqslant 10kR$	25°C	70	90	—	dB
Supply Voltage Rejection Ratio, PSRR	$R_S \leqslant 10kR$	25°C	—	30	150	μV/V
Output Voltage Swing, V_{OPP}	$R_L \geqslant 10kR$	25°C	±12	±14	—	V
	$R_L \geqslant 2kR$	25°C	±10	±13	—	
		0 to 70°C	±10	±13	—	
Supply Current, $I^\pm$		25°C	—	1.7	2.8	mA
Device Dissipation, P_D		25°C	—	50	85	mW

*Values apply for each section of the dual amplifiers.

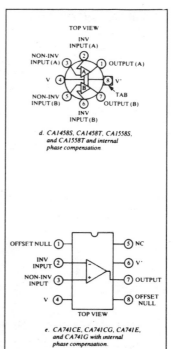

d. CA1458S, CA1458T, CA1558S, and CA1558T and internal phase compensation

e. CA741CE, CA741CG, CA741E, and CA741G with internal phase compensation.

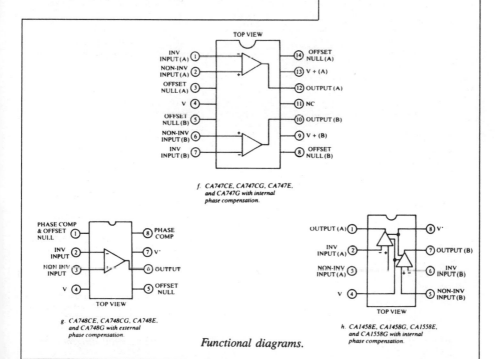

f. CA747CE, CA747CG, CA747E, and CA747G with internal phase compensation.

g. CA748CE, CA748CG, CA748E, and CA748G with external phase compensation.

h. CA1458E, CA1458G, CA1558E, and CA1558G with internal phase compensation.

Functional diagrams.

CA741, CA747, CA748, CA1458, CA1558 Types

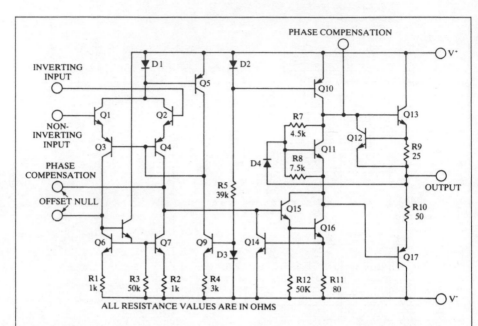

Schematic diagram of operational amplifier with external phase compensation for CA748C and CA748.

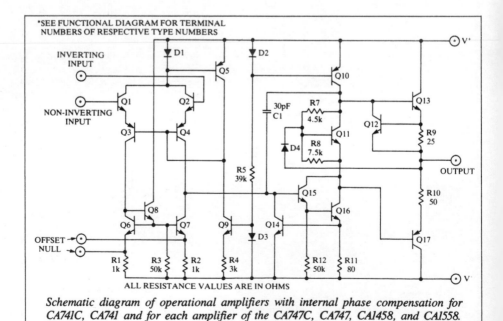

Schematic diagram of operational amplifiers with internal phase compensation for CA741C, CA741 and for each amplifier of the CA747C, CA747, CA1458, and CA1558.

CA741, CA747, CA748, CA1458, CA1558 Types

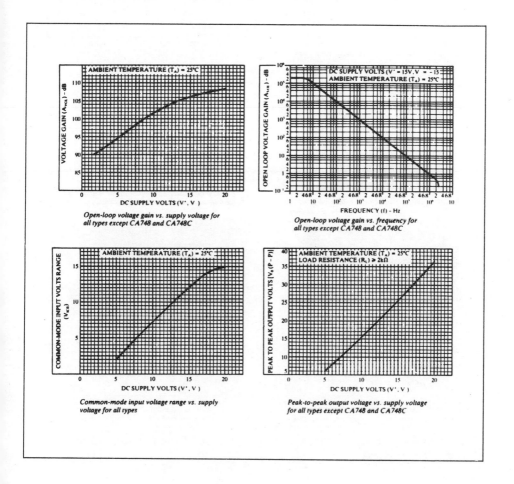

Open-loop voltage gain vs. supply voltage for all types except CA748 and CA748C

Open-loop voltage gain vs. frequency for all types except CA748 and CA748C

Common-mode input voltage range vs. supply voltage for all types

Peak-to-peak output voltage vs. supply voltage for all types except CA748 and CA748C

Electrical characteristics: *Typical Values Intended Only for Design Guidance*

CHARACTERISTIC	TEST CONDITIONS $V^+ = \pm 15$ V	TYP. VALUES ALL TYPES	UNITS
Input Capacitance, C_1		1.4	pF
Offset Voltage Adjustment Range		±15	mV
Output Resistance, R_O		75	R
Output Short-Circuit Current		25	mA
Transient Response: Rise Time, t_r	Unity gain $V_1 = 20$ mV $R_L = 2kR$ $C_1 \leqslant 100$ pF	0.3	μs
Overshoot		5	%
Slew Rate, SR: Closed-loop	$R_L \geqslant 2kR$	0.5	V/μs
Open-loop*		40	

*Open-loop slew rate applies only for types CA748C and CA748.

CA741, CA747, CA748, CA1458, CA1558 Types

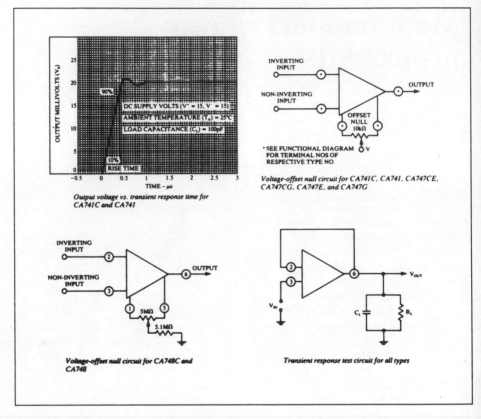

Output voltage vs. transient response time for CA741C and CA741

Voltage-offset null circuit for CA741C, CA741, CA747CE, CA747CG, CA747E, and CA747G

Voltage-offset null circuit for CA748C and CA748

Transient response test circuit for all types

Maplin model railway project kits

Maplin sells a range of kits for electronic projects for model railways. Some of these are ideally suited for beginners, while others are emphatically for experienced constructors. They contain all the components needed, including purpose-designed printed circuit boards, and detailed instructions. In the unlikely event of difficulties, Maplin's kits are covered by a 'Get You Working' service. A brief description of the kits listed in the March 1997 Maplin catalogue follows.

Control-a-Train (order code LK64U)
This is a pulse-width-modulated controller based around the CA3240E dual operational amplifier. One op amp is configured as a relaxation oscillator which generates constant-amplitude pulses proportional to its input voltage. The other is used as a buffer from the speed control circuit. Output is via a power Darlington.

The speed control contains a fixed level of inertia on both acceleration and deceleration. To allow for faster deceleration, a separate 'brake' push-button is provided which discharges the inertia capacitor more quickly.

The circuit requires a 15 V ac power supply, but can also be run from dc supplies; it has a built-in bridge rectifier and a voltage regulator. The voltage regulator is not strictly necessary in a circuit of this type, but its built-in current limiting eliminates the need for a separate overload protection system. It also helps to make the circuit's performance more consistent.

The kit includes a front panel with suitable legends, but not a case or console for the controller; one is available as an optional extra.

Digital Model Train Controller Mark II (order code LW61R and LW62S) and Receiver (order code LT29G)
These units form a 'command control' system (similar to Hornby Zero-1). The controller allows four out of up to 14 trains to be controlled individually on the same track, provided of course that each is fitted with a receiver unit. The controller delivers 18 V dc to the track and superimposes on this digital information to which the receivers on the trains respond by controlling the train's speed and direction accordingly. There are seven channels and two groups; each of the four train controllers can be set to operate on any channel and with either group.

As you might expect, this is a complex project. Furthermore, it makes extensive use of CMOS logic ICs. These have not been described in detail in this book. They perform logical operations as do TTL ICs, but their active components are MOSFETs which are highly susceptible to damage by electrostatic charges. For this reason, you are recommended to observe a number of simple precautions when handling them.

The controller itself requires five kits: four identical train control modules (LW62S) — which contain the speed/direction control circuitry for each train — and one common/power supply unit kit (LW61R) which contains the components common to the whole controller. A case for the controller is available as an optional extra. Power requirements: standard ac mains.

You will need a receiver kit for each train that is to run on the layout; unequipped trains cannot be run when the Digital Controller is in use. The current version of the receiver uses a PIC 8-bit microcontroller to decode the digital signals, while output uses four discrete power transistors in a bridge configuration. Each receiver must be set to its channel and group at construction time. Installing the receiver may present problems because neither terminal of the motor may be earthed to the chassis and the circuit board is comparatively large, measuring approximately 3.9 in × 0.75 in × 0.5 in. In larger locomotives, especially diesel or electric outline types, this size may not cause difficulties, but in smaller locomotives, especially tank locomotives, there may be no option but to mount the receiver in a coach or wagon permanently coupled to the loco.

Model Train Signal Lights (order code LT66W)

This unit provides automatic operation of a single two-, three- or four-aspect colour light signal which may use LEDs or tungsten lamps. Input is from reed switches, although a manual set switch is also provided. Choice of two-, three- or four-aspect operation is by means of links on the printed circuit board. Logic is CMOS throughout, the output stage for the LEDs or lamps being provided by the ULN2803 IC (an array of eight Darlingtons). Power requirements are 8–15 V dc.

This unit differs from those described earlier in this book in that it does not follow true signalling logic; it lights the aspects strictly by sequence. In four-aspect operation, therefore, the sequence is always red, yellow, double yellow, green and back to red. Control pulses from all the reed switches connected to the unit are effectively paralleled through a single OR gate; a pulse from any reed switch advances the signal to the next aspect in the sequence. Normally, if traffic is light, this will work well enough. But if traffic is intensive, the system will behave unprototypically; a train passing the signal at double yellow will change it to *green*, the next aspect in the sequence, instead of red. The manual set switch can be used to 'clock' the signal on manually to the appropriate aspect.

A further complication of this strictly sequential means of operation is that precautions have to be taken to handle contact bounce. The contacts of a longitudinally mounted reed switch close three times as a longitudinally mounted magnet passes over it. Without such precautions a loco passing a four-aspect signal at green would change it to red, yellow and then double-yellow probably in less than a second. The debouncing is provided by the CMOS 40106 IC in conjunction with resistors and capacitors.

The kit includes all electronic components, a printed circuit board, one reed switch and sufficient LEDs for a four-aspect signal. Magnets to operate the reed switch are available separately. The instructions with the kit include ideas on the construction of the signal itself.

Model Train Chuffer (order code LT39N)

The Model Train Chuffer generates a hiss of escaping steam while the train is stationary and a chuff rate that varies with train speed while the train is moving. Manual controls are provided for adjusting the chuff rate:train speed ratio and the volume of the audio output. Output is a nominal 1 V, suitable for connection to an audio amplifier. Power requirements are 15–36 V dc.

With its circuit board measuring approximately 2.5 in × 3.6 in, this is a unit for trackside rather than on-train operation. The technology is sophisticated, the white noise for the chuffs and steam sound being generated digitally using a voltage-controlled oscillator whose output pulses are manipulated in a shift register and a collection of XOR gates. A bridge rectifier connected to the track provides a control voltage roughly proportional to train speed to determine the chuff rate using another voltage-controlled oscillator. A voltage-controlled amplifier is used to modulate the white noise to produce realistic chuffs. A delightfully realistic touch is a delay circuit which reduces the hiss level after the train has been stationary for a while.

The kit contains everything needed for this project, except for a case, sockets, spacers and hookup wire, all of which are available as optional extras.

Steam Whistle and Two-tone Diesel Horn (order code LT61R)

Like the previously described kit, this uses digital techniques, but the sounds generated are in fact samples from recordings of 'live' locomotives, stored in a read-only memory (ROM) chip. This results in a more lifelike sound than can be achieved using 'synthetic' techniques.

The circuit contains the ROM itself, a 'clock' (oscillator) to step from one memory location to the next at the right interval and a digital-to-analogue converter. The contents of successive locations are presented to the converter which changes them to a fluctuating analogue voltage; this audio signal can then be fed to an amplifier for reproduction in the normal way.

The circuit also contains control logic which provide three input sockets: one triggers the steam whistle sound; another the diesel horn and the third triggers both sounds, one after the other (diesel horn followed by steam whistle). Both sounds are 2.73 seconds long. Reed switches are the recommended trigger devices. These are fitted to the track wherever a locomotive is required to whistle or sound its horn and are activated when a locomotive fitted with a suitable magnet passes by. Alternatively a manual push-button could be used, or may be wired in parallel with the reed switches. The unit also offers a choice of repeat or one-shot triggering.

The unit also has an external audio input allowing audio from another source (such as the chuffer described above) to be mixed with its own output; the combined sound can then be fed to an amplifier.

The circuit board size is 3.3 in × 3.75 in so this is essentially another trackside unit. Power requirements are 8–15 V dc.

Train Effects Generator (order code WE64U)

This is a very simple project consisting of nine components, excluding the battery or other power supply. It uses an unusual IC, the CIC82113, which comes already bonded to the circuit board and contains nearly all the electronics. The only other components are four push-button switches, two resistors, a transistor and a loudspeaker.

The sounds available, which are synthesised rather than sampled audio, are a whistle, a steam train chuffing, an American-style level crossing bell and crossing a bridge. Simply close the switch to activate the required sound. Reed switches could be used instead of the push-button switches to trigger the required sound at the appropriate place.

The circuit runs from two 1.5 V dry batteries which have a long life (the circuit shuts itself down when not in use). The printed circuit board size is approximately 3 in × 2 in, so this is still too large for on-train use, except perhaps in O gauge.

Other kits

Maplin offers kits for a diversity of other projects that may be of interest to railway modellers. For further details see the 'Projects & Modules' section of the Maplin catalogue.

Index